UNFADING HONOUR

UNFADING HONOUR

THE STORY OF THE INDIAN ARMY

1939–1945

by

MAJOR-GENERAL J. G. ELLIOTT

South Brunswick

New York: A. S. Barnes and Co., Inc.

Library of Congress Catalogue Card Number: 66-25032

A. S. Barnes and Co., Inc.
Cranbury, New Jersey

6459
Printed in the United States of America

TO THE
OFFICERS AND MEN
OF THE OLD
INDIAN ARMY

Preface

For many years now I have wished that the story of the old Indian Army in the Second World War might be written, so that the people of this country could learn what they owe to those soldiers who fought for them against the Germans, the Italians and the Japanese. Without their aid, the war could not have been won.

I am honoured, therefore, to have been asked to write this Preface. All the more so, because I had the privilege of serving for forty-four years with the men about whom this book has been written.

The author has, with great clarity and ability, set out what these soldiers were and what they did and has described the unique relationship between them and their British officers.

The differences between the various races and classes which made up the Army of the British Raj were marked indeed, but after a life-long association with them in war and peace, I am of the opinion that, given good officers, there is little to choose between them. When well led, they have proved themselves the equal of any soldiers in the world: well led they always were.

Today, the soldiers of India and Pakistan, serving now under officers of their own race, are to my personal knowledge maintaining to the full those qualities of loyalty, steadfastness, courage and discipline which are so convincingly described in this book.

PREFACE

It is well that we should remember our debt to them and try to retain that mutual affection and esteem which was so steadily built up through two centuries of service in many parts of the world.

Auchinleck
F.M

Contents

Maps

Illustrations

Foreword

My brief was to tell the story of the Indian Army in the years
1939–1945. Within the compass of one short volume a truly
comprehensive account could not be much more than a bare
catalogue of its achievements, so bare as to have little interest
or appeal to the readers at whom the book is really aimed:
those who know that there was an Indian Army, but little
more than that, and should therefore welcome the opportunity
to make good a gap in their education.

The alternative to extreme compression was to be highly
selective, which gave me the opportunity to expand the
stories chosen sufficiently to show the Indian soldier, and his
officers, in action; to show not only what they did, but what
they looked like while doing it. That has meant leaving out
far more than it has been possible to include, and for every
story taken there were others which would have done equally
well. So, those who feel they have been unfairly treated must
console themselves with the thought that the book sets out to
be a picture of the Indian Army as a whole and not of any
single part of it.

Primary research into military history is a task outside the
powers of the individual writer and I have relied almost ex-
clusively on official histories, and on those written for divisions and regiments. To strengthen the impression that the
picture is one of the army as a whole, I have adopted a system
of referencing the sources of my quotations which plays down
any emphasis on their identity. When a work is quoted for the
first time its title is given in full, followed by a number in

brackets; thereafter only the number appears. A key to all the works and their numbers is given in Appendix D.

I make grateful acknowledgement to the following authorities and individuals for permission to quote from the works shown against their names:

Her Majesty's Stationery Office for the official histories and books published by the War Office.

The Ministry of Defence, Government of India, for the Indian official histories and *The Tiger Strikes* series.

The Canadian Minister of National Defence, the director of the Australian War Memorial, and the War Histories Branch of the Internal Affairs Department, New Zealand, for their respective histories.

Regimental and divisional associations for their respective histories (all numbers 21–70).

Field Marshal Lord Slim and Cassell & Co.: *Defeat into Victory*.

Lieutenant-General Sir Francis Tuker and Cassell & Co.: *Approach to Battle—A Commentary*: *Eighth Army, November 1941 to May 1943*.

Mr Fred Majdalany and Longmans, Green & Co.: *Cassino: Portrait of a Battle*.

Major-General J. F. C. Fuller and Eyre & Spottiswoode Ltd.: *The Second World War*.

Mr Cyril Falls and Methuen & Co.: *The Second World War*.

The heirs of the late Brigadier-General C. A. L. Graham and Gale & Polden: *The History of the Indian Mountain Artillery*.

The Times for the extract in Chapter 4.

Lady Wavell for Lord Wavell's Foreword to *Fourth Indian Division* which closes this book.

I am indebted to the following who have supplied me with information or read chapters in draft form:

Field Marshal Lord Slim; Lieutenant-Generals Sir Francis Tuker and Kalwant Singh; Major-Generals D. R. Bateman, S. H. M. Battye, R. B. Clarabut, A. C. Curtis, H. L. Davies, B. P. Hughes, R. I. Jones, C. M. Maltby, D. W. Reid, J. B. Scott, and J. D. F. Steedman; Brigadiers A. R.

Barker, J. Bourke, H. K. Dimoline, C. I. Jerrard, R. S. Johnson, M. J. A. Sheehan, and H. Shuker; Colonels J. B. Church, C. C. Deakin, A. M. L. Harrison, J. L. Jones, C. C. J. Kellie, J. Hulme Taylor, J. Viney, and H. L. Westmorland; Lieutenant-Colonel S. K. Joshua, Military Adviser's Department, High Commission of India, and Lieutenant-Colonel M. I. Quereshi, for information from India and Pakistan respectively.

I thank:

The Librarians and staffs of the War Department, the Royal United Service Institution, and the India Office Libraries for their help and interest.

The director-general, the Imperial War Museum, for permission to use the photographs, and his staff and Mr A. E. Haswell Miller for their help in choosing them.

In the place of honour my thanks are due to Field Marshal Auchinleck, not only for reading every word and for much sound advice, but for giving me the opportunity to write the book. Let there be no misunderstanding: what I have written expresses, to the best of my ability, his determination to see full justice done to the army that owed so much to him.

J. G. Elliott

Kingston Magna
17 October 1964

CHAPTER ONE

Traditions

Having spent so many eventful years of my life in India, and having been so intimately associated with the Indian Army in peace and war, I think that no one is better able than myself to esteem that army at its proper value as regards what it has—with the help of British training and example—achieved in the past or to appreciate what it is capable of doing in the future under the same conditions... It is imperfectly known in England, and often insufficiently understood in India, how very diverse and divergent in many respects are the numerous races we enlist in our Indian Army.*

So wrote Field Marshal Earl Roberts, V.C., probably the greatest of that long line of distinguished soldiers who, over a span of almost exactly two hundred years, held office as commander-in-chief in India. He did not live to see his prophecy come true for, three years later, in 1914, he died in France in the very midst of the men he knew and loved so well. One may surmise that during the years 1939-45, from his seat in Valhalla, he watched with ever-mounting excitement as that army fought its way from strength to strength,

* Foreword to *The Armies of India*, Major G. F. MacMunn, D.S.O. A. & C. Black, 1911.

I

to emerge, when peace came, as a force in its own right in the affairs of nations; to the point, indeed, where imperfect knowledge and insufficient understanding of what it did are matters for concern and regret, not only in England, India and Pakistan, but all the world over—west of the Atlantic, for example, as this story quite clearly shows.

In 1962 the senior battalion of the present Indian Army celebrated its bicentenary and a former British officer of the regiment flew out for the occasion. He wrote, for the benefit of his friends, an account of his experiences. Space rules out a detailed recital of the honours the battalion paid him, the respect and affection shown; not, as he is careful to point out, to him personally, but to him as the medium through which they could express their regard for the British officers of the days of old. The parting scene at least must go on record. The farewell lunch lasted till 3.30 p.m. when it was time to leave for the airport, and it seemed as though the whole battalion knew about it, for he was followed out by a cavalcade of cars, jeeps and lorries.

> As I climbed the steps to the aircraft and turned to wave 'goodbye' they all broke into cheers and I admit that tears welled to my eyes at this spontaneous show of affection.
>
> The aircraft happened to be full of American tourists who had been visiting the Taj. They stared open-mouthed at the scene and in the aircraft I heard one of them say, 'I thought those goddam British had been pushed out of India. I guess some of us in the States have been mightily misinformed.'

The Indian Army differed so considerably from the other armies of the British Empire that the story of its doings will be the better appreciated if a little space is devoted to sketching in the background.

In the first half of the eighteenth century, as the interests and wealth of the Honourable East India Company increased, the directors found it necessary to recruit locally what were at first little better than armed guards for the protection of their warehouses and settlements. But, about 1760, finding them-selves in direct conflict with the French who had put their forces on a regular footing, they were compelled to follow suit.

With the crumbling of the Mogul Empire the British, the French, Tippoo Sultan and the Mahratta chiefs were all jostling for power, and for years the country was a happy hunting ground for adventurers of all colours, classes, races and religions, concerned only to sell their swords in the most exciting market.

Between 1838 and 1848, after a lull of thirty years, there were three campaigns which profoundly affected the whole future of the Indian Army: the first Afghan War, and the two Sikh wars. The hard fighting that took place undoubtedly shook the spirit of the Bengal Army, which was already suffering from the insidious effects of some years of peace, but it was the extension of our territories that followed which had even more far-reaching consequences. We were now in contact with the tribes of the North-West Frontier and it must have been clear from the very start that they would at best be uneasy neighbours; and if we had to fight them on their own ground, which in itself imposed considerable hard-ships on men from further south, they were likely to prove an enemy of sterner quality than any, barring the Mahrattas, the army had had to face before.

Then came The Mutiny. The outbreak was confined almost entirely to the Bengal Army, indeed regiments from the Bombay and Madras Armies helped to suppress it. It is true that those affected had been corrupted by men who aimed to break the power of the British, but it is also true that corrup-tion had set in where sloth and inefficiency were already at work. The Mutiny left a legacy of bitterness to bedevil relations between British and Indian for the next ninety years and led to sweeping changes. The European regiments and batteries then in the service of the East India Company passed to the Crown and thereafter, although British and Indian battalions always fought side by side in formations of the Indian Army, the British regiments no longer formed an integral part of that army, but served in India on a system of reliefs.

3

The immediate need, of course, was to fill the gaps left by the regiments which had mutinied, and to fill them with men whose loyalty was beyond question. The occupation of the Punjab and the frontier tracts had opened up wide new fields for recruitment and for several years past, either to control the tribesmen, or indeed to help put down The Mutiny itself, officers like Hodson, Sam Browne, Brownlow, and Coke had been raising irregular corps, often with rather less formality than today attends upon the launching of a troop of scouts. Jats, Sikhs, Dogras, Punjabi Mohammedans and Pathans, they had been drawing on the yeoman manpower of the newly extended territories. They found it first-rate material, brave, hardy, independent and loyal, so that it is hardly to be wondered that these same classes were taken to fill the empty ranks of the Bengal Army. From then on it was a matter of the survival of the fittest, and only those who stood up to the test of war could hope to be enlisted.

During the next forty years the Indian Army saw service in Abyssinia, Afghanistan, Burma, and China. There were perhaps half a dozen battalions that failed the test, broke the link with their old classes and were reconstituted with men from the Punjab, but it was the appointment of Lord Kitchener as commander-in-chief in 1902 that set the seal on the system of selective recruiting. He came out convinced on two points: that the danger to India lay in an invasion by the Russians through Afghanistan, and that it was not the business of the army to defend India against the Indians.

The abolition of the Presidency Armies in 1895 and their unification under Army Headquarters was a half-hearted reform that was never pressed to its logical conclusion, and regiments and battalions continued to be stationed in the areas from which they were recruited. The Punjab Frontier Force would no doubt have resisted any attempt to move them from their stamping grounds along the border; on the other hand, no officer with a spark of fire or ambition was content to serve out his days in single battalion stations in the enervating climate of the Madras Presidency. Only the dead wood remained there, with disastrous effects on the morale and efficiency of their men.

4

In a drastic reorganization designed to fit the army for its major role, Kitchener ruled that all units must be prepared to serve on relief in India wherever the needs of the service dictated. In his view it was clear that the units of the old Madras Army were not fit for duty on the North-West Frontier, and with complete ruthlessness he ordered the disbandment of no less than fourteen battalions, which were reconstituted with men from the Punjab. After that the pattern changed very little until 1940. Gurkhas, Garwhalis, Madrassis of the Sappers and Miners, Mahrattas, Rajputs and the men from the Punjab and Frontier Province had proved their worth, and they were the ones to be taken.

These various classes differed considerably in temperament, but they had three things in common which gave the Indian Army its peculiar quality. They came from small yeomen farmer families, and were frugal, hardy and unsophisticated— men to whom it was second nature to move with certainty by night over ground that held a thousand pitfalls for the townsman reared in a world of lamp-posts and pavements Then, although they generally enlisted from economic necessity, they were not, in the strict sense of the word, mercenaries. In England, military service is still regarded with some of the suspicion that has filtered down from Cromwell's major-generals; in India, the profession of arms is an honourable one. Lastly, they had those innate characteristics of the countryman; good manners, humour and a regard for authority. The standard of discipline was inherently high and owed little to well-filled conduct sheets and the stamping of orderly-room feet. From this general absence of fuss sprang a mobility that was a priceless asset in war.

A young officer, holding a wartime commission, visited the district from which the men of his company were recruited to inquire into the well-being of those who had been wounded and discharged on medical grounds, and to offer such consolation as he could to the relatives of those who had been killed. He wrote:

There were no tears; no recriminations. They were very sorry: it was 'kistmet ki bat' [a matter of fate]. I met a

5

pensioned havildar who had been wounded in the first
World War. He said of his eldest son, a V.C.O. who had
died of wounds at Myingan: 'It is a great honour that
my son should die fighting bravely'. It was refreshing to
get back to a life where courtesy, hospitality and loyalty
meant so much, and where the little things of life were
appreciated.

What sort of a person was the British officer who went out
to lead these men? In the early days, no doubt, there were
some who lacked the price of a commission in the British
Army; but over the years there were more who sailed in
search of wider horizons than anything the Horse Guards or
Aldershot had to offer. Quite a few went in the footsteps of a
father or an uncle, setting a fashion that was to continue to
the end. There was, for example, Major Alexander Gordon
of 1st European Infantry who retired and died in Boulogne-
sur-Mer in 1851. His brother James, surgeon to 24th Native
Infantry at the battle of Sitabaldi, led a party of the regiment
to spike and capture two large brass cannon from the Arabs.
Alexander had a large family, even by Victorian standards.
Five sons commanded cavalry or infantry regiments of the
Indian Army and all saw service in places as far apart as
Kabul and Peking. The seventeenth and youngest child, a
daughter, married a major of the Royal Artillery and sent her
two sons to the Indian Army; the elder was killed on Gallipoli.

The bond between these officers and the Indian soldier
is something that the outsider may find hard to understand,
though the experience of the officer who revisited India for
the bicentenary celebrations may be a help. He wrote:

> After breakfast I met all the pensioners. This was prob-
> ably the highlight of the visit because their obvious
> delight at meeting again an old British officer was spon-
> taneous. Some of the older ones were much affected and
> many a tear appeared as they talked about old officers.
> One old pensioner, Wazir Singh, who enlisted in 1901
> and rattled off the names of old officers, many of whom
> I had only heard of but never met, openly cried when in

6

answer to his questions about them I had to tell him that many of them were dead.

It was that tie, let there be no mistake about it, that was the mainspring of the whole machine. It went beyond the relationship between officer and man in the British Army, and that, in all conscience, is something that the rest of the world is envious of; and it is because it had its foundations in absolute confidence that in spite of differences in race, religion and customs it was somehow so intimate, informal, and permanent.

The young British officer joining the Indian Army found two guardian angels lined up to guide his feet in the way that he should go. The first was the spirit arising from the well-nigh bottomless fund of goodwill built up over the years by those who had served before him; it was assumed, as a matter of course, that to his dealings with his men he would bring that straightforward, disinterested and entirely predictable approach that they knew they could rely on. The second was the Indian officer. Akin to the warrant officer of the British Army, he held the Viceroy's commission which entitled him to be saluted by his men, a point of some significance in assessing the esteem in which he was held; it gave him just that bit more authority. In the early days of the East India Company, units were commanded by their Indian officers, but after the reorganization of 1760 European officers were introduced to counter a similar measure by the French, the enemy with whom we were then most concerned. These officers were at first attached to units and employed in what was little more than a supervisory role, but it does not seem to have been a satisfactory arrangement and in 1796 a permanent cadre of British officers became part of each unit. This put them on a footing with the officers of the European regiments, that is, they exercised command, and the Indian officer was relegated to a subordinate footing. Thus, by chance rather than design there came into being the man who through the years has played so great a part in the fortunes of the Indian Army: native officer, Indian officer, Viceroy's commissioned officer—the change of name has never worried him. Dignified, yet never standing on his dignity, his wide experience and influence have been tactfully and unreservedly at the service of all, from the colonel downwards, and to none more willingly given than to the newly joined subaltern. Each relied on the other: the British officer knew he could never hope to command his men direct, the V.C.O. looked for the backing and guidance he needed from his squadron or company commander.

In the years between 1940 and 1950 the V.C.O. rendered two outstanding services to the army. Claiming no credit for his achievements, he quietly but firmly shepherded the wartime commissioned officers during the days when they were learning their job; and he steered the newly constituted regiments and battalions of India and Pakistan through the troubled waters of Partition.

No finer type of soldier has ever existed and there is no more eloquent tribute to his worth than that, as the junior commissioned officer, he continues in the armies of today.

The army had just about time to benefit by the reforms introduced by Kitchener when the First World War was upon them. The divisions who arrived in France in 1914 at a most critical moment fought through a bitter European winter and won eight V.C.s before being withdrawn to other theatres of war: East Africa and Mesopotamia, where the forces were predominantly Indian; and Palestine where both cavalry and infantry played a decisive part in Allenby's final victory.

The Indian soldier emerged with great confidence in himself, and with the foundations truly laid for his triumphs twenty years later; the record of the army in the years between the wars did nothing to shake those foundations. In 1919, when the British Army, in the pangs of demobilization, was settling down as the army of occupation in Germany, the Indian Army had two small wars on its hands. The first, against Afghanistan, was not a very serious affair, but the fighting against the Mahsuds in Waziristan was as bitter as anything the Frontier has ever known. Nor was it conclusive, for three years later there were large-scale operations to establish Razmak as a permanent garrison in the heart of Mahsud territory. In 1926 an Indian brigade was the first to come to the help of Shanghai; in 1930 there was wide-spread trouble around Peshawar; two years later a brigade and a half were in Burma. In 1935 there was fighting in Waziristan and on the Mohmand border, where Captain Godfrey Meynell, adjutant of The Guides, won the V.C. In 1936, when the Italians invaded Abyssinia, a company of Indian infantry earned international thanks and respect for their defence of the diplomatic community in Addis Ababa.

Nothing very much to make a fuss about perhaps; a couple of hundred casualties here, no more than a handful there, but all the same, that number of homes to which a man did not return. And in the larger picture not such a heavy price to pay for keeping the army on its toes, and that, beyond all shadow of doubt, is where it stood on 3 September 1939.

Time and again the record shows that an Indian brigade or battalion captured a position against very little opposition, with the implication that this was really rather an unsporting thing to do. An examination of the details too often reveals that success was due to the unexpected: a move by night, over the impossible approach, or at a speed which beat the enemy to it.

The reader must decide for himself whether indeed that was not the outstanding characteristic of the Indian Army; its ability to move fast and far, and to snatch the fleeting opportunity.

It only remains to review the British soldier's place in the formations of the Indian Army. The general practice was that one battalion in a brigade would be British, and the other two Indian or Gurkha. The gunner regiments were nearly all British, although all mountain artillery was Indian; the sappers were Indian. Signals and the administrative services were mostly Indian with a leaven of British N.C.O.s in the technical appointments.

There may remain, buried in some long-forgotten adjutant-general's file, the minutes in which it was decided that the inclusion of a British battalion in an Indian brigade was a good thing: in brief, it was probably felt that the rather more phlegmatic British character would contribute qualities of stability and determination when things were not going too

9

well. But times have changed and there are available two points of view on this matter, written by outside observers, which are worth quoting. Cyril Falls, summing up generally at the end of his book *The Second World War*,* writes:

> Again, the theory upon which the composition of infantry brigades of the Indian Army was based was that the single British battalion normally included would set a standard and provide an example to the Indian battalions. Good as were many of the latter in the First World War this was how things commonly worked out in practice. That was also the case in the Second World War to start with, but here the British battalions did not as a rule remain at their best as long as the Indian and Gurkha battalions. By 1944 it could not be said that these were in any need of an example set by Europeans.

Fred Majdalany, in his book *Cassino*,† devoted several pages to an analysis of just what made 4th Indian Division tick. In the context we are discussing he offers this suggestion:

> They [the Indian soldiers] loved everything about soldiering, they enjoyed showing off their prowess as marksmen, signallers, or in the exercise of the fieldcraft which came to them naturally.
> Because of this they automatically imposed on their British officers the necessity to live up to these standards.

And from that it followed that:

> The Indian's joy in soldiering not only kept his officers up to the mark but affected in precisely the same way the British regiment who served at his side. The British battalions in an Indian brigade had a compulsion to excel that was infinitely more powerful than the voice of any sergeant-major or martinet of a commanding officer.

* *The Second World War: A Short History* (76).
† *Cassino: Portrait of a Battle* (74).

From the inside, there is the view of General Tuker who commanded 4th Indian Division for over two years.*

It was a most successful mixture because each race borrowed qualities from the other, while the fortunate Divisional Commander was able to plan so that each was employed where it could exploit to the full its peculiar characteristics. One of the most valuable contributions that the Gurkha and Indian made to our British element was to set a standard of frugality so that everyone learned to expect hard times and to make the best of them. We moved light. Tommy brought among us his priceless gift of easy bonhomie. All three races of fighting men came together naturally because all were possessed in liberal measure of that unfailing catalyst—a sense of humour.

To watch them working alongside each other or sitting on the sand drinking 'char' together gave one a sense of looking upon a microcosm of our British-India wherein Indians lent spiritually to us British as much as we ever lent to them, and where both races emerged the better for their daily commerce. There was a tolerant and kindly recognition of racial differences and a cheerful exploitation of their similarities. No British, Gurkha or Indian soldier ever passed through the lines of the others at brewing-up time without being offered a place and a mug in the circle round the flickering half-petrol-tin, where Tommy-Urdu and Johnny-English made do for banter, for talk of home and for recollections of battles they had fought together. The tongues wagged and they laughed. This fellowship was the most inspiring of all worlds to live in—the world of service that each man rendered to his brother. There was, therefore, nothing strange when our British anti-tank gunners took it upon themselves to act as porters or coolies for our Gurkha and Indian infantry, humping on their backs over the crags

* In *Approach to Battle—A Commentary: Eighth Army, November 1941 to May 1943* (72).

right up to the front line the infantry's ammunition and its signal sets; and there was nothing odd when Indian infantry set to dig the gunners' emplacements for them.

The finest thing that emerged from the days of the British in India was this spirit of mutual service.

CHAPTER TWO

Growth

However high the morale of the army, the picture behind the scenes was far less reassuring. Quite shortly after the end of the First World War the Legislative Assembly of India passed a resolution defining the role of the army as being 'the defence of India against external aggression and the maintenance of internal peace and tranquillity'. As with the self-governing Dominions, any further commitments were to be for negotiation and agreement by the Assembly. Both the Indian Government and the British Government accepted the resolution, and if in the field of domestic politics it is hard to fault, it proved even harder to put into effect. To start with, the final arbiter of India's destiny was the Secretary of State in Whitehall and, resolution or no resolution, Indian troops were kept in Imperial garrisons overseas, and Indian formations were sent as reinforcements when Imperial emergencies arose. And what was meant by external aggression? For over sixty years it had been understood as the threat of invasion by Russia, moving through Afghanistan. The task of the army in India was to be no more than to delay the attack pending the arrival of Imperial reinforcements, a role for which, for some reason, a lower standard of equipment and armament was considered acceptable. With the expansion of air power it became clear that the defence of India began on the airfields of Iraq and Iran, and events were to prove that the capture of these areas was a task the Indian Army was well placed to carry out. Anyway, by 1939 the Indian Government had accepted the commitment to send troops to both the Far East and Middle East to secure areas that would contribute towards the defence of India proper.

In 1923, on the recommendation of a committee which had been reviewing the whole field of defence expenditure, the annual budget was summarily cut from £48 million to £42 million. It was a cruel blow and a setback from which the attempt to keep the army's equipment up to reasonably modern standards never recovered. In less than five years arrears amounted to as much as £8 million, and although there was a project for finding the money over a period of four years the financial crisis of 1930 put a stop to that, and a couple of years later there was a further drastic cut.

The Assembly resolution referred to reflected pretty accurately the feeling of the Indian politician. Moreover the army was recruited from classes for whom he felt little sympathy— a sentiment that was cordially reciprocated—so it is hard to blame him for failing to vote money for the modernization of an army that was being used in defiance of his wishes for purposes of which he did not approve. The British Government, which was at that time busy cutting its own armed forces to the bone, could hardly be expected to help India, and it should have surprised no one when a committee under Lord Chatfield in 1938 recommended that no less than £33 million were needed to equip the army up to modern standards, almost exactly the sum of the annual budget. The Home Government, awake at last to how serious the position really was, offered to find the money, but the offer came too late.

A random selection of a few of the things which the army was short of will give some idea of just how unfitted it was to fight a modern enemy. The cavalry regiments were still mounted on horses; the infantry had no anti-tank weapon, no mortars, no carriers and no trucks; engineer and signal units lacked up-to-date equipment, and there was a serious shortage of mechanical transport companies. It was quite normal in the early days for units going overseas to receive and learn to fight with these modern refinements on their arrival in the theatre of war; but when the history of a cavalry regiment records the receipt of their armoured cars no more than a matter of days before going into action, it will be realized how far peace-time parsimony can cost men's lives and lose the early battles of a war.

When war was declared, the leaders of the Indian National Congress, predominantly Hindu and the largest and most important political party, although by no means in favour of substituting German for British dominion over their country, declined to give their support to the war effort till they received what they considered to be a satisfactory pronouncement on the extension of self-government once the war was over. With more give and take by both sides something might have been done, but as it was they got no such pronouncement, and they held aloof. Their rivals, the Muslim League, anxious not to miss a trick, at once authorized their leader to assure the government of their support. In view of their aspirations Congress could not perhaps have been expected to do otherwise, but when one considers the months of tortuous manœuvring that went on before Independence was finally granted, it is surely clear that it was not practical politics to embark on such negotiations and try to fight a major war at one and the same time. Any pronouncement that could have been made must have been couched in the most general terms, and would have stimulated demand after demand for clarification and further concessions, the nuisance value of which would have far outweighed any advantages that might have accrued. Regrettable though it was, we did therefore fight the war without the support of the Congress Party. It is difficult to assess the result of this abstention. It certainly had an adverse effect on the recruitment of officers, particularly for the medical services. The educated were the most politically conscious and, in sympathy with the stand taken by their leaders, many who might have made good officers did not come forward.

The recruitment of officers was in fact a difficulty that could and sometimes very nearly did slow up the whole rate of expansion. It was a difficulty that might have been less formidable if there had not been such grudging progress made in the grant of the King's commission to Indians between the wars. As early as 1917 ten vacancies were reserved each term for Indians at the Royal Military College, Sandhurst, and many of these early entries rose to high rank in the armies of India and Pakistan. After the war came the opening of the Prince of Wales's Royal Military College, where those who aspired to enter Sandhurst could go to be accustomed to the rigours of the life of a gentleman cadet, but it was not until 1923 that the first step forward was taken. Two cavalry regiments and six infantry battalions were then chosen for Indianization, which meant that all newly commissioned officers posted to them would be Indians. There followed resolutions in the Assembly, and committees which reviewed the whole problem, but it was always a very long time before resolutions or recommendations were put into effect. There was an increase in the Sandhurst places, and the grant at the same time of six vacancies at Woolwich and at the Royal Air Force College at Cranwell, but it was not until after the Round Table Conference that, in 1932, the Indian Military Academy was opened in Dehra Dun. The entry for each term, thirty by competition and thirty from men already serving, was more than enough to fill the increase, announced at the same time, in the number of Indianized units, which was raised to a brigade of cavalry and an infantry division of all arms. By the outbreak of war the sum total of all this activity was that there were fewer than 500 Indian commissioned officers, while there were still nearly 3,000 British officers. The officer strength in the Indian Army averaged no more than half that in comparable units of the British service, and it is an indication of the magnitude of the problem that by the end of the war there were 8,300 Indian and 34,500 British officers.

A more liberal attitude in the years between the wars would have opened up the possibility of a military career to a wider circle of young Indians, and would surely have increased the numbers of suitable applicants for war-time commissions. As it was, the quality of those who did offer themselves was disappointing. Candidates were first interviewed under provincial arrangements, and only those thought likely to make the grade went before the military selection boards, but between them the two were rejecting as high as eighty-five per cent of the total.

There was inevitably a very severe drain on British man-power. British businessmen in the East and British units in India provided enough to meet the early needs, but over the five years the great majority of British officers came out from England, some as officers, but mostly as cadets to be trained and commissioned after arrival; and of the latter no less than one thousand young men of a very high standard came direct from the public schools. It is worth pausing to consider the difficulties these young temporary officers faced and over-came: the Indians called on to display qualities of leadership and to shoulder responsibilities for which neither upbring-ing nor education had done anything to prepare them; the British, serving in a strange land, often under appalling climatic conditions, leading men whose language and customs they were only just beginning to understand. The record of the army under their leadership is tribute alike to the resolu-tion with which they accepted the challenge, and to the sureness of the foundations built by those who went before them.

There were also plenty of problems to be solved in the recruitment of the other ranks of the army, particularly in the demands for tradesmen, and for men with sufficient intelli-gence and education for the more skilled categories. In the main, however, the difficulty was to train those who had been enlisted, and to form units from men who had been trained. It has been suggested that these difficulties were accentuated by the policy of restricting peace-time recruitment to the favoured 'martial' classes. There is truth in the claim, but it is not quite as simple as all that. The martial classes found about forty per cent of the total numbers enlisted, and they mostly went to make good wastage or raise new units in the fighting arms, where, in fact, they were best suited to serve; but this effort drained their resources and the remaining sixty per cent came from provinces and districts, mainly in Madras and Bengal, where there had been little or no enlist-ment, at any rate for very many years. This meant, in a country the size of India, that the army was taking men speaking new languages and dialects, even with new customs. The problem was to find the instructors to teach them, and then to find Viceroy's commissioned officers and N.C.O.s to form the framework of the new units. The difficulty was most acute in corps where there was most expansion, such as signals, supply and transport, and the ordnance and medical services. The argument runs that if pre-war recruiting had been on a true all-India basis it would have been easier to find both instructors and suitable leaders for the new units. The crunch comes when consideration is given to how exactly this spread-over could have been effected. Enough has been said in the opening chapter to throw doubt on the wisdom of weakening the fighting arms for no better reason than to provide cadres for the increase of the administrative services in war-time. The real weakness of the army was that it was unbalanced. For its role in peace it needed a number of fighting units of high standard operating from fixed bases; there was no call for the elaborate administrative 'tail' that modern warfare demands and, since there was not enough money to pay for both, the administrative services suffered. If the modernization programme recommended by the Chatfield Committee had had time to get under way, there might well have been an extension of the recruiting basis to fill the new units.

Napoleon rated the value of the moral to the material as three to one. If his estimate had still held good, the central and most intractable of all India's expansion problems might have been easier to tackle than it was, but unfortunately the odds had shortened considerably over the previous fifty years. India was not a manufacturing country, and the output of her ordnance factories was geared to the level at which her army was equipped, which, as has been explained, was not a very high one. There was no motor industry, and virtually no factories turning out such essentials as electrical and medical equipment. Thus, the crucial fact remained, and nothing could be done in India in war-time to alter it, that the bulk of the units raised could not be put in the field until they had received arms, vehicles and equipment from abroad; and when the necessary priorities had been established, it was a long sea voyage to India through dangerous waters from the factories in the United Kingdom, the United States and Australia. For none was frustration more bitter and prolonged than for the Indian Armoured Corps. A big tank battle in North Africa could wreck a delivery programme, and even when at long last it seemed as though an order must be fulfilled, the verdict might be that experience in battle had rendered that particular model obsolete and production had been discontinued.

In short the pace of expansion was in the last resort governed by a factor over which India had no direct control. The voice of him who cries from afar is always the one that is answered last, and on more than one occasion it was only a point-blank refusal to send units out of India until they had been properly equipped that brought about some improvement in the supply position.

Even before war was declared India had begun to honour her Imperial obligations.* During August 1939 an infantry brigade left for Malaya and another for Egypt, and the latter were followed in September by a second brigade and a divisional headquarters, to achieve fame as 4th Indian Division, The Red Eagles. It may be mentioned here, for the want of a place elsewhere, that there went to France at this time a detachment of four animal transport companies of the R.I.A.S.C., complete with their own supporting services. They returned to India in 1941 but not before their steadiness and discipline during the evacuation from Dunkirk, and later when they were stationed in the United Kingdom, had attracted the most favourable attention from all who were fortunate enough to meet them.

The dispatch of these immediate, and incidentally quite invaluable reinforcements, virtually exhausted India's reserves of modern equipment: the ball was now in the other court. Were these troops to be replaced by fresh raisings? Would further formations then be needed overseas, and if so, what prospects were there of getting the necessary equipment? If these questions were in fact ever addressed to the

* An outline Order of Battle of the Indian Army is given at Appendix B.

British Government, it seems that no satisfactory reply was ever received. Against the general background of apathy that hung over England in the first nine months of the war, the view may well have been taken that any encouragement given to India to replace or expand would have provoked demands for equipment; equipment that just was not there to be given.

Apathy is one thing, positive discouragement is quite a different story, and although it matters not whence or how the rumour started the lamentable truth is that in the opening months of the war it was commonly said, up and down India, that the Indian Army would never be needed to fight the Germans in Europe. There was no general mobilization; no general recall of reservists; recruits, and there was no lack of them, were turned away with tokens for their call-up if they should ever be needed. Only an army with truly resilient morale could have recovered from these initial disappointments; but if the army never lost heart, it lost nearly a year of valuable time.

With no incentive to break fresh ground, Army Headquarters seem to have filled in time by taking a new look at an old problem, the North-West Frontier. By the surprise treaty of August 1939 Germany and Russia were now allies, and it was at least reasonable to suppose that the latter might feel free to stir up trouble in Afghanistan. Accordingly, a plan was sent to the War Office in May 1940 suggesting that one armoured and five infantry divisions be raised to meet this contingency. The effort would absorb all India's resources till the following spring when, if these formations were not needed for the purpose for which they were to be raised, they would be offered for service overseas. The infantry divisions were accepted, and by mid 1941 had all gone overseas, but the first hint of disappointment in store for the Armoured Corps came with the refusal of the offer of the armoured division on the grounds that the supply of the necessary tanks would interfere with the armament programme at home.

A further examination in March 1941, with the threat to Afghanistan unresolved and the truculence of Japan increased, made it clear that there must be further expansion, and steps were taken to raise one more armoured and four more infantry divisions. They were to be ready in 1942, and the War Office gratefully accepted the conditional offer to make them available for employment overseas.

Once again this meant that they had to be replaced, and planning began to raise one more armoured and four more infantry divisions. However, the entry of Japan into the war, and the premature dispatch of troops under training to Malaya and Burma, brought the whole programme under review. The project for this third reinforcement of four divisions had been embarked on in all good faith, but the strain was proving too much. Brigades and divisions were taking shape on the ground but they were a very long way from being ready to go to war.

It was very clear that any fresh raising in terms of divisions was out of the question. The formation of an airborne division was put on the stocks against the day when there might be brigades available, but plans for a third armoured division were abandoned as there was no prospect of armour to equip it. For all that, 1942 and 1943 saw the raising of a vast host of non-divisional units destined for the lines of communication in Burma. In 1943, also, two demands were met that imposed a drain on India's slender resources of specialized manpower: General Wingate's Special Force, and the headquarters of South-East Asia Command. The Corps of Indian Electrical and Mechanical Engineers was formed, and the various medical services were consolidated into the Indian Army Medical Corps.

The only new arrival of the years 1944–45 was the airborne division which after some vicissitudes was incorporated into Ist Airborne Corps on 1 August 1945.

With supplies of acceptable manpower running low, the record of these last two years is one of the maintenance, consolidation and improvement of what had already been done; and it was no mean achievement either. By August 1945 just over two million men had enlisted in the army.

Every one of them was a volunteer.

CHAPTER THREE

North Africa

August 1939–December 1940

The Italian colonial province of Libya, consisting of Tripolitania on the west and Cyrenaica on the east, extended from the frontier with French Tunisia, about 100 miles west of Tripoli, to just short of Sollum in Egypt, a stretch of some 750 miles as the crow flies; and from Sollum to Alexandria is another 250 miles. As a point of geographical accuracy, only this last stretch could strictly be called the Western Desert, though once war began the term was applied generally to the whole vast battlefield that extended up to about 150 miles south of Benghazi, the high water-mark of our first two attempts to drive the Italians and Germans out of North Africa. The salient feature, which had a dominating influence on all the fighting, was that there was only one through line of communication, a metalled road that followed the general line of the coast: there was a rather one-horse railway from Alexandria to Matruh, about 130 miles short of Sollum; there were good harbours at Tripoli and Benghazi, and rather less good ones at Tobruk and Sollum.

The security of Egypt as a base of operations was at the mercy of a veritable tide-rip of political cross-currents, whose direction and intensity were never constant. In Egypt itself nationalist feeling was strong, and under a treaty signed in 1936 our troops were being withdrawn to the Canal Zone. Alexandria was of considerable importance as being the only port on the Mediterranean east of Malta that could be used as a naval base. In war Egypt was to be our ally, but the degree of her enthusiasm for our cause would wax and wane as rival politicians came to power, and according to the success or otherwise of our armies fighting elsewhere.

Against attack by the Italians from the west there was only one definite defensive position, later to become famous as Alamein, which was a truly formidable obstacle if we had the troops to man it; in practice it was the length of the enemy's lines of communication which effectively ruled out an advance into the Nile Delta. The long Libyan coast line, with the Italian mainland to the north, flanked our sea lanes through the Mediterranean, and very much reduced the value of Malta as a naval base. On the other hand, while the French were still in the war the Italians had to keep a considerable army watching their western frontier with Tunisia. To the south of Egypt lay the Sudan and, beyond that, Eritrea and Abyssinia, both in Italian hands. To the northeast was Palestine where our mandate still ran, and where we had nearly two divisions of infantry committed to keeping the peace between Arab and Jew. East from there were Iraq and Iran, the source of so much of our oil; to the north, Syria, where there were two French divisions ready to move to the defence of Egypt; ready, that is, till the fall of France, when Syria became just one more headache for the commander-in-chief in the Middle East. North again was neutral Turkey, the very keystone in the arch of our defences against a German move through the Balkans, or a Russian threat to the Caucasus; and beyond Turkey, Greece.

In June 1939 the post of General Officer Commanding in Chief, Middle East, was created, and General Wavell* came out to fill it with instructions 'to take command forthwith of the troops in Egypt, the Sudan, Palestine, Transjordan and Cyprus. He was to prepare plans for them and for any troops in Iraq, Aden, British Somaliland and the Persian Gulf. He was to collaborate, as necessary, with the French, the

---

* The late Field Marshal Earl Wavell, G.C.B., G.C.S.I., G.C.I.E., C.M.G. M.C.

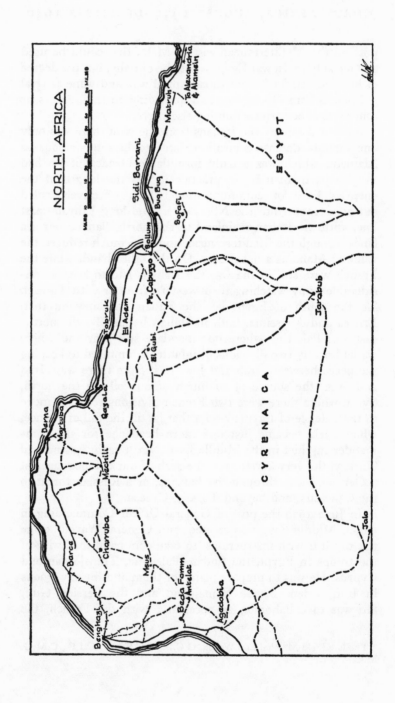

Egyptians and any other allies'. He found that the accepted policy of trying to keep Italy out of the war for as long as possible, with the inevitable attitude of falling over backwards to avoid giving offence, bred a defensive approach to all plans and preparations, and he at once ordered his commanders to think ahead to the day when there might be troops available to take the offensive.

By the end of the year the troops he could expect to have available for active operations consisted of the Mobile Division, later 7th Armoured, formed in 1938 from units already in Egypt; 4th Indian Division, less one brigade still in India, which had arrived after the outbreak of war; and 16th British Infantry Brigade from Palestine. There were a lot more British troops, mostly infantry, in Palestine, Egypt and the Sudan, but they were tied up on internal security tasks, and protecting docks, railways and base installations. 4th Indian Division, which was to become famous under its sign of the Red Eagle, was a reinforcement of particular value as it provided a fighting headquarters for the conduct of operations in the field.

The first brigades of the Australian and New Zealand divisions reached Egypt in February 1940 and moved off to training areas; the second convoy disembarked in May, but when the third contingent sailed in that same month it was not considered safe to pass it through the Red Sea, and the convoy was diverted to the United Kingdom; the missing brigades did not rejoin their divisions till some months later.

After the fall of France it was for some time not certain what would be the attitude of the forces in her colonial possessions. In the end, of course, our hopes came to nothing and we were left alone, sandwiched between two large Italian armies, one in Libya, the other in Eritrea.

The overall strength of the Italian forces in Libya was known with some accuracy to be nine regular divisions, three Blackshirt divisions, and two divisions of Libyan national troops, but there was some doubt as to the distribution between *5th Army* facing the French in Tripolitania and *10th Army* deployed in Cyrenaica against ourselves. They were thought to be up to strength though there were large numbers of recruits; the artillery and tanks were below the best modern standards, and they were short of transport which, in view of the length of the lines of communication, was a real weakness. Except among the Blackshirts, morale was probably not very high.

By August 1940 the troops in the Western Desert amounted to 7th Armoured Division, consisting of two armoured brigades and a support group which had been there for some time, and 4th Indian Division with two of its own brigades and 16th (British) Infantry Brigade. The third Indian brigade, the 7th, arrived in September and at the same time, from the U.K., came a most invaluable reinforcement, 7th Battalion, The Royal Tank Regiment. Troops moving into the desert found little

of the traditional soft, burning sand of the Sahara, save in the Great Sand Sea far to the south. But there were vast stretches of hard sand and of stony ground raddled with black basaltic slabs; there were bony ridges and ribbed escarpments and deep depressions; there were flat pans which held water after the rains, where gazelles cropped the coarse grass in midsummer. There were wadi-fed flats which sprang overnight into flowery glory in the spring; there were endless undulating sand and gravel dunes whose crests marched in rhythm, like waves at sea.

To the tyro these wastes held no landmarks, but desertworthy soldiers used their compasses only to check their navigation. They steered by the *birs*, the curious cisterns of antiquity, the *alems*, the Senussi direction cairns, the *gabirs*, the reputed tombs, the *ghots*, the circular potholes and the *mengers*, the kopje-like mounds which the mirage sometimes lifted into mid-air. These features gave the desert character and, harsh habitation though it remained, there are few who lived and fought there who have not forgotten its worst and remembered its best. On many it cast a spell that did not pass. The days of burning heat and intolerable glare, while the mirage blocked the horizon with Braille-like formations;

the cool dark nights with the incomparable pageant of the heavens wheeling overhead; the choking sandstorms, the marrow-sucking *khamsins*, the intolerable pestilence of flies, the clammy fingers of the night mists, all played their part in moulding the character of the desert soldier. Skins might burn, lips might crack, eyeballs might sear, throats might parch, but amid the sandy wastes life flowed with riotous vigour.*

On the outbreak of war our information was that the frontier posts from Bardia down through Capuzzo to the oasis of Jarabub were lightly held but were being reinforced, and that there were two divisions behind them moving forward. From the very beginning a policy of the utmost aggression was adopted, consistent with the size of our forces and the state of their equipment and vehicles. The Western Desert Force was ordered to dominate the frontier, cut the enemy's communications with Jarabub, and, by the selection of a wide variety of objectives, to puzzle and harass the enemy. They crossed the frontier on the night of 11 June 1940 and discovered that the voice of Mussolini calling his people to war from the balcony of the Palazzo Venetia had not carried as far as the troops in the front line; the outposts were taken by surprise. Three days later we captured Capuzzo and Maddalena, though the former was shortly afterwards retaken. But the results of these forays, which were all the work of 7th Armoured Division, went far beyond the immediate gains. We had acquired invaluable experience and shown that we could use the desert to our advantage, whereas the enemy seemed reluctant to venture away from roads and tracks, and we succeeded in giving him an exaggerated impression of our numbers. However, by the middle of July the wear and tear of all this activity was beginning to have a serious effect on vehicles, which had been very far from new when the war started and, to conserve our strength for a counter-stroke in case the enemy attacked, it was decided to draw in our horns.

* *Fourth Indian Division* (21).

About the same time Mussolini, who had been expressing dissatisfaction with the excuses for inaction reaching him from Graziani, gave orders that, preparations completed or not, the marshal was to move forwards on the day that German troops set foot in England. On 7 September, impatient of the tardiness of his ally, he issued a peremptory order that the advance was to begin on the ninth.

The enemy's air activity began to increase appreciably, and:

> Early on the 13th September a spectacular artillery barrage opened on Musaid, which the enemy then proceeded to occupy. This was followed by heavy shelling of the airfield and empty barracks at Sollum, and when the dust had cleared the enemy was disclosed to the westward with his motor-cycles, light tanks, and other vehicles drawn up as if on parade awaiting the order to advance.
>
> . . . The enemy's close formation presented excellent targets to the artillery and air, but it was not long before the 1st Libyan Division was in possession of the barracks and was beginning to trickle down the escarpment towards Sollum.*

Without allowing our rearguards to become engaged, we succeeded by tactics of opportunity in inflicting considerable casualties as we withdrew, and eventually his advance ground to a standstill on a line running south from Sidi Barrani. The triumphant tone of his broadcasts at first gave the impression that a further advance was imminent, but it soon became clear that he had halted to build up stocks, and that an attack in the immediate future was improbable.

As early as 11 September, just before the Italians advanced, General Wavell initiated a study of the problem of our advancing into Cyrenaica. In the first instance it was directed at the preparation of a plan for a devastating counter-attack should the enemy move on Matruh, but as the weeks passed

---

* *History of the Second World War: Mediterranean & Middle East*, Vol. I (1).

it became clear that there was no need to wait for the enemy to move before attacking him; the problem then became how to make a long approach march across the desert and attack one or more of the chain of defended camps that he was constructing on a line running forty miles south-west from Sidi Barrani. The proposal was at first for a short, sharp attack followed by the withdrawal of most of the forces to railhead but, as the details were developed and confidence in the superiority of our own troops increased, the plan expanded considerably.

As so often happens, the first problems to be solved, and the first steps to be taken, were administrative. The battle would be fought 100 miles from railhead at Matruh, and there just was not the transport to lift the troops forward and keep up a daily maintenance run of that length. It was accordingly decided to establish two dumps forward in the desert about forty miles short of the enemy positions; each was to hold five days' supplies and an equivalent stock of ammunition and petrol, and great care had to be taken to conceal their existence from those who must not know they were there, and their purpose from those who did. The ability and willingness of our troops to live and fight hard may be gauged from the fact that the accepted basis for the operation was that they must be ready to operate non-stop for four days and expect up to fifty per cent casualties, while the reserve of water for the whole operation amounted to one gallon for each man.

A great deal of thought was naturally given to the actual method of attack. Valuable tactical lessons had already been learnt, but there had been no test of attack on a strongly held perimeter camp, nor had the 'I' tanks been used in the desert. To try out these methods, a training exercise was held at the end of November with objectives marked on the ground that were replicas, though few knew it, of the positions to be assaulted.

By then General Wavell was so well satisfied with the progress made that, although the administrative plan provided for operations lasting no longer than five days, he was expressing his belief that 'an opportunity might occur for converting the enemy's defeat into an outstanding victory'. 'I do not entertain extravagant hopes of this operation,' he wrote, 'but I do wish to make certain that if a big opportunity occurs, we are prepared morally, mentally and administratively, to use it to the full.' (1)

Starting on the coast, the enemy defences consisted of a large camp at Maktila, some fifteen miles east of Sidi Barrani, garrisoned by a Libyan division with a large number of guns and some tanks. There was then a gap to a group of camps manned by another Libyan division; pt 90, Tummar East and Tummar West. Just to the south lay Nibeiwa, the strongest of them all, held by the Maletti Mobile Group totalling some 4,000 men and a battalion of medium tanks. Twenty miles to the south-west, across the Bir Enba gap, was a further group of camps on the escarpment based on the old Egyptian frontier cantonment of Sofafi. Patrols reported that 'all these camps swarmed with busy workers, erecting entanglements, digging trenches and dugouts, emplacing guns and constructing vehicle shelters'. There were perhaps three more divisions disposed behind, in Sidi Barrani and between there and Sollum. Thus, seven enemy divisions, albeit weak ones, were about to be attacked by one infantry division, 4th Indian, supported by 7th Battalion, Royal Tanks, 7th Armoured Division, and a column made up from the garrison of Matruh which was to move on Maktila to prevent troops from there taking any part in the fight going on to the south. 4th Indian Division moved at dawn on 6 December and, when they halted next day, were told that this was the real thing. They remained well dispersed in the desert about thirty miles south-west of Matruh, and on 8 December made a long move of sixty miles to a rendezvous only fifteen miles from Nibeiwa. Further to the south-west from there was the armoured division whose role in the battle was to move into the Bir Enba gap and prevent any reinforcements from Sofafi, or the direction of Sollum, from taking part in the fighting. During the night of 8–9 December, the Royal Navy bombarded Maktila and Sidi Barrani.

The first objective was the camp at Nibeiwa, a rough rectangle of between one and one and a half miles, protected by a perimeter wall with a tank obstacle of a bank and ditch.

It was known that mines had been laid, but as the enemy supply lorries were in the habit of entering the camp at the north-west corner a patrol was sent to verify that this entrance was, in fact, clear. Acting on their report, a final rendezvous six and a half miles south-west of Nibeiwa was chosen, leaving one battalion on the eastern face to engage the enemy's attention and persuade him that the attack was coming from that direction.

The attack was made by 11th Brigade.

> . . . the divisional artillery began to register. Simultaneously the British armour moved forward with a battery of 25 Field Regiment under command. Only then did the Italians come to life, rushing to man their weapons. It was too late: rank on rank of tanks came rolling out of the desert, with Bren carriers out-riding on their flanks, their machine-guns uptilted in high angle fire. Gathering momentum as it closed, this modern commando charge thundered into the north-western gap in the defence.
>
> The rush won home with unexpected ease. No guns had been laid to cover the western approaches to Nibeiwa, the perimeter in that sector was unmined, the ramps and ditches easily negotiable. The heavily armoured British tanks burst upon the Italian light and medium tanks in leaguer outside the perimeter, while they were warming up their engines. Within minutes the British tanks smashed them to scrap metal; billows of black smoke arose. . . . Frightened, dazed or desperate Italians erupted from tents or slit trenches, some to surrender supinely, others to leap gallantly into battle, hurling grenades or blazing machine guns in futile belabour of the impregnable invaders. Italian artillerymen gallantly swung their pieces on to the advancing monsters.
>
> Fifteen minutes after the tanks struck the camp, a shout over the radio: 'CAMERONS—GO!' The Highlanders' carrier platoon shot ahead . . . the infantry tumbled out and raced in hotfoot with the bayonet; above the noise of battle shrilled the skirl of the pipes as

the gravely pacing pipers played in the charge. . . .
1/6th Rajputana Rifles, riding hard to the hunt, followed
in, passed through the Camerons, and began to mop up
in the northern and eastern expanses of the camp. Here
and there brave or hysterical handfuls refused the
summons and fought till shot down, but within an hour
resistance was over. Some hundreds of dead and wounded
lay among the debris and litter; more than 4,000 prisoners,
including 80 officers, huddled in sullen and shaken
groups. 23 tanks, together with some scores of lorries and
guns, represented material captures. (21)

5th Brigade had been waiting for the success of this first
assult to move on Tummar West when 3rd Battalion 1st
Punjab Regiment took part in the attack.

Artillery concentrations began at 1.35 p.m. Twenty
minutes later the infantry tanks penetrated the camp,
followed by 1st Battalion Royal Fusiliers, who cleared
the first half of it. The Third debussed 500 yards away
from the camp and followed, preceded by the carrier
platoon, to capture the other half of the fortification.
Much greater resistance was met in this half of the
camp, but all went well till the troops reached the
north-eastern and south-eastern corners, where a stubborn resistance was encountered. The situation was
further complicated by the fact that they had taken over
2,000 prisoners and men had to be detached to guard
them.*

Just as the north-eastern corner was being cleared an
Italian column of six light tanks followed by a considerable
infantry force launched a counter-attack, part of which
reached the south-eastern corner of the camp where it was
repulsed by the machine-guns of 1st Battalion Northumber-
land Fusiliers and the headquarters of 3rd Battalion. The
attack cost the Italians over 400 casualties.

* *The First Punjabis* (51).

During this action Havildar Kalyan Singh won a well-merited Indian Order of Merit for rescuing the machine-gun from his blazing carrier, and showed great daring in helping his platoon commander by leading his crew and gun into action against an enemy strong point.

The battle of Sidi Barrani was not yet over. Although the Italian counter-attack had been defeated, the attack on Tummar East which was to follow was delayed and the Italians made good use of this respite to retire to pt 90. An attempt to obtain the unconditional surrender of the garrison there having failed, 'the battalion at 2 p.m. on the eleventh, supported by five infantry tanks, advanced in skirmishing order and arrived at pt 90 to find 2,000 Libyans lined up with kit-bags and suit cases packed for travel'. (51) Honour had been satisfied.

This affair at pt 90 was in fact the final action in the clearing up of the whole system of camps north of the Bir Enba gap. The day before 16th Brigade had been directed against Sidi Barrani, and, by nightfall, with some assistance from 11th Hussars of the armoured division, all resistance had been wiped out.

There remained only the Sofafi camps, away to the south, to be dealt with, and on the afternoon of the eleventh the two Indian brigades were ordered to concentrate close on Nibeiwa in preparation for a night advance. By 10 p.m. the division was on the move but at the last moment the news arrived that the enemy had fled.

> This last manœuvre was probably the most brilliant performed by the division; without a single written order, after three days of continuous fighting and moving in a thick duststorm, the units disengaged themselves from the aftermath of a battle, replenished with petrol, food and water, and moved through the dark for 25 miles over previously unreconnoitred country.*

Summarizing the results of the battle, the official history

---

* *The Tiger Strikes: India's Fight in the Middle East* (15).

comments that 'to the 4th Indian Division the operation had several novel features, yet the confidence and enthusiasm of the troops, when they had learnt what they had to do, could not have been greater. The execution of the plan bore witness to sound training and good leadership, and to a fine fighting spirit in the troops'. (1)

The divisional history allows itself a little more colour. 'It was a tonic such as the free peoples craved. . . . Nowhere was its effect more profound than in the United States . . . "The Old Country is in there, pitching!" exulted Walter Winchell, the most widely read of columnists. . . . American correspondents poured in spate into Cairo.' (21)

In their own short history 7th Armoured Division, with characteristic brevity, covered the battle in a single sentence: 'After a short action against Italian artillery in the sandhills in which one squadron of 3 Hussars suffered heavily, being caught in a salt marsh in front of the enemy guns, acres of Italians surrendered.'

Fourth Indian Division does not allow such modesty to pass.

It was 7th Armoured Division which reconnoitred the camps minutely and found the entrances and weak spots on the perimeters. It was 7th Armoured Division that cordoned the battlefield and held reinforcements from the hapless enemy garrisons. Fourth Indian Division feel also that their bays should be shared in full by 7th Royal Tank Regiment, whose magnificent work in the van of the advance proved a decisive feature in the battle. (21)

The troop-carrying transport had been provided by the New Zealand division, the start of a long and friendly association in battle.

As early as the eleventh, General Wavell had decided to go ahead with the plan he had had in mind to withdraw 4th Indian Division and send it to reinforce General Platt in the Sudan. When it became clear that the attacks on the Sofafi area were no longer necessary, the division was withdrawn to the camps from which it had started the operations, and four days later was concentrated near Cairo. Its place was taken by

6th Australian Division which in the next six weeks, in co-operation with 7th Armoured Division, completed the rout of the Italian armies with all the dash and fire with which it had been begun.

CHAPTER FOUR

Italian East Africa

4th Indian Division pulled out from their lightning campaign in the Western Desert just in time to move 1,250 miles to the eastern frontier of the Sudan where, side by side with 5th Indian Division, the Ball of Fire, they were to fight the one seriously contested battle that was the turning point in the campaign that led to the eviction of the Italians from the Horn of Africa.

Starting in a small way in 1870, with the lease by a private shipping company of a coaling station at the southern end of the Red Sea, Eritrea was, by 1890, established as an Italian colony, duly proclaimed by royal decree. Shortly afterwards it was promoted to the dignity of a Province of Italian East Africa. There was inevitably contact, and conflict, with Abyssinia, just emerging from the mists of time. She was an elusive country to treat with as successive rulers could not be counted on to honour agreements made by their predecessors. It was in 1896, in an attempt to enforce a treaty, that the Italians suffered an ignominious defeat at Adowa, where 4,600 white and 3,000 colonial troops were cut to pieces.

Nothing daunted, they persisted over the next thirty-five years in their attempts to secure concessions and extend their stake in the country. In 1923, Abyssinia joined the League of Nations and, under the mistaken impression that having joined the club he would be secure against the more unscrupulous of his fellow members, the Emperor felt strong enough to resist further Italian demands, which by 1933 were becoming totally unacceptable. At the end of 1934 there occurred the carefully engineered geographical dispute over the obscure village of Wal-Wal on the Eritrean border. After nine months of protracted reference to the League, a period that gave Italy time to concentrate her forces for attack, she invaded the country. Even by the most ruthless air attacks and the use of poison gas she took seven months to reach the capital, Addis Ababa, and was then still a very long way from having conquered the country as a whole. She was forced to maintain there a large standing army for internal security, and the Draconian measures resorted to did not in fact achieve their purpose. A number of Italian settler families were sent out, after the traditional Roman pattern, but the fair prospects held out to them were far from being realized.

The position in September 1939, therefore, was that, with the exception of the two narrow coastal strips of British and French Somaliland, the Italians were established, albeit none too securely, in a sprawling empire that covered the whole of the north-eastern corner of Africa. Taking the most optimistic view, the best we could hope to do would be to contain them within the boundaries of their empire, encourage in every way the activities of Patriots and guerillas, and leave them to die of inanition. But it would be a lingering death, and would make protracted demands not so much on our fighting troops as on our always meagre resources of transport, petrol and air support.

There would, moreover, be one detachment of their armed forces which we could not afford to ignore: in the harbour of Massawa the Italian Navy had a force of eight submarines and seven fleet destroyers. Operating against our lines of communication through the Red Sea, they would threaten the passage of reinforcements from India, and of convoys from the United Kingdom routed round the Cape. Nor was that all. Because of this threat, the Red Sea had been declared a 'combat zone', closed to American merchantmen carrying lease-lend materials to the Middle East.

It had, therefore, always been accepted that at the earliest

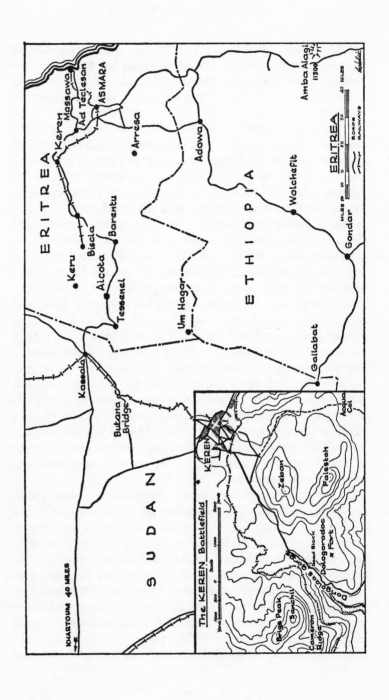

opportunity we should have to capture Massawa and gain control of sufficient depth of territory in Eritrea and Abyssinia to deny to the enemy the airfields from which he could attack convoys in the Red Sea. On the assumption that we should have the support of our allies, the operation was to be based on Jibuti, in French Somaliland, and to ensure that Jibuti would still be there when we could find the troops to attack Massawa, we decided that we would resist any attack on British Somaliland that might be made before we were ready.

On the fall of France General Legentilhomme, the commander of the troops in French Somaliland, announced that he would fight on in the allied cause, and it seemed at first that he could count on the support of his colleagues and brother officers. However, under pressure from home and from the Italian armistice commission, they turned against him, and on 5 August he was forced to withdraw to Aden, though not before his delaying tactics had won us a valuable breathing space.

The French contingent in Somaliland which would have been available amounted to seven battalions with some artillery, tanks and armoured cars, a total of about 7,000 men; not a very large army, but in the circumstances a serious loss, and we had to decide whether or not to fight. There was little hope of preventing the enemy from capturing the port of Berbera, if he chose to attack, but General Wavell felt that, rather than withdraw and leave the way clear, we should put up some show of resistance, and agreed that he could make available the five battalions which the local commander considered to be the minimum to give a reasonable chance of making a fight of it. When the force came to be mustered it consisted of two African battalions from East Africa with a section of pack artillery, a contingent of the local camel corps, two Indian battalions from Aden and, to round off the language problem, a battalion of the Black Watch, General Wavell's old battalion.

The Italians put into the field three Italian and twenty-three colonial battalions, twenty-one batteries of artillery, perhaps thirty tanks of different sorts, some armoured cars and fifty-seven aircraft.

It is bare waterless country, the stony hillsides covered in places with scrub and small thorny trees, but there was one position which the enemy had to attack, the point where the only good road to Berbera passed through a low range of hills. The extent was far too wide for there to be any depth to the defences, but as the Italians attacked they suffered very heavy casualties before our companies were forced to withdraw. It was reported that the Italian white troops could be seen, emulating if not improving on the tactics of the Duke of Plaza Toro, moving well in rear of the colonial battalions whom they kept up to scratch by picking off laggards with rifle fire. Their first attack was made on 11 August and on the seventeenth the enemy were in contact with the last rearguard position some eight miles back. Here they were so roughly handled by counter-attacks made by The Black Watch that the embarkation at Berbera was completed on the eighteenth without interference, and when the Italians arrived there the next day the town was empty.

The news of yet one more defeat, this time at the hands of the Italians, no doubt made bad reading in the morning papers at home, but the fact remains that this resounding victory cost them over 3,000 casualties, and an expenditure of precious war material that could have been used to better purpose later on.

The Italians now held uninterrupted control of the coast line from the southern frontier of the Sudan on the Red Sea to the northern limit of Kenya, facing the Indian Ocean. Under the terms of the armistice, the French were obliged to allow them the use of the harbour and port of Jibuti and of the French section of the railway running to Addis Ababa. They had plenty of troops. There were twenty-nine colonial brigades with two pack artillery batteries attached to each, and seventeen independent colonial battalions. In these, the officers and senior N.C.O.s were Italians. There were sixteen Italian battalions of high quality, Bersaglieri, Carabinieri and Savoy Grenadiers, and ten groups of Italian artillery.

The infantry were supported by a hundred armoured cars, sixty tanks, and close on two hundred aircraft. But there were limitations. The army was in the country primarily for purposes of internal security, a fact which the inhabitants did not allow them to forget; the colonial troops, when they stood to fight, fought magnificently, but they were only recently raised and, if they could be manœuvred into a withdrawal, they would lose heart. Above all, there was the precarious supply position: what they had, they had, and when it was gone there was no replacement.

When Italy came into the war our forces on the western and southern borders of this mighty Italian empire were very small. In the Sudan were three battalions of British infantry, stationed for the protection of Khartoum, Atbara and Port Sudan, while the Sudan Defence Force, totalling some 9,000 men, was watching 1,200 miles of frontier. In the south in Kenya there were two East African brigades, two West African brigades had just arrived by sea, and one South African brigade, forerunner of 1st South African Division, was near Nairobi. The standard of training was low, there was no field headquarters higher than a brigade to control operations, and until these deficiencies were made good there was little prospect of taking the offensive.

By the end of August, the position in the Sudan had improved considerably. The Emperor of Abyssinia had flown in to Khartoum, and a mission was on its way into the country to reconnoitre a plan to raise Patriot forces which would rally the inhabitants to his standard. 5th Indian Division had been assembling in India for a move to Iraq to protect our interests in the Iranian oilfields, but after the move had been ordered the chiefs of staff decided that there were better uses for the division elsewhere. It was accordingly sent to Port Sudan and from there moved south to the Sudanese frontier east of Khartoum. There were only two infantry brigades, each of three Indian battalions, and the three British battalions already in the Sudan were drafted into the division which then had three brigades each of one British and two Indian battalions.

One of these brigades was held in reserve in the Port Sudan area. With the other two, the divisional commander was given the task of preventing an Italian advance on Khartoum on a line extending a mere 200 miles north from Gallabat. 10th Brigade was in the south watching Gallabat,

9th Brigade about Butana Bridge was watching Kassala. With so few troops to watch so great a front, the obvious course was to strike at the enemy's initiative by convincing him that we were in much greater force than was in fact the case, and the task was given to Gazelle force. A group of Sudan Defence Force machine-gun companies, carried in 15 cwt Fords, had been employed on a mobile role in the Kassala area, and they were now reinforced by Skinner's Horse, the 5th divisional 'cavalry' regiment, mounted in 15 cwt Chevrolets, a battery of field artillery, and perhaps a couple of companies of lorry-borne infantry, depending on the task in hand. The base of operations was the Gash delta, a trackless waste of high grass north of Kassala. Gazelle was commanded by Colonel Messervy.*

'Gazelle' was a misnomer for that fleet-footed animal of the desert, which is essentially a timid creature, whereas the 'Gazelle' as welded and wielded by Messervy had the cunning and ferocity of a man-eating leopard. Messervy was charged with the task of dominating the 'Gash' delta and deceiving the enemy. In both respects he succeeded admirably. By great mobility, daring, and an enterprise that often amounted to impudence, Gazelle Force led the Italians to believe that at least two divisions faced them—there were scarcely more than a thousand men. Messervy's columns harassed and ambushed enemy maintenance convoys, and raided behind Italian outposts—the Sudan Defence Force officers' mess supplied itself with fresh fruit and vegetables from Italian gardens in Kassala itself. Characteristic of their day-to-day achievements was the rounding up of a party that was repairing the telephone line from Kassala to Tesenei; when a small enemy force came out to search for the missing line party, it, too, was destroyed.†

Early in November, 10th Indian Infantry Brigade attacked

---

* General Sir Frank Messervy, K.C.S.I., K.B.E., C.B., D.S.O.
† *Ball of Fire: The Fifth Indian Division in the Second World War* (22).

Gallabat in the Sudan with the object of recapturing the fort, and also the village of Metemma which lay on the far side of a dry river bed with steep banks. The two Indian battalions of the brigade captured the fort, but the tanks supporting them suffered heavy casualties from boulders hidden in the long grass; at the same time the R.A.F., who had been operating from forward airstrips, met enemy machines of very much superior performance and lost two thirds of their fighter strength. The enemy was then free to bomb the fort at his leisure and in the face of repeated heavy attacks it was decided to withdraw to a position affording some cover three miles back. Even though the operation did not achieve its declared object, the Italians were unable to reoccupy the fort and the news that they had been engaged by forces with modern equipment had an encouraging effect on the Patriots.

On 1 December General Wavell held a conference of his senior commanders. General Cunningham in Kenya was ordered to advance on his right up to the Somaliland border in readiness to capture Kismayu in May when the rains were over; on his left he was to operate in the Lake Rudolf area to encourage the Patriots in southern Abyssinia. General Platt in the Sudan was to capture Kassala preliminary to an advance directed on Asmara. 4th Indian Division was, of course, completely committed to the forthcoming operations in the Western Desert, but it is characteristic of the more favourable outlook that General Wavell was even then planning to move it at the end of the month to reinforce 5th Division for the battle in the incredibly difficult country that lay ahead.

> Seven thousand feet up among the mountains lies Asmara, the capital, a town with a pleasant equable climate and more than 70,000 Italian inhabitants. On the coastal plain is Massawa, a well-developed and strongly defended port and one of the hottest places on earth. . . . There is only one railway in Eritrea, of a gauge different to any other in the world. From Massawa this line climbs the 7,000 feet to Asmara and thence drops down 5,000 feet to Agordat. The only road from the plateau down to

the western plains is at Keren, where road and railway wriggle their way through a narrow gorge into a long valley. To the traveller in the days of camel and mule transport the plateau seemed as remote and impregnable as a fastness of the gods, for the mountains rise like a great wall, grim and even threatening in the barrier they present. Between these mountains and the Sudan frontier lies an arid, almost waterless desert; dusty, flat ground lying between precipitous hills, covered with gaunt thorn scrub and tamarisk in the wadi beds, down which for three months in the year tear wild torrents to lose themselves in the sand. The climate even in the winter is hot, while in the summer it is almost unbearable. (21)

Kassala is a focal point of communications and while it remained in enemy hands we were denied the use of the direct railway line from Port Sudan for the maintenance of our forces. From the Sudanese frontier, running east from Kassala, there were two roads; a good road, the Via Imperiale, through Tessenei, Aicota and Barentu to Agordat, Keren and on to Asmara; and an indifferent dry-weather track, through Keru to Biscia, which was the western terminus of the railway. There was a cross track from Aicota to Biscia. From Gallabat there is a very much longer approach to Asmara passing through equally difficult country, via Gondar, Wolchefit and Adowa.

The original date for the attack on Kassala had been fixed for 8 February but, by early January, 4th Division had arrived from Egypt, moving by sea, river, rail and road, the news of their victory at Sidi Barrani had gone before them and it was felt that the enemy might be starting to withdraw. It was accordingly decided to advance the date to 19 January when it was thought the enemy might be caught on the move. 4th Division, with Gazelle Force under its command, was ordered to capture Sabderat on the northern road and to press on to Keru as soon as the supply situation allowed; 5th Division was to secure Aicota and then be ready to move east on Barentu, or north-east on Biscia.

But by the eighteenth the bird had flown, and on the

following day 4th Division, with Gazelle in the van, was hot
on their trail. During the afternoon contact was made with
the Italian rearguards forty miles away, but they slipped
away during the night, and the following evening Gazelle was
held up short of Keru where the track passed through a
narrow gorge with commanding heights on either side. It
was while the force commander was considering the position
early next morning that there occurred the only cavalry charge
of the African campaign.

> . . . a nearby patch of scrub erupted. With shrill yells a
> squadron of Eritrean horsemen, 60 in number, raced on
> the gun positions in front of Gazelle Force Headquarters.
> Kicking their shaggy ponies to a furious gallop, the
> cavalrymen rose in their stirrups to hurl small percussion
> grenades ahead of them. With great gallantry they
> surged on, but the gunners manned their pieces in time
> to blow back the horsemen from the muzzles of the guns.
> Clerks and orderlies opened fire from slit trenches and
> from under thorn bushes; a troop of Skinner's Horse
> joined the scrimmage, thrusting the audacious intruders
> from the camp. Only a handful of the raiders regained
> the shelter of the scrub. 25 dead and 16 wounded were
> left on the ground. (21)

The infantry of the leading brigade was called forward to
deal with the opposition but it was not until after dark, over
thirty-six hours later, that a patrol reported that the enemy
were thinning out, and by dawn next morning the hills were
clear. In fact, success was due not so much to the frontal
attack as to the approach of the brigade of 5th Division from
the south which threatened their line of withdrawal.

Two brigades of 5th Division had reached Aicota without
much difficulty; from there the leading brigade was ordered
to advance direct on Barentu, while the other turned north-
east along the track to Biscia to outflank the enemy who were
holding out at Keru. 4th Division now passed through Biscia
and on to Agordat, while, its task completed, 10th Brigade
turned back to take part in the battle of Barentu, coming down

from the north. The hills guarding the town were occupied by most of *2nd Colonial Division*, and despite the converging attacks they fought with great tenacity.

The commander of one of the leading companies of the Highland Light Infantry reached his objective with

no more than a dozen men at his back. He attacked nevertheless, drove off the enemy, and destroyed the artillery observation post, but the enemy put down a heavy barrage covering a strong counter-attack. Hollis, who was mortally wounded, then ordered Sergeant-Major McMillan to withdraw with the six or seven men remaining, but the sergeant-major demurred. He was indeed in an awkward position. At what moment does authority depart from a dying leader? 'Never, while I live,' said Nelson in the cockpit of the *Victory*, as the paralysis crept towards his heart. Mark Hollis was of the same opinion, and McMillan then asked for the order in writing. This Hollis wrote out on one of his visiting cards, exhibiting at the moment of death a flash of the sense of humour which had always distinguished that excellent fellow. So McMillan and the others left him on the objective. He was recommended for a posthumous Victoria Cross and Sergeant-Major McMillan was awarded the Distinguished Conduct Medal. The Italians were greatly impressed by the valour of this small detachment, and were chivalrous enough to bury the dead with such military honours as were possible to accord under the circumstances.*

Both our brigades suffered heavy casualties, and once again it was not until 4th Divison captured Agordat behind them that the enemy withdrew.

One of the remarkable things about the battle of Agordat was that it was fought as early as it was, on 28 January. In ten days the division had advanced 150 miles against opposition on what was no more than a fair-weather track. Some

---

* *Proud Heritage: The Story of the Highland Light Infantry* (32).

of the credit goes to the relentless pressure maintained on the retreating enemy by Gazelle, but a great deal to the efforts of the R.I.A.S.C. transport companies who completed the concentration of 5th Brigade after its arrival from Egypt 250 miles further forward and five days earlier than originally planned. The position covering Agordat was held by the Italian *4th Colonial Division* who occupied field defences among some formidable mountainous country, and once more it was only after three days' hard fighting by both brigades that the enemy was driven out.

As things had turned out, the advance from Kassala had, of course, progressed very much more rapidly than the high command had foreseen. Keru, Barentu, and Agordat had all fallen inside a fortnight, but until the position had cleared up it had been advisable to keep touch with the enemy detachments to the south at Um Hagar and Gallabat so that these alternative lines of approach would be open if a hold-up in the north made it necessary to use them. However, the enemy, seeing that his retreat was threatened, abandoned Um Hagar on the twenty-sixth and was pursued by a battalion of the Mahratta Light Infantry, with a detachment of Spahis and men from the Sudan Defence Force; among the more unusual spoils of war they captured a gold mine in good working order. Further to the south at Gallabat the enemy stood fast until 31 January. Then, early on the morning of 1 February, routine patrols sent forward to draw the enemy's fire, and so confirm his presence, found that he had gone, and a small mobile force of all arms set off in pursuit.

An Indian Sapper officer, Second Lieutenant Premindra Singh Bhagat, rode in the leading carrier as being the best place to spot mines. His company commander has contributed a few sidelights on the events of the next four days.

On the first day his section cleared five minefields and he was blown up once. The score for the second day was about the same, then early on the third day his carrier was blown up and his driver killed. Having cleared the way, he changed into another carrier and again led the advance. Early on the fourth day he ran into an ambush and used the anti-tank rifle on the carrier to kill a sniper. Summarizing his impressions, he has written: 'After being blown up on the third day, Bhagat was still very alert and I was most impressed by the way the British infantry section followed in his footsteps unquestioningly through the mines. There was no doubt that he was the key man in this little pursuit, and all, from the column commander to British and Indian ranks, recognized it.'

For his 'cold, calculated courage' Bhagat won the V.C., the first Indian holding the King's commission to do so.

With affairs in the north going so well, further pursuit was unnecessary and 9th Brigade concentrated back at Gedaref.

At both Barentu and Agordat the enemy had made the most of the advantages that the terrain offered to the defender, he had fought with great determination for several days, and had finally retired only when his line of retreat was threatened. It was thus becoming clear that if we should find ourselves up against a position that we could not turn, the courage, fortitude and determination of our troops would be tested to the very limit. Gazelle followed up the enemy after the battle of Agordat but, twelve miles to the east, they found a four-span steel bridge so damaged as to be unsafe for traffic, and it was not until the morning of 2 February that they were in contact with the first outposts of the Keren defences, two miles south of the entrance to the gorge.

> From the canyon came dull booms; clouds of smoke and dust curled upwards in the still hot air. The last Italian rearguards had passed through and on a stretch of several hundred yards demolition squads were blowing away the retaining walls which pinned the road to the cliffsides. Two 'I' tanks crossed the valley to reconnoitre and reported the ravine to be blocked by barricades of huge boulders covered by anti-tank and machine guns. The eastern gateway of the Eritrean fortress was bolted and barred. (21)

The irresistible force had met the immovable object.

The traveller along the Via Imperiale bound for Keren and

Asmara motors up the Ascidera valley with grim forbidding mountains towering two and three thousand feet above him, and closing in on either hand. Rather more than two miles short of the watershed, dominated by Sphinx (5,590 feet), the road swings north and north-east to enter the Dongolaas Gorge, climbing up the eastern side of the last four miles to the plateau on which Keren stands; up the western side, in places no more than 500 yards away, runs the railway. The mountains everywhere block the view ahead to the man toiling up from the valley, but offer a hundred observation posts from which the defender above can watch his every movement. The hills are steep, covered with a thick prickly thorn and immense boulders and rising to knife-edge false crests; in places there are unscalable cliffs running for hundreds of yards. The mere physical effort of climbing such hills would have taxed the fitness of an unencumbered man.

> The exertion of men laden with equipment, rifles, ammunition, shovels, was wearing on even the stoutest, and it is no wonder that those soldiers who did reach the almost unclimbable crests were momentarily too exhausted to make further effort. It was this moment of breathless exhaustion and strain that the Italians were so often to choose for delivering a counter-attack from their points of physical and moral vantage. (22)

The enemy had been at work on these defences for months, if not years. The tangled hillsides were sown with wire and mines and machine-gun posts; paths ran to every sector, even water was laid on, and above all the Italians had one thing the Indian army had left behind in India, they had mules. Not only had we no mules, we had no mountain artillery either— the ubiquitous 3 in howitzer with its steeper trajectory which can reach targets on reverse slopes that are secure from the field-gun, and can get into action in places which cannot be reached by tractor-drawn artillery.

At times the attacking strength of the infantry would be reduced by a quarter to find the porters to carry the loads the fighting men had to have. It was recorded that during one period of eight hot, dusty days every round of ammunition, every mouthful of food, every drop of water had been carried up by hand. It was a galling thought for troops who for years had fought on the North-West Frontier over hills less formidable than these, supported by the best mountain artillery and the finest mule transport of any army in the world.

Dominating the gorge to the left rose Sanchil and Brig's Peak, each no more than a shade short of six thousand feet and of particular importance because they gave observation all the way down to Keren. Five hundred feet below and a thousand yards short of them was Cameron Ridge; further to the left were Saddle, Flat Top and Sammana. To the right the hills were slightly lower but no easier to climb: Fort Dologorodoc standing on a tangle of under-features, behind it Falestoh, joined to Zeban; 2,500 yards to the south-east across a tangle of ridges was Sphinx, and across those ridges, over the precipitous Acqua Col, a track ran north to Keren.

To man these defences the Italians had deployed a colonial brigade, three battalions of the Savoy Grenadiers from their general reserve at Addis Ababa, and one more fresh brigade arrived before the battle started. To the north were two colonial brigades that had not been in action, and there were also in reserve behind the position the remains of the six brigades that had fought at Keru, Barentu and Um Hagar.

It was an unpleasant prospect but there was no way round it; the only way of reaching Asmara was by means of a head-on attack, and on 4 February 2nd Battalion Cameron Highlanders opened the battle for Keren. Four hours later, with great determination and by skilful use of broken ground, the battalion had won its way to the ridge which was to bear its name, and had secured a jumping-off place for the assault on Sanchil and Brig's Peak.

That night 3rd Battalion 14th Punjab Regiment passed through the Camerons and without meeting very much opposition captured Brig's Peak. Next morning they were looking east across the valley to the white walls of Keren and, of more immediate significance, they could see that Sanchil, a thousand yards away, was beyond all doubt the bastion on which the whole of the defensive system depended. Proof of its importance to the enemy came at once in the form of an overwhelming counter-attack, supported by a heavy artillery bombardment, along the hog's back that connected the two summits. The Punjab Regiment was driven back to Cameron Ridge, and for a time it seemed doubtful if even that could be held. 1st Battalion Rajputana Rifles, Wellesley's Rifles, came up to reinforce the Camerons, joined later by 3/1st Punjab Regiment, and the enemy's attacks were beaten off, but the struggle lasted for ten days. There is the story of a young lance-naik of Wellesley's Rifles, only just promoted, who was left in command of a platoon reduced to seven men. During a night attack when the neighbouring platoon was overrun, he beat off two attacks and then with two remaining men chased the retiring enemy with the bayonet. In the morning eleven dead lay outside his post.

When the battalion was withdrawn for a brief rest, after a long stretch when they had endured extreme discomfort and suffered heavy casualties, the divisional commander recorded that 'the morning after leaving the line, every man turned out as smartly dressed in clean shirts and starched shorts as if he were on a party at Cairo'.

With such clear proof of the determination of the enemy to hold Brig's Peak and Sanchil, and of the strength he had concentrated in that area for the purpose, it seemed possible that Acqua Col, with its track running north to Keren, might be less strongly held. On the night of 7 February 5th Brigade, with 4th Battalion Rajputana Rifles leading, set about the task. As they arrived at the top they came under heavy mortar and machine-gun fire, the company commander was wounded, and Subedar Richpal Ram headed the rush that carried the leading platoons over the crest. They beat off five counter-attacks but an hour before dawn, their ammunition exhausted, they had no choice but to fight their way back to where the rest of the battalion had dug in on a low ridge below the col. There were only ten survivors. Before the attack could be renewed it was decided that some attempt should be made to neutralize the enemy artillery that had been supporting the defenders, and this necessitated the establishment of a gunner observation post on Brig's Peak, across the valley, to overlook the gun positions on the plateau west of Keren.

On the afternoon of 10th February . . . 3/1st Punjabis swarmed upwards from Cameron Ridge. Bitter fighting followed. By nightfall the leading companies had established themselves on the upper slopes of Brig's Peak and were investing the pinnacles. At dawn they struck again. They swept over the spires, destroyed the garrisons, rushed across the low hollow, up the easy hog's back and seized the near slopes of Mount Sanchil. This splendid feat of arms might have proved a prelude to victory had 11th Brigade been able to consolidate and to provide sufficient garrisons for the summits, and had pack trains been available for their replenishment. Unfortunately men were scarce and mules non-existent. (21)

Heavy counter-attacks during the day forced them back onto Brig's Peak, and under further overwhelming pressure from two directions that developed just before midnight they were compelled to fall back on Cameron Ridge. Casualties had been heavy. Two commanding officers, three company commanders and 280 other ranks had fallen. It is worth noting that just three months later this battalion, together with the battalion of The Rajputana Rifles, that was battling so staunchly across the valley at Acqua Col, were fighting with apparently undiminished vigour at Kissoue and Mezze near Damascus.

Equally serious was the loss of the gunner observation parties that had been on Brig's Peak; however, the Acqua Col attack was made as planned. Once again the Rajputana Rifles led the assault, and again Subedar Richpal Ram led his battalion. Once more they reached the crest but 'these indomitable handfuls were submerged in a sea of enemies'. Among those struck down was Richpal Ram who, as he lay dying, kept command and cheered his men on. His superb gallantry won him the V.C. On their right 4th Battalion Sikh Regiment was attacking Sphinx, but there also the task proved too much for them and they withdrew after the loss of over one hundred men.

Given one or two more battalions, or had one of the brigades had pack-mule transport, Keren might have fallen within the week; as it was there was nothing to do but to take stock and set about the necessary preparations that would give a better chance of success when the time came for the attack to be resumed. 5th Division was still at Barentu, but as there was not the transport to maintain them there, much less any to spare for stocking the forward areas for the coming battle, they withdrew to railhead at Kassala and set about intensive training for the particular task that confronted them.

4th Division had been living under active service conditions for over six months and badly needed a rest. Instead, under an ever-mounting thermometer, they set to work to prepare for the next round. The plan was to put supplies of all sorts, ammunition, and petrol for fifteen days into the forward divisional area and, as most of it lay as open as the palm of a hand to the Italian observers on the heights above, a great deal of the work had to be done by night. The infantry kept a standing garrison of two battalions up on Cameron Ridge where '. . . all movement by day was quite impossible. . . . Rations of water had to be carried up by men of the reserve company from the dump over a thousand feet below. Both food and water were therefore extremely short. By day it was very hot and there was no shade; by night it could be bitterly cold. The smell of the old battlefield and the flies made life almost unbearable. . . .'*

The R.I.A.S.C. were driving heavy lorries as much as 120 miles a day over shocking roads in blinding clouds of dust. Artillerymen 'snatched precarious sleep' beside guns that were spotted and shelled as soon as they opened fire. Signal lines were laid and protected; and as casualties were averaging fifty a day from wounds and sickness the doctors were never idle. If the Sappers never claimed to have worked longer hours than anyone else, they could at least boast that they tackled a wider variety of jobs. In addition to their normal

---

* *Always a Fusilier: The War History of the Royal Fusiliers* (31).

tasks of specialized engineer work in the battle area, they were boring water holes, clearing wells, and repairing and operating sabotaged machinery of all sorts. However, pride of place for versatility must surely go to the field company which repaired and ran a stretch of the little railway, making daily deliveries right into the rear areas of the battalions up on Cameron Ridge.

Just below the ridge was a tunnel, which was the forward terminus; fifteen kilometres away down the hill was the war-time station of Hummet West. Clearance of the line was no more than an initial difficulty, there were plenty of goods wagons for the task in hand, but there were no locomotives. Wagons were cut down to flats and each one was towed by a 15 cwt Morris truck, its wheels on the ballast astride the lines. Steering called for skill and strength of wrists and, although the line was continuously under fire, drivers were seldom changed and did their two trips a day without relief.

There was no turn-round at the tunnel so the truck would be reversed up a ramp onto its flat; gravity then powered the return journey. The train of six flats would lift as much as ten tons, take three hours over the round trip, and do two journeys a day. Loads forward were the standard essentials of infantry in contact with the enemy; water, rations, ammunition, wire, the post orderly; wounded travelled on the return journey. There were also two special services; a trolley powered by a motor cycle which was used mostly by officers visiting the forward battalions; and the Night Hawk, a powered railway flat constructed from an old Fiat lorry, which, as it ran on the lines, could travel during the hours of darkness.

While these preparations were going on a reconnaissance was made to see if the road to Arresa, thirty miles to the south, could be made into a main route. The divisional cavalry regiment, the Central India Horse, wrote that

> they actually drove to a spot 17 miles from Asmara where they were held up by a precipice with only a camel track leading to the top which in most parts was only 3-4 feet wide. As this progress was the result of two and

54

a half weeks concentrated patrolling it was a great disappointment to be foiled at the last fence. It was strenuous mobile work with some mountaineering all well done, netting of stragglers and supplementing rations by venison, bustard, partridge and guinea fowl. Sandgrouse got off as cartridges were limited and the table came before the game book. It was during this period that 'Boggy' Howson while reconnoitring through the mountains towards Asmara sent back for security reasons a message which became well known throughout the Division: 'Have passed back six prisoners under escort, am proceeding to recce forward towards BUMBEATON.'* This message was understood without hesitation although there were no codewords in use at the time.†

The enemy had spent these weeks in improving his already very strong defences—in places he had erected as many as ten parallel lines of barbed wire—and owing to the very broken nature of the ground it was generally impossible to detect the wire or the other defence works from artillery observation posts: nor did they show up on air photographs. They were holding the position with nearly forty battalions of infantry, giving them a superiority of roughly two to one. The R.A.F., who were now operating from forward airfields, had been carrying out sustained attacks against the Italian Air Force and had reduced it to almost complete inactivity; one of the few bright patches on an otherwise stormy horizon.

The general plan for the attack, which opened on 15 March, was for 4th Division to secure Brig's Peak and Sanchil, and, when it had succeeded, 5th Division, which had come forward during the previous week, was to capture Fort Dologorodoc. 4th Division was confronted by a task the difficulties of which it knew only too well, and in addition it extended its objectives to take in the hills up to 2,000 yards to the left, partly with the idea of making it more difficult for the enemy to counter-attack Brig's Peak, if we

---

* The reader must ask some Indian Army officer to decode this for him.
† *Central India Horse Newsletter* (41).

succeeded in reaching it, and partly to block any attempt the enemy might make to raid round our extreme left and get among the gun positions in the valley below. Two diversions were planned on the flanks: to the south a detachment of Skinner's Horse with units of the Sudan Defence Force were to pretend that they were a very much larger force; and in the north 7th Brigade Group were to attempt a further advance and thus prevent enemy troops in the north being released to help the southern front. 7th Brigade, with two Free French battalions, half a battery of artillery, and a company of sappers, had left Port Sudan during the first week in February. The line of advance south was virtually roadless, the supply problems were formidable, but by 8 March, over-coming some enemy detachments on the way, they were no more than fifteen miles from Keren. There they were held up by fully manned defences every bit as formidable as the main position.

The fresh attack on Brig's Peak and Sanchil was made by the Camerons who, although suffering heavy losses, were only partly successful; and the Royal Fusiliers, passing through them, were also held up short of Sanchil. To the left, 1st Battalion Rajputana Rifles, 2nd Battalion Mahratta Light Infantry and 4th Battalion Sikh Regiment, in that order, had been attacking the heights to the north-west. After very severe fighting they more or less gained their objectives, but could do no more than hold their own against counter-attacks. Across the gorge 2nd Battalion Highland Light Infantry led the 5th Division attack and attempted to capture two under-features below the Fort, but they were caught in a withering fire from their left flank from below Sanchil and had no choice but to lie out all day among the rocks in the burning heat, unable to move. It was not an auspicious start, but it was the first step in an operation that was to prove the turning point of the whole battle.

Just as it was getting dark, 3rd Battalion Mahratta Light Infantry, with two companies of 3rd Battalion Frontier Force Regiment under their command, set out to capture Pinnacle, towering a thousand feet above them, the nearer of the under-features.

Twice 'B' Company, commanded by Subedar Shrirang Lawand, were forced back and yet a third time, encouraged by the example of their indomitable leader, they pressed forward until the saddle was reached. Fifteen minutes later they were on their objective. The divisional commander has placed on record how, in the darkness, the first intimation he had of the capture of the Pinnacle was hearing from across the valley the triumphant Mahratta battle-cry 'Shivaji Maharaj ki jai*'.†

The companies of the Frontier Force Regiment passed through to take Pimple, and 2nd Battalion West Yorkshire Regiment, who had been moving up behind to exploit success, now advanced along a knife edge, which the enemy seemed to have thought impassable. By daylight Fort Dologorodoc was in their hands. Their task had been made that much the easier by the fact that some of the garrison had left for a counter-attack to drive off the Mahrattas; they found a rude welcome awaiting them on return to base. The following night a second brigade was passed through the Fort in an attempt to take Falestoh and Sphinx. The opposition was very severe, they were caught in the flank by artillery fire from Sanchil, and the supply difficulties were so great that at one stage an improvised air drop had to be arranged. It was accordingly decided, when it was seen that the attack could make no more than limited progress, to withdraw and maintain a line about half a mile beyond the Fort.

The Fort itself was found to consist of a concrete trench enclosing perhaps an acre of hill top, and it was the hill top and not the Fort which mattered to the enemy. Over the next week he made half a dozen most determined attempts to recapture it and suffered crippling casualties, and there can be no doubt that the loss of these reserves, coupled with the psychological effect of failure, very much weakened the Italian will to resist over the whole front. On the more positive side, possession of the Fort feature enabled us to take a

* 'Victory to the Great Lord Shivaji'.
† *History of The Mahratta Light Infantry* (53).

closer look at the extent of the road blocks in the gorge. After two most gallant engineer reconnaissances, carried out by night, the Sappers reported that the damage was less extensive than had been supposed, and that they could clear it after forty-eight hours' work. A further point which emerged was that, although Sanchil dominated the whole of the area to the left of the gorge, it did not command the road blocks or the passage of the gorge itself; the key feature at this point was Railway Bumps, situated below and out of sight of Sanchil, where the railway loops away from the road to cross a network of valleys coming in from the north.

The final phase was planned in four stages: the capture of Railway Bumps and some corresponding ground on the right of the gorge; the clearance of the block and the repair of the road to take tanks; a final attack to clear the ground commanding the last stretch of the gorge from the right; and the pursuit.

The troops who were to capture the Bumps, Highland Light Infantry and 4th Battalion Baluch Regiment, assembled in the railway tunnel below Cameron Ridge:

The scene was like some Rembrandt painting, as the men waited in the darkness that was pierced by an occasional light and the glow of cigarette ends. From time to time tea and rum were served out. The Indians remained silent by contrast with the 'Jocks', who chattered away and suddenly burst into the strains of *Annie Laurie*. Brigadier Rees* walked to the end of the tunnel to see whether the sounds could be heard, but all was well. . . . At 3 a.m. the troops tiptoed forward. Brigadier Rees waited anxiously, watching the seconds tick by on his watch. As each minute passed he knew that the men had reached a certain distance without being discovered. What troops the enemy held on Railway Bumps was unknown. The moment was tense, and in no man's mind was there any sense of an easy attack, still less of a walk-over. . . . Each battalion had two companies to

* The late Major-General T. W. Rees, C.B., C.I.E., D.S.O., M.C.

fight, and one to carry stores, ammunition, rations and water. (22)

The enemy was surprised and the attack succeeded.

By half-past five most of the objectives had been gained. Some five hundred prisoners were taken. Several admitted that they had never seriously considered that anyone would risk an attack along the railway track. The colonel of the Bersaglieri battalion surrendered with his headquarters in their dugout. . . . He was almost speechless with rage at having been surprised. (22)

The other attack across the gorge met with indomitable resistance, and it was only after another equally determined attack by the Mahrattas that they succeeded.

By 6.30 a.m. the first Sapper company was at work on the road block. They had asked for two nights and a day for the work, they were given two days and a night. Although the next day both divisions reported that there were signs that the enemy might be withdrawing, the work on the block was repeatedly attacked. It was on that day that General Wavell visited the battlefield. After viewing the situation from 5th Division headquarters at Fort Dologorodoc, he expressed a wish to visit the forward brigade and was most emphatically advised not to do so.

But General Wavell was stubborn, and was already edging down the spur towards the roadway when five Savoias flew overhead and dropped bombs, as anticipated, on the mountain battery position. The bombs straddled the road. The officers and men in and around divisional headquarters who stood within splinter range of this attack threw themselves down in cover of the rocks. Wavell smiled, and only then was persuaded to give up his intention of going forward. Instead he sent a message of good wishes for 29th Brigade's attack next morning. (22)

The Sappers were working their companies in five-hour shifts round the clock. Toiling at intense speed, taking no heed of the battle raging around and above them, they blew up great rocks and falls from the hillside above, but most of the work was done 'with pick and shovel and even with hands'. By dusk on the twenty-sixth they had cleared a twelve-foot roadway, and worked on through the night to widen it for tanks.

At 4.30 next morning the last attack of all went in to clear Zeban, but the enemy had fled. As the leading vehicles of the pursuit force made their way up the gorge a white flag appeared on the crest of Mount Sanchil. Troops of 4th Division made contact with those of 5th Division climbing the hill from Railway Bumps to the east and took the surrender of the Bersaglieri garrison. Among the tumbled rocks at the summit they found the bodies of perhaps half a dozen infantrymen, British and Indian, who in pairs or perhaps even singly had fought their way to the top: for these men the sky had been the limit.

An extract from *The Times* of 17 May 1947 expresses a fitting tribute to the men who fought at Keren from a man who knew just how much they had achieved.

EARL WAVELL

The viscountcy and earldom of the United Kingdom conferred on Field-Marshal Viscount Wavell and his heirs were gazetted last night by the name, style and title of Viscount KEREN, of Eritrea and of Winchester in the County of Southampton, and Earl Wavell.

The pursuit column, Fletcher Force, commanded by the colonel of the H.L.I., consisted of the C.I.H., eleven 'I' tanks, and thirty-six infantry carriers drawn from different battalions in both divisions. The most urgent task was to seize Ad Teclesan, about thirty-five miles away and rather over half way to Asmara, as it was known that a defensive position had been prepared at that place and it was hoped to capture it before the enemy could reorganize his retreating forces and occupy it. However, Fletcher Force soon ran into trouble and 29th Brigade was brought forward to help. It was essential to maintain the momentum of the advance as it was of the first importance to complete the capture of Eritrea before the rains broke. 9th Brigade was brought forward and passed through to fight the battle of Ad Teclesan, giving place in turn to 10th Brigade which actually took the surrender of the town. A great deal of the credit for this rapid advance must go to the administrative services: the supply lorries were covering over 200 miles from railhead at Kassala over roads which in many places were still bearing the marks of demolitions and damage left behind by the enemy, while the repair services were working at pressure to ensure that broken-down vehicles did not check the flow of traffic.

After Asmara, it was the turn of Massawa. One of the main preoccupations of both victor and vanquished now was the feeding of the Italian settler population and their protection from the vengeance of the natives. Consequently, the Italian admiral at Massawa was encouraged to surrender the port by the threat that if he did not do so we should accept no responsibility for the care of these civilians. It seemed that fear of Mussolini's displeasure weighed more heavily with him than the safety and well-being of his compatriots: he appealed to Caesar, and was told to refuse our terms.

Given resolute defenders the capture of Massawa might have proved a difficult task but the operation was completed on 7 April, fifteen days after the fall of Keren. Four days later President Roosevelt proclaimed that the Red Sea and the Gulf of Aden were no longer combat zones; American merchant ships could now transport their cargoes direct to Suez.

Elsewhere the Italians had been under continuous pressure on both their western and southern fronts. In August 1940 Colonel Sandford had entered Ethiopia from west of Lake Tana, and over the next five months, in co-operation with Colonel Wingate, had so organized Patriot forces that the Emperor was able to re-enter his country on 21 January and set up his first headquarters at Belayu, 100 miles south of Gallabat. The bulk of the fighting which followed was done by Wingate's Gideon Force, with a hard core of 800 men of

the Sudan Defence Force, and by a masterly stroke of timing
they were within striking distance of Addis Ababa simultaneously with the arrival of the African brigades, coming in
from the south and from Berbera, who entered the capital
on 6 April.

The advance from Kenya had opened with operations by
1st South African Division in the Lake Rudolf area, designed
to encourage the Patriot movement south-west of Addis
Ababa, but the main advance northwards was by the two
African Divisions, first to Kismayu and Mogadishu, then
north to Diredawa, where they were joined by a force that
had landed at Berbera from Aden on 16 March. This advance
from the south covered 1,700 miles in eight weeks and is a
classic example of what can be done by a force flexible
enough to adapt its plans as the situation changes and by
troops ready to take risks, move fast and live hard. Supporting the force were two Indian mountain batteries who
had been in East Africa from the early days of the war. Confronted at the start with the problem of converting themselves from pack to motor transport, they solved it with the
aid of the local railway workshops; later, for the advance on
Gondar, they changed back again at even shorter notice, and
went into action with Abyssinian irregulars carrying two
rounds of ammunition apiece in nosebags. At the end of the
campaign the battery commander put it on record that:

> It was a gunner's dream. The battery was always un-
> brigaded . . . and we were left to ourselves. Artillery was
> so scarce on the ground that any gunner got a royal
> welcome from the infantry and we learned to know and
> appreciate the South Africans and the K.A.R., Gold
> Coast, and Nigerian battalions which we supported.

Typical of the British officer's reluctance even in time of
war to be separated from his rod or his 12 bore, the report
concludes that 'during the period 1st November 1939 to
4th January 1942, the four British officers in the battery killed
by rod, gun or 3·7 howitzer 1,239 head of game. This large
figure comprised most things from a buffalo to an Italian cow,

also 463 trout, francolin, guinea fowl, geese, duck, snipe and many of the species of East African deer'.*

Three days after the fall of Keren Rommel attacked in Cyrenaica, where the Western Desert Force had been stripped to the last margin of safety to find troops for Greece, and General Wavell's most pressing concern became to get troops back to the point of greatest danger. Leaving a brigade behind, 4th Division was shuttled back to Egypt immediately after the capture of Massawa, and General Platt was told that in his plans for clearing up outstanding Italian resistance and generally restoring law and order in Ethiopia priority must be given to opening up the Addis Ababa—Asmara road to facilitate the transfer of troops northward.

After meeting the call for troops for various duties in Asmara and Massawa, 5th Division had available no more than Fletcher Force, 29th Brigade and two other Indian battalions, a commando battalion, and two and a half regiments of artillery. At the same time increasing demands were coming in for the protection and general care of Italian civilians, to the point that it became necessary to represent to the Duke of Aosta that if he really wished us to accept this responsibility he had better lay down his arms and have done with it. This he was not prepared to do, and assembled his remaining reserves and such troops as had survived the fighting around Keren for a last stand at the Toselli Pass nearly 200 miles south of Asmara. The road there crosses a mountain barrier at a height of over 10,000 feet, with Amba Alagi at 11,186 feet only a mile from the pass. We had a superiority over the enemy in artillery but in infantry there was probably not much to it. The position had been wired and fortified, tunnels and shelters had been constructed and there were rations for three months and an adequate water supply. If his troops chose to defend themselves with real determination it was only too clear that their eventual defeat might be costly in both lives and time. Fortunately 1st South African Brigade was fighting its way up from the south and, after the decisive defeat of an enemy force at Dessie, they

* The History of the Indian Mountain Artillery (34).

reached the Amba Alagi area little more than a week after the battle had started, in time, in fact, to make a decisive attack from the south at a moment when 5th Division's battalions had been stretched to the utmost.

The Italians had had to attack this position themselves in the course of their own advance on Addis Ababa five years before, and we had in our possession a report written by Marshal Badoglio in which he concluded that the correct method of attack was via the Falaga Pass, seven miles west of Toselli. Our plan, accordingly, was to encourage them to expect their own solution by making a strong feint on the left flank, a secondary one in the centre, and then to deliver the real assault round our right.

The reader whose physical ceiling has probably never risen above a ski slope at 5,000 feet can have little idea of the physical effort involved in just climbing to twice that height: how much greater the demand on resolution and physical fitness when burdened with weapons and equipment, having to seek out and destroy an enemy sitting in comparative comfort in carefully concealed and protected positions. The trip by porter or locally impressed donkey corps from the roadhead below to the battalions above took eight hours. General Mayne, the divisional commander, tells a story that illustrates the camaraderie that existed between the units in his division:

> I had puffed and panted my way to the top of a sheer peak which afforded the best available observation of the enemy's position at Toselli. The Garwhali tactical head-quarters were there, and so was an important O.P. from 28th Field Regiment. As I arrived exhausted at my destination, a party of British gunners caught me up and were hailed with obvious enthusiasm by some Garwhali signallers, who were brewing tea in a dug-out. I stopped for a breather before scaling the last fifty feet to the look-out and saw out of the tail of my eye much hand-shaking and then the Englishmen squatting down beside the Indians and accepting the tea and cigarettes they offered.

Frontier Force Regiment, Dogra

Rajputana Rifles, Rajput

TYPES OF TRAINED SOLDIERS

Mahratta Light Infantry, Mahratta

Indian Corps of Signals, Madrassi

RECRUITING TYPES

Punjabi Mohammedan, Awan

Medical examination

Punjabi Mohammedans from Shahpur

Madrassi M.T. drivers arrive to enlist

Field-Marshal Auchinleck talking to India's youngest V.C.,
Sepoy Kamal Ram, a jat of 8th Punjab Regiment

Hillside at Keren

MARETH LINE   Before the battle
6 pdr anti-tank gun in action

Stretcher-bearers
Interrogating German prisoners

Troops searching houses in Sfax Harbour

Having finished my own business in half an hour or
so, I began stumbling down the hill again, only to be
stopped by the same Garwhali signallers and led into
the dug-out. There I, too, was given tea, biscuits and a
cigarette. I took them thankfully, but with mild protest,
knowing that every half-pint of water and morsel of
everything else had to be carried by hand from a water
point over a mile away and nearly a thousand feet lower,
and I asked the Garwhalis whether it was their habit to
entertain every Tom, Dick and Harry who came their
way. Their answer was a flat denial. Not a bit of it. It was
business enough to keep their own tummies full, and
normal hospitality had to go hang. But in my case it was
different. I was after all the divisional commander, and
a very old man too! Then what about the British soldiers,
I asked. 'Oh, that's quite different,' they replied, 'they
belong to the 28th. They belong to us.' (22)

The opening moves were made by Fletcher Force on
29 April and up to 2 May they had a series of small successes.
One position captured could be reached only by means of a
rope let down from a tree on the summit, inviting the comment that 'inevitably, evacuation of casualties had become a
matter of extreme difficulty'. On the afternoon of 3 May the
Garwhalis began to move forward for their feint in the centre,
and by a carefully worked out display of vehicle lights in the
valley below, and by the most intrepid patrol work in scaling
the heights above, completely deceived the enemy into thinking that here at last was the real thing. In consequence, he
moved reinforcements to meet it, thus facilitating the main
attack by troops of 29th Brigade which went in next morning. This last attack was finally held up early the next day,
having reached a point about 3,000 yards west of the main
road, where it encountered wire defences across a knife-edged
ridge. Fletcher Force on the left was now reinforced and the
attack was renewed there on 8 May. At the same time the
Frontier Force Rifles made a wide sweeping movement which
won them possession of two heights deep in the enemy
position south of the Pass.

They had orders to carry out a silent attack at first light.
. . . Throughout that night, in heavy rain and over extremely difficult country, this body moved to within assaulting distance of Castle Ridge. The men had to descend two thousand feet into a narrow valley. From here they climbed up to their starting line. The approach along this steep and unreconnoitred route had taken eight hours. Their attack was launched silently a few minutes after four o'clock on the morning of May 8. (22)

In a message of congratulation from the brigade commander he said: 'How they reached their objective is beyond my comprehension.'
Words could say no more.
It was, of course, bitterly cold by night at that height, and some of the troops had been fighting for six days with very little sleep, so that it was with considerable relief that the divisional commander on 11 May flew over to make contact with the South Africans and co-ordinate a joint attack from both north and south to begin on the thirteenth. The operation on the thirteenth and fourteenth was successful, but while the final plan for the last assault of all, on Fort Toselli, was actually being hatched, the enemy threw in his hand. A lucky shot from a 6 in howitzer the night before had struck a fuel dump from which oil and petrol flowed down into the last remaining source of fresh drinking water.
The opening stages of the negotiations for the surrender were delayed when the Patriots, who were proving to be somewhat erratic allies, waylaid and slew the first party of envoys just as they emerged from their positions. Subsequently, matters were discussed at Italian headquarters, and some time seems to have been devoted to the rejection of a novel, face-saving formula which would allow the enemy to remain as non-belligerents in an enclave at the top of the hill, thus saving the Viceroy the humiliation of actual surrender. The idea was, of course, turned down, but the vanquished were permitted to surrender with all the honours of war.

At 11.15 a.m. on May 19th the defeated remnant of the

Italian Army marched out of Amba Alagi and filed eight abreast down the hill. As they passed, a guard of honour of one officer and twenty-five men drawn from each battalion of the Fifth Indian Division, presented arms. General Mayne* stood beside the road, a slim and impeccable figure in service dress, and took the salute. The pipe band of the Transvaal Scottish played *The Flowers of the Forest*. (22)

The Viceroy and commander-in-chief, the Duke of Aosta, surrendered with his immediate personal staff to General Mayne the following day.

No one pretends that the Italian was a fighter of the calibre of the German or the Japanese, but at Keren he deployed his finest troops in a position of great natural strength, and for six weeks they fought with great determination. His will to fight cracked when, in spite of the tactical advantages he enjoyed, he was driven out of Fort Dologorodoc by the temerity and dash of Indian infantrymen, advancing, as they did at Sanchil and Amba Alagi, by night, and over ground that was as formidable as anything our armies met anywhere throughout the war.

Our troops had magnificent support from the R.A.F., and the success of the troops and Patriots in the south and west all contributed to weakening the enemy morale. The campaign, however, was won at Keren. The 4th and 5th Indian Divisions fought their way through to Asmara and Massawa because they were tough, fit, and resourceful; they were fighting against time and they won a victory of no small strategic importance.

* The late General Sir Mosley Mayne, G.C.B., C.B.E., D.S.O.

CHAPTER FIVE

Iraq—Iran—Paiforce

Baghdad
20 January 1941

Your Excellency,

England, that relentless and subtle enemy of the true liberty of peoples, has never ceased from forging for the Arab peoples chains to enslave and subjugate them, sometimes in the name of the perfidious League of Nations, and sometimes by the placarding of false and hypocritical sentiments of humanity for others, but always in truth for the most imperialistic designs, camouflaged behind the principles of a mendacious democracy and internationalism.

The Arab peoples have found themselves, by a geographical coincidence, in the centre of land and sea cross-roads, which form according to the English the principle knot of British imperial communications.*

So wrote Mohammed Amin El Husseini, Grand Mufti of Palestine, who four years before had made his home town of Jerusalem too hot to hold him, and had recently withdrawn to the politically more congenial climate of Baghdad.

The rather fulsome letter from which this extract comes ran

* Quoted in *Official History of the Indian Armed Forces in World War II.*

in all to some 1,500 words and was addressed to that well-known champion of all the freedoms, Adolf Hitler. It leaves one in no doubt that, although we were officially on friendly terms with Iraq, influential circles outside the government were busy trafficking with our enemy; and it may well be that the Grand Mufti with his implacable hatred of the British was the driving force behind those intrigues. The letter probably travelled in the Italian diplomatic bag.

A glance at the map shows that Iraq, an area of great strategic importance, did indeed stand at the very knot of our Imperial communications. To the north Turkey and Russia; to the east Iran and Afghanistan; to the south the Persian Gulf on the flank of the sea approaches to India; to the west Syria, Transjordan and Palestine, the right flank of our forces in the Middle East. It was a region that the Government of India had never allowed to pass into the hands of the enemy. As early as 1800 the presence of Napoleon in Egypt and Palestine prompted the East India Company to establish an agent in Baghdad to counteract his influence. Since then, the growth of communications—first cables, then air bases—and above all the discovery of oil in south-west Iran and north-east Iraq, had combined to enhance its importance.

Before 1914 Iraq was part of the old Ottoman Empire and it was to protect the Persian oilfields from the Turco-German threat that the Indian Army fought there for four years between 1914 and 1918. When the war was won, Great Britain accepted from the League of Nations the mandate for setting the country, under King Feisal I, on its feet. Under Turkish rule there had been three separate vilayets, Mosul, Baghdad and Basra, and as the population was largely agricultural or nomad there was virtually no ruling class other than the officials appointed by the Turks. When we took over, the country was fortunate to have the services of some unusually capable British administrators, and remarkable progress was made; docks and railways were built, and by 1930 the mandate came to an end and a treaty of alliance was signed. It contained two important military provisions, the retention of R.A.F. bases at Habbaniya, which lay seventy miles west of Baghdad, and at Shaiba, ten miles west of Basra;

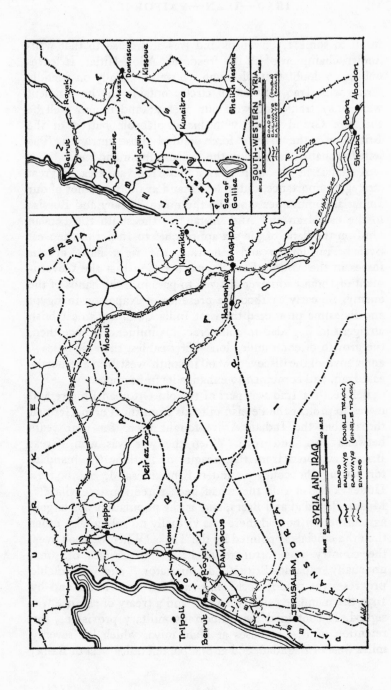

SOUTH-WESTERN SYRIA

MILES 10 20 30 40 MILES
ROADS (DOUBLE)
RAILWAYS (SINGLE)

SYRIA AND IRAQ

MILES 50 0 50 100 MILES

ROADS
RAILWAYS (DOUBLE TRACK)
RAILWAYS (SINGLE TRACK)
RIVERS

and the right at any time to move troops in transit through the country.

From quite early days Hitler seems to have been alive to the strategic importance of Iraq, and in a country struggling to stand on its own feet the Germans did not find infiltration too difficult. By 1939 they had established clandestine relations with elements hostile to the government and had contacts in the army. When war broke out they suffered a setback as, under the terms of our treaty, they were forced to close their legation in Baghdad. The hospitality extended them by the Italians, however, did much to mitigate this disadvantage.

Even before the war relations with Iran, of which more later, had so far deteriorated that plans had been under consideration for the dispatch from India of a force to protect our interests in the oilfields and at the great refinery at Abadan. When the war began there was to be faced the additional threat of a move southward by Russia, still on paper in alliance with Germany.

With France out of the war and an Italian Armistice Commission established in Syria the situation deteriorated even further; Iraq was now threatened from three sides. Middle East Command, with the Italians, and indeed the Germans, almost on their doorstep, were with some justification not worrying overmuch about the possibility of trouble further afield, the more so as they had no troops to spare to deal with it. India was not so complacent and early in 1941 made an attempt to force the pace and sort out the various projects which had been under discussion for so long. In March 1941 a conference was held between India and Middle East Command to discuss the move of a force of one Imperial and two Indian divisions to meet the danger.

There were now two problems: the more immediate was to keep the friendly government in Iraq in the saddle, which in practice meant locating a small force in the Baghdad area; the other was to establish a base area in Basra for the maintenance of the larger force which would be needed to meet external aggression from the north. The Baghdad force might come from Palestine or from India, but it would have to be maintained through the port of Basra. G.H.Q. India had prepared and submitted to H.Q. Middle East a plan under which India undertook the whole responsibility, including operational control, for establishing ourselves in Iraq while it was still possible to do so without meeting serious opposition.

The proposals were accepted in principle and, with the blessing of the Chief of the Imperial General Staff who had recently been in Cairo, India was invited to send a representative to discuss them. However, on arrival, he seems to have been persuaded that something far less ambitious was all that was necessary, or perhaps feasible—amounting to no more than steps to strengthen the security of the two Iraq airfields, and a reconnaissance for the dispatch of a small force from Palestine to Baghdad should it become necessary, though just how the troops would be found does not seem to have been settled.

The Commander-in-Chief India reacted very sharply to what seemed to him to be a complete departure from the plan he had sent his C.G.S. to discuss, and recalled him for further consultation.

At that moment the balloon went up.

King Feisal I had died soon after the treaty was first signed and his son, King Ghazi, who succeeded him, was killed in a motor accident just before the war. He left a four-year-old son, destined to be murdered in Baghdad some twenty years later, in the care of a cousin, who, as Regent, continued to maintain friendly relations with the British. There was at any rate one leading politician with pro-German sympathies, the ambitious Rashid Ali, who, although he had been Prime Minister for a short time the previous year, was not in power in March 1941. His most effective support came from a military clique, known as the Golden Square, consisting of four officers holding the key commands of two of the infantry divisions, the armoured division and the air force.

The Regent, who can have been under no illusion as to the fate of himself, the young King, and indeed the whole country if it fell under German domination, decided that to avert this possibility he must break the Golden Square, and on 25 March gave orders for its members to be posted to districts remote from the capital. They not only refused to obey this order but hatched an immediate plot to assassinate the Regent. Luckily he was warned of the danger and was flown from Habbaniya to Basra where he was given refuge by the Royal Navy. Rashid Ali's moment had come; compelling the press to publish a bogus letter of resignation from the Prime Minister, he announced that by the wish of the army he had assumed office.

On his way down to Basra the Regent met briefly, at Habbaniya airport, the incoming British Ambassador, Sir Kinahan Cornwallis, who had been for some years adviser to King Feisal and was therefore well placed to size up the situation. By 5 April he advised the Foreign Office that in his view the country as a whole was sitting on the fence waiting to see what the British would do. He saw no prospect of putting any sort of squeeze on Rashid Ali, and there was not the least chance of the Regent returning to power unless we put him back. In fact, there were only two courses open: armed intervention, which, if undertaken at once, would be opposed only by those units in the army under the personal influence of the Golden Square; or the recognition of Rashid Ali, which was tantamount to handing Iraq over to the Germans.

The chiefs of staff asked the commander-in-chief, Middle East, what forces he could make available for the task suggested by the ambassador. They got a pretty bleak reply, but in fairness to General Wavell it must be emphasized that before the end of August when the situation in Iraq and Iran was finally stabilized Middle East Command was actively concerned with operations in Eritrea, Greece, Crete, Syria and North Africa. The general said he could, in case of the most extreme urgency, spare one battalion to move from Palestine to Baghdad, but he favoured instead a strong declaration of policy, backed by a demonstration of air power. Neither of these suggestions offered much chance of success so on 8 April an approach was made to India. By great good fortune an infantry brigade, with a supporting regiment of artillery and a Sapper and Miner company, was at that moment actually embarking at Karachi, bound for Malaya. G.H.Q. India offered to divert it to Basra. They further proposed to fly 400 men of the King's Own Royal Regiment to Shaiba, synchronizing their arrival with that of the seaborne convoy. For good measure, they also suggested sending a divisional headquarters and, in the immediate future, two more infantry brigade groups to complete the division. On 10 April the chiefs of staff accepted the offer and on 12 April, four days after the request had first been made, the convoy sailed.

We had under the treaty the right to move troops through the country, but something of a crisis arose after the ships had actually sailed because of a suggestion that we should first test Rashid Ali's protestations of neutrality by giving him formal notice of our intention to take advantage of this clause and arrive at an agreed date; in the meantime the convoy could wait in Bushire. As the original destination of the convoy had been Malaya, all baggage and equipment was stowed as for a peaceful disembarkation, and the troops were not in any state of readiness to have to fight their way ashore. G.H.Q. India accordingly protested in no uncertain terms at a suggestion that threw away all chance of effecting surprise, and the plan went forward as originally made. On 17 April the King's Own Royal Regiment flew 400 men into Shaiba, and on the next day 20th Indian Infantry Brigade, together with the headquarters of 8th Indian Division, landed at Basra. They landed unopposed. Rashid Ali had been informed only the evening before and was told that the troops were in transit to Palestine. He had no immediate alternative but to accept the story but he stipulated that the troops must in fact move on and, if they were to be followed by others, then the total force in the country must not at any one time exceed a brigade group. Accordingly, when he was told on the twenty-eighth that another small convoy, which in fact contained only administrative units, was due on the thirtieth, he seems to have decided that he must do something before it was too late. Encouraged no doubt by the promises of help he had been receiving from the Germans, he forced a showdown by moving a strong brigade group of all arms to the plateau south of Habbaniya, thus blockading the R.A.F. station. He also delivered an ultimatum forbidding all further flying, even for training purposes.

This was the turning point of the whole operation. The R.A.F. had at Habbaniya some sixty-four machines, practically all training types, but they had during the past month succeeded in converting them to some sort of operational standard. The air officer commanding, heartened equally by an encouraging signal from the Prime Minister and a reinforcement of eight Wellingtons operating from Shaiba, took the very bold decision to attack the blockading force. The Iraqi troops showed no great liking for being bombed from the air, and by 5 May he had succeeded in driving them off the plateau. The garrison of Assyrian Levies had been reinforced by 300 men of the King's Own Royal Regiment flown up from Shaiba and by Colonel O. L. Roberts,* G.S.O.1 of 10th Division, sent up to co-ordinate the ground forces. Taking advantage of the success of the bombing he moved out, dominated the immediate surroundings of the station, and was even able to lay plans for an advance on Baghdad as soon as reinforcements arrived.

The second infantry brigade arrived in Basra from India on 6 May, and the next two weeks were spent in restoring law and order which involved some desultory fighting mostly against a hostile civil population. It was of course essential to secure control of the docks, and the safety of Shaiba, before moving up-country, and indeed the metre-gauge railway north to Baghdad had been cut by rebels. However, the advance began at the end of May and the leading brigade was concentrated in Baghdad by the middle of June.

On 7 May H.Q. Middle East had dispatched a column from Palestine, Habcol, to the relief of Habbaniya. It consisted of 1st Cavalry Brigade carried in 15 cwt trucks with a battalion of infantry and some artillery. It had a gruelling time crossing the desert in the intense heat and arrived on 18 May, passing over a flooded canal south of the lake by a bridge built by a detachment of Madras Sappers and Miners flown up from Basra. 2/4th Gurkha Rifles, part of the second brigade to land at Basra, were also sent up by air. The whole force, under the commander 1st Cavalry Division who had

* General Sir Ouvry Roberts, G.C.B., K.B.E., D.S.O.

75

arrived from Palestine, advanced on Baghdad. They met with no very serious opposition and on the evening of 30 April, as they reached the outskirts of the city, they received a welcome signal from Cairo telling them that a convoy, no doubt with an eminent divine in the leading car, and containing Rashid Ali and his supporters, had that day crossed the border into Iran. The next day the Regent returned to Baghdad and an armistice was signed.

By mid June a total of five Indian brigades, with a second divisional headquarters and a considerable force of base troops, had landed, and the situation was for the moment secure. The advance to Baghdad was made along both the river lines, and a force was established at Mosul with a battalion on the oilfields at Kirkuk.

Prompted perhaps by the letter quoted at the beginning of this chapter, the Germans had sent an emissary to Syria in January, to report on the situation in that country and in Iraq. By the end of March they had decided to give active support to the Arab cause, and early in April the Grand Mufti was so informed, but in fact they had not decided what support to give, nor how to send it. Their indecision cost them dear, for from then on they had to dance to our tune, and they were generally a step behind. On 6 May, the day when the threat to Habbaniya was more or less over, they had got as far as agreeing with the Vichy French in Syria for the release of stocks of arms and equipment sealed under the armistice agreement, and on 11 May three German aircraft landed at Mosul airfield. A trigger-happy Iraqi, who was no doubt put back for further training in aircraft recognition, fired at the leading machine and killed the pilot, Major Axel Von Blomberg, son of the field-marshal, commander-designate of the air reinforcements that were on their way. During the next fortnight twenty-one German and twelve Italian aircraft, all of types more modern than anything the R.A.F. had in the country, arrived at Mosul and made attacks on our columns and on Habbaniya, but their action was not co-ordinated, they suffered considerable casualties, and before the end of the month the survivors had withdrawn.

The Germans failed because Rashid Ali was stampeded

into action before they were ready to support him. It may be that Iraq was all part of a deliberate plan, Greece, Crete, Syria, Iraq, which fell behind hand after the losses they suffered over Crete; it may be that, like the Commander-in-Chief Middle East, Hitler had other things to think about. Whatever the cause they lost the initiative because it was wrested from them by resolute action on our part.

On 18 June overall responsibility for Iraq passed from H.Q. Middle East back to G.H.Q. India and it was at once apparent that there was every intention of exploiting the advantages secured by gaining control of an area of such strategic importance.

On 8 June, forces from the Middle East had invaded Syria, and on 19 June G.H.Q. India ordered Iraqi Command to send two brigades to take Deir-es-Zor, a crossing over the Euphrates, and so threaten the French flank and rear. This operation was to have priority over all others of purely local significance. On 22 June the Germans attacked Russia. The rapid advance on their southern flank opened up the possibility of a German advance through the Caucasus, and then either through Turkey or down the Caspian Sea into Iran. This brought very much to the fore the question: 'What is to be done about Iran?'—or Persia, as the Prime Minister still preferred to call it.

In 1919 there had been an ambitious and really rather unscrupulous attempt by the then Foreign Minister, Lord Curzon, to enforce a treaty with Iran, which would to all intents and purposes have added the country as one more jewel in the Imperial crown. Negotiations broke down and came finally to an end on the intervention of 3,000 Persian Cossacks who rode into Teheran. At their head was one Major Reza Shah, a ranker officer, who two years later became the Shah of Persia. Our popularity and prestige declined sharply and, despite our oil concessions in the south, we were given little or no part in the drastic modernization of the country which the new ruler undertook. The Germans, who made a speciality of helping newly developing countries on favourable financial terms, stepped into the breach, and by 1939 Iran was riddled with Germans holding key positions in communications and industry: many of them doubled the part with their fifth column activities. The numbers increased when we occupied Iraq and in July 1941 probably totalled between two and three thousand. There was, therefore, a very real threat of sabotage to our vital oil installations in the centre and south, or of guerrilla operations against the Russian rear in the Caucasus in the north.

As early as 9 July the Viceroy of India was urging His Majesty's Government to put pressure on the Shah to get rid of the Germans, and over the following weeks there was a good deal of abortive diplomatic activity, with the Iranian government playing for time. At length, on 25 August, our patience exhausted, we invaded the country from the south-west and west, in conjunction with an advance by the Russians both east and west of the Caspian.

The operations in the south-west were carried out by 8th Indian Division and had as their main purpose the security of the refinery at Abadan. There were in fact three columns: one directed on Abadan travelled downstream in boats and landed from the river; one motored across the desert from Basra and came in from the north; the third was sent to Ahwaz where there was a garrison of the Persian Army, while a detached battalion moved by air to the oilfield at Haft Khel to protect the British staff and their families. The division suffered about sixty casualties and resistance ended with the surrender of the Ahwaz garrison on orders from Teheran.

There was even less resistance offered to 10th Indian Division in the north, where there were two objects to be achieved: the security of the Naft Shah oilfields, some forty miles south of Khanikin, which was effected by a battalion of the 7th Gurkhas moving independently; and the advance along the main road to Kermanshah and Teheran. This road crossed the Pai Tak pass, some fifty miles inside Iran, which might have presented a formidable obstacle in the hands of a determined defender; however, just inside the frontier the road forks and a second mobile force was sent by the longer route to the south which joins up again at Shahabad. The southern column reached Shahabad with little trouble and sent a force back along the road against the rear of the

Pai Tak pass, only to find that the enemy, discouraged by some effective bombing by the R.A.F., had melted away. All hostilities ceased on the fourth day but, as the Shah seemed unable or unwilling to get rid of the Germans in the country, it became necessary a fortnight later for columns of both allies to advance on the capital.

A treaty was signed in Teheran on 9 September and on the sixteenth the Shah abdicated, being succeeded by his son who expressed his intention of co-operating with the allies. The war, if it really amounts to that, had not been directed at the Iranian people: its object was to install a government that would eject the Germans and allow us to take such action as might be necessary to prepare defences against an invasion by German armies from the north-west.

The present Shah has since the war maintained that our real object was to gain control over the country's ports, roads and railways for the purpose of delivering aid to Russia; and that had this object been made clear to his father some agreement could have been arrived at. It is true that the delivery of this aid did become the main preoccupation of Paiforce, as the command was later called, but it is certain that in August 1941 no one foresaw the extent to which it would grow. If, and it is a big if, we allow that the Shah wanted to get rid of the Germans who had such a stranglehold over his country, it is quite certain that he was powerless to do so until we intervened and did it for him.

So, within five months, the decision to enter Iraq had twice justified itself. We had been able to wind up the loose ends of the Syrian campaign; and we had removed from Iran the Germans who, if they had been left unmolested to pursue their nefarious designs, would most surely have inflicted serious damage to the allied cause during the highly critical year of 1942 that lay ahead.

There were now two long-range problems to be tackled.

The first was to plan to the best of our ability against a German break-through in the Caucasus, a contingency that until the end of 1942 could never be written off as impossible. We had in rather uncertain terms a common flank with the Russians in Iran, extending over about 200 miles at the south-west corner of the Caspian Sea, and from there we now had uninterrupted control over the vast area extending west through northern Iraq and Syria to the Mediterranean. But it was a front of 750 miles, there were never more than half a dozen divisions in sight to hold it, and there was an almost complete lack of armour. As commanders changed, and the situation in Burma and North Africa deteriorated, draining away troops that might have been available, plan followed plan into the waste-paper basket and this is not the occasion to seek to retrieve them from their resting place. In the most general terms, the intention always was to have tank-proof localities prepared in the Mosul area from which reinforcing divisions, if they ever arrived, would be able to operate.

For the troops it was a long, hard and thankless task, in a climate of extremes, where the thermometer may range from 15° F in winter to 125° F for weeks on end in the summer.

> The plan involved a huge programme of digging; in one sector alone twenty-four miles of anti-tank ditch had to be cut through solid rock. Engineer and Pioneer companies were in short supply, so that the infantrymen—jacks of every trade and masters of many—found themselves operating compressors. No bulldozers were available. The thousands of coolies who were hired for the work had to be housed and administered in camps. Once more the soldiers of whom no one ever heard were suffering nearly all the hardships of battle.*

The other problem was the delivery of aid to Russia which merits a book in its own right. Starting with what, in the light of the eventual tonnage handled, seems like a modest amateur effort by the Government of India to dispatch stores and food by the land route through Baluchistan, there was almost continuous development to the point where the Americans alone had over a dozen major projects of their own on hand. Aircraft, stores, lorries, ammunition, food, petrol, there was

* Paiforce: The Official Story of the Persia and Iraq Command 1941–1949 (18).

no end to the list of what the route would carry. Perhaps the outstanding contribution made by the Indian Army was the work of the transport drivers of the Royal Indian Army Service Corps.

When Paiforce was formed, aid to Russia was run by a civilian transport organisation—the United Kingdom Commercial Corporation—with Persian civilian drivers. In November 1942 the Germans were driving down from Rostov towards Baku, threatening the vital oilfields of the Caucasus. Facing the Germans was the Russian Caucasian Army, cut off except by way of the Caspian Sea and through Persia. Guns, tanks, ammunition and supplies of all kinds were being sent to Russia as fast as road and rail services permitted; but at the height of the crisis, the Russians urgently required ammunition and they asked that it should be sent as quickly as possible. It could not be entrusted to civilian drivers and, to meet the emergency, six-wheeled lorries were transferred to 203 and 204 Companies of the R.I.A.S.C.

From Andimeshk to Tabriz was 730 miles over some of the most mountainous country in Persia; high passes had to be crossed, one nearly 8,000 feet above sea level; and, save for 150 miles, the road was of rough shingle. The Russian 'S.O.S.' was for 5,000 tons of 75 millimetre ammunition which had to be delivered within one month. On the morning of the 19th November, 'A' Platoon of 204 Company left Andimeshk and later made a spectacular entry into Tabriz welcomed by a Russian Officer and a guard of honour. 203 Company's first convoy left Andimeshk on December 3rd, clad in shorts and shirts, in a temperature of 126 degrees. Three days later, at Hamadan, they shivered in 19 degrees of frost, sleeping in the vehicles on top of the ammunition.

During January 1943 the winter began in earnest and the convoys had to face severe conditions. Sometimes they were engulfed in blizzards; sometimes they waited a day or more, keeping warm as best they could, while the road ahead was cleared with bull-dozers. Every load, however, was delivered to Tabriz and no convoy was more than two days late in arriving.

Owing to the amount of traffic, the road was always dangerous; every convoy required great mental and physical effort; but the accident rate, with a good company, was only in the region of one accident for every 150,000 miles.

204 Company was the first R.I.A.S.C. Company to drive ten-ton vehicles which, in fact, weighed 11 tons unloaded and 21 tons loaded. The road was difficult and dangerous enough with smaller lorries, but to take over the big lorries in winter—with snow and ice for hundreds of miles, frequent blizzards and temperatures around zero—was enough to daunt the hardiest driver. The Shibli Pass, for instance, 6,400 feet above sea level, descends on the north side in many hairpin bends, and a sheer drop of hundreds of feet from the road edge called for nerve and good driving. On two sharp bends, the driver, who might be a Madrassi weighing 140 lbs, had to stop his loaded Mack and, holding the whole 21 tons on the handbrake, reverse uphill to complete the turn.

Figures are impressive—275 convoys carried direct aid to Russia; 52 were loaded with bitumen; 35 with petrol; and 66 with other supplies, a total of 428. The number of lorries loaded was 11,739; 42,840 tons of supplies had been sent to Russia and R.I.A.S.C. drivers had covered 18,000,000 miles.

To mark Russian appreciation two men—Subedar Narayan Rao Nikkam and Havildar Gajendar Singh— were awarded the Order of the Russian Red Star.*

The Iraq–Iran venture attracted less than its fair share of attention because it all seemed so deceptively easy. To appreciate its true worth it must be set against the accepted German policy, which was to reinforce success and abandon failure. Due to the rapid and decisive action taken from India

* *R.I.A.S.C. in World War II.*

in April 1941 the German effort was stillborn, but the issue was, for a month, too nicely poised in the balance for comfort. If the first enemy reinforcements had been allowed to develop unchecked, they would quite surely have been extended; and in the face of a hostile Iraqi army, backed by even a small detachment of the Luftwaffe, an opposed occupation of the country might well have been beyond our slender resources. And because we had Iraq, Iran presented no real difficulty; but if Iran had remained in the hands of well-organized German saboteurs, we should have been faced with very serious trouble; the loss of our oil supplies, intervention against the Russian flank in the critical days around Rostov, and, of course, no aid to Russia.

In an examination of the gains and losses in the Middle East during the spring and summer of 1941 the Prime Minister concluded that on the whole the balance was in our favour. He attributed this satisfactory outcome to determined and farsighted action in both London and Cairo. He might, fairly, have added that both were lucky to have had so much of their home-work done for them in Delhi.

CHAPTER SIX

Syria

The Syrian campaign, which was fought over what comprises the modern states of Syria and Lebanon, lasted only thirty-five days. Like Iraq, Syria was part of the old Ottoman Empire and in 1920 the League of Nations' mandate for setting the country on the road to independence was given to the French. It was at the time not very clear just what justification there was for the decision and, in fact, an independent American Commission which looked into the whole question advised against it; but it was the outcome of some hard political bargaining which had been going on behind the scenes during the war, and the French won the day.

It is doubtful if the population anywhere really welcomed them, even in Lebanon where there was a Christian majority; elsewhere they at once ran into serious opposition because the mandate ran counter to hopes that Syria would become an Arab state under an Arab king. Feisal I had indeed been ruling in Damascus under British supervision since the end of the war, and the first thing the French did was to compel him to leave by force of arms.

It was not an auspicious beginning. The stormy course of Syrian politics over the past fifteen years is a pointer to the difficulties the French were up against, and it is certain that they have never been given full credit for the material advance the country made under their guidance; but, when that has been said, the fact remains that they failed to discharge their essential responsibility under the mandate which was to bring into being one or more independent states. It was not till 1936 that they even got as far as the preparation of the necessary treaties: one with the new state of Lebanon; the other with Syria, centred on Damascus and including as somewhat reluctant partners the Jebel Druz in the south-east and Latakia in the north-west. There was ample provision for the protection of French interests, and for the retention of considerable numbers of French troops over the period of transition, but the treaties came to naught because the French Chamber refused to ratify them. Thus, on the outbreak of war France was still ruling Syria without having secured very much agreement or support from her subject peoples.

After the fall of France, the Germans, in a moment of generosity, allowed the Italians to supervise the armistice arrangements, which followed the pattern of the package deal concluded for all the overseas possessions. A Polish brigade which had been in Syria, together with a small contingent of Free French with some colonial troops, crossed the border into Palestine where they came under the command of General Catroux. In Syria the basic pattern of discord was now further complicated by divisions of loyalty among the French who remained: all were neutral, but some were very much less neutral than others.

As early as September 1940, Catroux, with the characteristic optimism of those who shared his political opinions, was assuring us that the moment had come for him to overthrow the Vichy government in Syria, and asked for our help in doing so. The proposition was not without its attractions, but there were two serious drawbacks. If it failed, and it was really anyone's guess as to what the chances of success were, the Vichy government, which at that moment was not transgressing the reasonable borders of neutrality, might well turn nasty; and, whatever the outcome, there was always the chance that the local population, who would be watching affairs with the keenest interest from their ringside seats, might take advantage of any hitch to take part in a general free-for-all. Should this happen we had absolutely no troops available to restore order, so the Free French were told that they must restrict their efforts to propaganda.

Shortly afterwards a new high commissioner, with strong pro-Vichy sentiments, General Henri Dentz, was appointed; more and more Germans were reported to be entering the country, and by the end of the year it was clear that any sort of political coup was out of the question. That did not alter the fact that a friendly French government in Syria would relieve General Wavell of a lot of anxiety about his right flank; the trouble was that it was never very clear just how to set about making the change, or where to find the troops for what would now plainly have to be an operation of war. In the opening months of 1941 the problem was the source of almost unceasing diplomatic and political activity in Free French circles, and there was never any lack of ideas as to how other people, meaning ourselves, should set about the task. Their first suggestion was that if we entered the country in absolutely overwhelming force, honour would be satisfied, and General Dentz would lay down his arms. Unfortunately no troops, let alone a strong force, were available. A little later, after our withdrawal from Greece, it was at least on the cards that the German airborne offensive, which in the event descended on Crete, might be directed against Syria and we were then urged to send reinforcements to General Dentz to enable him to resist; but as there was no reason to suppose that General Dentz had any intention of resisting, it was hardly wise to open negotiations which would have shown him how very slender our resources were.

In May the Axis aircraft that had been attempting to intervene in Iraq were known to have been refuelling on Syrian airfields where the R.A.F. had been attacking them on the ground, and it was perhaps this activity which brought home to those in Middle East Headquarters the fact that Axis bombers based on Damascus, and attacking the Suez Canal, would be closer to their target than if they were operating from Mersah Matruh. Once again General Catroux stressed the advantages of immediate action, but the only possible troops which might have been sent into Syria at short notice were on their way to relieve Habbaniya, so he suggested that his force in Palestine should cross the frontier and make a stirring appeal to their countrymen to rally to the cause. All he needed from us were lorries, drivers and air support; he might as well have asked for the moon and the stars as well, for all three were in chronically short supply. Even when assured that increasing German pressure on the country was resulting in a reversion of feeling towards ourselves, General Wavell still resisted all proposals made to him for intervention, partly because he did not have the resources to allot, partly because he disliked the idea of demonstrations he could not support; demonstrations which, if they failed, would leave matters worse than they had been before.

On 18 May Catroux arrived with a highly circumstantial story to the effect that the Vichy French were about to withdraw into Lebanon and hand the rest of Syria over to the Germans; here, he said, was the very last opportunity, for, until the Germans arrived, the eastern road to the north lay clear, and Damascus lay, like a plum, ripe for picking. By then a force for intervention in Syria was actually being assembled, but it was nowhere near ready, and, as there was no confirmation of the story from other sources, General Wavell once again refused to intervene. Catroux finally whittled his plan down to a proposal that his Free French force should be moved to the Palestinian frontier opposite Deraa, where they could test the reaction of French and Arabs to the idea of invasion, but even this modest excursion involved the provision of 300 lorries. General Wavell, with something of a suspicion that these plans were being hawked round diplomatic circles in London behind his back, asked for a categoric decision from the chiefs of staff: was he to comply with this demand? He was told that he must do so; whereupon he replied that he refused to be dictated to by Generals de Gaulle and Catroux, and that if his judgement was not trusted, he must ask to be relieved of his command. He received a soothing reply from the Prime Minister: the decision had been based on an all-round survey of the war in all theatres, and if the Germans could pick up Syria and Iraq with petty air forces, tourists and local revolts, we must be prepared to run equivalent small-scale risks and face the political consequences of failure.

Providentially, at this critical juncture General Catroux reported that his information was totally inaccurate, and that, on the contrary, the Vichy French had already manned the prepared positions in which they intended to fight for the defence of Syria.

The enemy were known to have at their disposal some five regiments of cavalry and twenty battalions of infantry with reasonable artillery support; of greater significance, they had about ninety tanks in good running order, and a force of not far short of a hundred aircraft, which incidentally received a fifty per cent reinforcement during the campaign. General Wavell had estimated that to conquer and occupy the whole of Syria he would need two divisions and an armoured brigade. On 20 May, when the plans for Exporter, as the operation was called, were sent to London, he had available 7th Australian Division, of which one brigade was missing, six battalions of Free French troops, and part of 1st Cavalry Division. With this force he hoped to secure the line Damascus –Rayak–Beirut, but he would not be able to deal with the enemy if he withdrew north to the Aleppo area. We had no armoured troops and, perhaps the most serious weakness of all, no more than three and a half squadrons of aircraft.

In submitting his plan General Wavell asked if he was to act when ready or wait for some further provocation, such as the arrival of German reinforcements. He was told that he was free to move at a date to be fixed by himself, and by the time he was ready his force received a reinforcement that was to play a significant part in the campaign; 5th Indian Infantry Brigade arrived from the fighting at Keren. He was also able to make some initial moves of units of the British 6th Division who provided much needed reinforcements after the battle had started.

Exporter was launched therefore against a somewhat chequered political background. Although it may well have been the fear of German air forces operating from Damascus which finally decided General Wavell that the threat from Syria must be dealt with once and for all, in fact the Germans, after their failure in Iraq, and with Barbarossa, their attack on Russia, no more than three weeks away, had withdrawn from the country. Secure in the thought that we always fought according to the Queensberry rules, they decided that they would give us no excuse for getting rid of the Vichy French, who might come in useful to them later on.

By means of leaflets and broadcasts the people of Syria were informed that the Free French were entering the country to put an end to the mandate and establish their unfettered independence. Up to the very last moment the Free French seem to have cherished the hope that the enemy, their countrymen, might parley and lay down their arms. The hope was rudely shattered as soon as we crossed the frontier, the buttons were off the foils and the fight was on: and nowhere was it to be more bitterly contested than in the sector where Frenchman fought Frenchman. In the very best British tradition Operation Exporter was fought by a force scratched together at the last moment, inferior in numbers, and lacking, notably, aircraft, tanks, anti-aircraft artillery and transport. It was matched against a determined and well-equipped enemy who knew the ground and had had ample time to prepare his defences.

Geography and communications are above all the factors which determine strategy, and in Syria they left the attacker little choice. There are only three roads by which to advance into the country from the south: along the fringe of the desert from Deraa to Damascus, and northwards to Homs; from the head of the Sea of Galilee to Merjayum, then up the valley of the Litani to the railway junction of Rayak, and again on to Homs; and along the sea coast from Haifa, through Tyre and Sidon to Beirut, and on to Tripoli. Mount Hermon and the Anti-Lebanon range stand between the two easterly roads; Lebanon, with spurs running down to the Mediterranean, forces the westerly road to hug the coastline.

General Wilson,* who was by then commanding in Palestine, was ordered to capture first the line Damascus–Rayak–Beirut, and subsequently to advance to the line Palmyra–Homs–Tripoli. An advance along the coastal road could be

* The late Field Marshal Lord Wilson, G.C.B., C.B.E., D.S.O.

supported by the Royal Navy, and by a commando battalion which was on call in Cyprus, so he decided to make that his main line of advance, with Beirut, the seat of the Vichy French government, as the objective. He allotted the coast and central roads to 7th Australian Division. The advance by the easterly road on Damascus was to be headed by 5th Indian Infantry Brigade who, after capturing Deraa, would hand over to the Free French, reduced because of shortage of transport to a brigade group.

During the first week in June, 5th Indian Infantry Brigade commanded by Brigadier Wilfred Lloyd* concentrated just short of the frontier, with the Royal Fusiliers south of the Sea of Galilee, the remainder of the brigade south-west of Deraa. The Royal Fusiliers were to send one company to command the railway line while the main body of the battalion was to advance on Kuneitra, the capture of which would deprive the enemy of all east-west communications south of the main road from Beirut to Damascus. Crossing the upper waters of the Jordan—there no more than a brawling stream—at Jisr Benat Yacoub, the Ford of Jacob's Daughters, they approached Kuneitra where, in deference to the Free French, an officer was sent forward to demand the surrender of the town. There was a prolonged parley but 'at length a French officer came out and, like a herald in a mediaeval war, announced that hostilities would begin again at midday; and at that hour the guns opened fire'. There seemed likely to be considerable opposition, but at that juncture a Free French officer arrived at battalion headquarters with the information that the town was undefended on the north and east. As he had been stationed there only a fortnight before, it was felt that he should know, and a wide sweeping movement through the night brought the troops about dawn into the town from the opposite side. Surprise would no doubt have been complete had not the enemy withdrawn two hours before, leaving the Fusiliers to take over the sleeping town in peace.

The illusion of manoeuvres was thus fully maintained,

* The late Major-General W. L. Lloyd, D.S.O.

the enemy again being imaginary, though no one would deny that it was a first class scheme. (31)

The advance on Deraa was made in two columns. The 4/6th Rajputana Rifles were to move north to secure an important railway viaduct which was known to have been prepared for demolition, and then come down on the town from the north-west while the main body, with 3/1st Punjab Regiment, attacked from the south. The bridge had been a target for Lawrence's Arabs in 1918, but on that occasion the Turks had been alarmed when one of the raiders dropped his rifle; this time there was to be no mistake. The company commander started forward alone to deal with the Vichy post on the far side of the dry ravine, but his company havildar major insisted on going with him. They cut the wire round the picquet and crept inside.

Then the sentry's attention was attracted but he apparently thought the intruders were dogs. He picked up a stone and threw it. Presumably because they did not howl or run away his suspicions were well and truly aroused. The bolt of his rifle clicked and Murray and Goru Ram waited for no more. They charged the tent and sentry at once with their tommy guns in action, and wiped out the whole post. The sound of the shots was the signal for the rest of the platoon to rush the two guard posts on top of the viaduct and capture them; and so the Chehab viaduct was saved. (15)

By 3 a.m. the Sapper detachment had removed the demolition charges, and the battalion continued its difficult march across country to be in position north-west of Deraa by daybreak. The advance of the main column from the south was headed by a car wearing a white flag, but the engine was wrecked by a shell from an anti-tank gun, which luckily failed to explode, and when further *pourparlers* had been rejected, the guns of 1st Field Regiment opened fire and the Punjab Regiment had little difficulty in capturing the town.

At 11 a.m. the Rajputana Rifles set off for Meskine, fifteen miles away to the north, which was found to be strongly held. A flank attack was successful largely owing to the determination and gallantry of a naik who led his platoon forward, when his commander and havildar had become casualties, and wiped out a machine-gun post manned by the Foreign Legion. By morning the enemy had gone and the brigade, having given the operation a rousing start, moved slightly to the south-east to guard the desert flank while the Free French, who had crossed the frontier the day before singing the 'Marseillaise', moved through and took the lead in the advance on Damascus. By the eleventh they had reached Kissoue, ten miles south of Damascus, but there their attack, which was resumed the following day, was halted and 5th Brigade was called forward to deal with the situation.

The village of Kissoue lies surrounded by hills on three sides. To the right of the main road, before reaching the village, towers Jebel Maani, 3,300 feet high; further on is the Jebel Kelb. Immediately to the north is Tel Kissoue, and to the north-west, just under 3,000 feet, Jebel Madani. The Free French had gained a footing on Jebel Maani but had avoided a frontal attack, declaring the position to be impregnable. Viewed artistically the picture was attractive enough: a small stream looped the village, the low ground along its banks being heavily cultivated, while a maze of small streams intersected the cactus *zarebas* and tiny orchard enclosures of lemon, nectarine and fig trees. 'Green woods and bines made the village look very attractive, with its mud houses and mosque peeping over the tree tops.' Tactically it was the very devil. Among the orchards was a maze of wire defences covered by machine-gun posts, and in front of the whole had been dug an anti-tank ditch, thirteen feet deep and thirteen feet wide. A company commander wrote:

> While the conference between commanders was in progress, we company commanders were given the opportunity of liaison with the Free French battalions which had carried out the attack the night before and which were licking their wounds in a woody area immediately to the east of the hill. Our impressions of our allies were not

very good, particularly as, when the suggestion of an attack against Kissoue cropped up, we saw these semi-naked, unshaven and ragged Legionnaires shake their heads in argument with their own officers and reply: 'Les Anglais sont fous!' (21)

The brigade commander decided after reconnaissance that a night attack without artillery support afforded the best chance of success and it appears that the senior officers of our allies, if less outspoken, were equally sceptical of the success of such an undertaking.

'A direct attack without artillery preparation, tanks or air bombardment?' They shrugged their shoulders. 'And with one battalion?' They raised their hands and looked significantly at each other. It was surely only their innate politeness that prevented them tapping their foreheads to indicate the insanity of the plan. (15)

In the darkness of the Saturday night the Punjab battalion moved up to the start line in lorries.

The night was as quiet as the tomb as the men crept forward, equipped with hastily constructed scaling ladders to aid them across the ditch. At 3.20 a.m. the stillness was suddenly broken by the clatter of machine-guns and the explosions of bursting bombs. The firing rose in a crescendo, to die away and then flare up again. Suddenly success signals went up and the firing died away in the village as the first grey of dawn appeared in the east. The Punjab Regiment had completely surprised the Vichy troops and after some heavy hand to hand fighting in the village had captured the whole of it. The impossible had been achieved, though luck played its part. The garrison was in the middle of a relief; no attack was expected and many of the defenders' weapons were already loaded into lorries waiting for the arrival of the relieving troops. (15)

By nine o'clock Kissoue was in our hands and 'numbers of

dripping prisoners had been fished out of the irrigation ditches where they had hoped to be overlooked by the mopping-up squads'. It was now the turn of the Rajputana Rifles to capture Tel Kissoue which they did supported by the artillery which had been ranging on it since daylight. The attack succeeded but the Free French, after an initial success on the right, were held up short of the Jebel Kelb. There were two fierce counter-attacks on Tel Kissoue and on the village itself but they were twice beaten off and when they had failed

> Vichy had recourse to more spectacular, though much less effective, tactics. A trumpet sounded, and from behind the shelter of a covering ridge a squadron of Spahi horsemen wheeled out and came forward at the gallop. It was gallant, it was picturesque, and it was quite futile.*

The whole operation was a remarkable, indeed an amazing, achievement, and the brigade commander perhaps felt that it deserved the tribute expressed in the words of a captured Vichy officer: 'Ce que vous avez fait, c'est incroyable. Vos Indiens sont vraiment formidables.'

But that was not all. Appreciating the importance of exploiting the success he had gained, the brigadier called on his two battalions for one more effort, the capture of Jebel Madani, the commanding height to the north-west, before it could be reinforced from the north. They responded magnificently. Once again attacking in the dark, they took the enemy by surprise and by daylight were 'looking northwards across gardens, orchards and streams upon the minarets of Damascus gleaming in the sunshine only nine miles away'.

Despite the overwhelming success of the capture of Kissoue the news reaching the brigade commander and General Legentilhomme from elsewhere gave less cause for satisfaction. Progress generally had been less rapid than the optimists had hoped for, and everywhere the enemy were resisting far more bitterly than even the pessimists had foretold.

* *Five Ventures* (14).

At this stage the cause of General de Gaulle was far from attracting universal support from his countrymen, rather did many feel that by his attitude he was embarrassing the efforts of the Vichy government to secure reasonable terms from the Germans; and by their rapid withdrawal from the country when they saw their cause was lost, the Germans had put us in a false position. Hypocrites as always, we were claiming to have come to drive out the Germans, when everyone knew that the Germans had already gone. Couple these factors with the French professional soldier's pride in fighting for a cause he regarded as just, and it is not surprising that until the Senegalese and the Foreign Legion lost their stomach for the fight we were faced by a skilful and determined enemy.

The news from the Australian division was that, after some rapid initial progress, they had bumped into a strong position south of Sidon. The commander had ordered the central brigade, which had taken Merjayun, to leave a battalion to watch the enemy who were blocking the road north to Rayak, and then to advance across country to Jezzine to threaten the left flank of the Sidon defences.

At that moment General de Verdilhac, the Vichy commander, launched three shrewd and well-directed counter-attacks which for some time caused us considerable anxiety. On the Australian front, the battalion commander who had been left behind at Merjayun, impatient at finding himself out of the hunt, attempted to outflank the enemy facing him, leaving no more than a weak holding force behind. The Vichy commander promptly attacked, and the advance on Jezzine had to be abandoned while a battalion from the brigade was sent back to restore the situation.

In the centre, a strong force of some 2,000 infantry with eleven tanks attacked the Royal Fusiliers in Kuneitra.

At 0400 hours the noise of tanks was heard. The battle had begun. Effective resistance was hopeless for the lack of proper weapons. Anti-tank rifles were useless even at ten yards, grenades had no effect, and of 'molotov cocktails' there were very few. There were no 'sticky bombs', and the only useful anti-tank weapon, a captured

95

Italian Breda gun, broke down after firing a dozen rounds. The result was that the Vichy tanks broke into the town at about 0600 hours. Infantry attacks were at first repulsed, but the tanks attacked and overwhelmed one section post after another, until, at 1130 hours, the commanding officer decided to collect his remaining troops for a last stand at battalion headquarters, sited in three strong granite houses with an anti-tank ditch behind it. There were many gallant deeds that day. Towards evening it looked as if the enemy infantry had withdrawn as there was a lull. At 1820 hours a French officer appeared in an armoured car, waving a white handkerchief. The officer explained that the battalion was surrounded by a vastly superior force of tanks and other armoured fighting vehicles. He hoped they would surrender now as he hated shooting Englishmen. After consultation with the second-in-command and Regimental Sergeant-Major Gardner the commanding officer decided that to give in was the only alternative to the massacre of the remainder of his men. At 1900 hours he surrendered with thirteen officers and 164 other ranks. (31)

News of the perilous situation at Kuneitra had reached brigade headquarters, but the two Indian battalions were fighting the battle of Kissoue, and no help could be sent. Nor was that the whole tale of woe. On the right a small enemy column, emerging from the Jebel Druz, captured Ezraa and cut the communications of 5th Brigade, but a rapid counter-stroke by an improvised force retook the town. Nothing daunted, the brigade commander decided that to halt would be to play the enemy's game. If reasonable precautions were taken to protect the flanks of a further advance, the resumption of the attack to capture Damascus was the move most likely to restore the situation. But let there be no under-estimate of the courage needed to make the decision: the enemy were astride two roads in his rear, his British battalion was lost to him completely, his Indian battalions were well below strength from casualties and detachments, they were tired, and they would certainly be outnumbered. The Australian official history records 'that the enterprise was bold in the extreme, typical of the irrepressible leader who conceived it'. (8)

Two miles to the west of Damascus near the aerodrome lies the village of Mezze; to the west again is a ridge with a line of forts guarding the approaches to the city; and further on, to the north-west, is the Barada gorge through which pass both road and railway to Rayak. Brigadier Lloyd's plan was for the two battalions to attack by night, fight their way through the tangle of gardens and orchards, capture the airfield and village, and press on to block the Barada gorge, thus cutting the escape route of the forces in the city. The Free French on the right were to advance from the Jebel Kelb direct on Damascus. A British battalion from Egypt was known to be moving forward. The Australians, having by-passed Kuneitra, were driving up from the south-west, and it was hoped that these reinforcements would arrive in time to take the shock of the French efforts to break out. At 8 p.m. the Punjab battalion formed up to lead the advance of 5th Brigade.

The first objective was the fortified village of Mouddamiya, five miles from Mezze, on the approach to Damascus airfield. Captain Harley led a determined attack against the machine-gun posts, armoured cars and strong points in Mouddamiya. In pitch darkness, lit up by intense shelling, the men pushed on to the far edge of the wood. Yard by yard the gardens were cleared. One tank after another was found and destroyed. In this attack Jemadar Bhagat Singh set an example of gallant effort and confident leadership by destroying four strongly held machine-gun pill-boxes in spite of his platoon having suffered heavy casualties. In the assault on the fourth pill-box he was killed. By midnight Mouddamiya was captured, but twenty-seven men only remained on their feet. (51)

The battalion pressed on. The company on the right became involved in rescuing from a Vichy road block the transport, belonging to both battalions, carrying anti-tank guns, reserve ammunition, land mines, tools, food and water which had by mistake kept to the main road. It was a costly mistake for the battle of Mezze House was fought without these vital loads. The other two companies at midnight decided to ignore all minor objectives and move directly on Mezze. Only one of two small forts on the ridge above them was taken, and the advance was held up. The main body, The Rajputana Rifles, had by then arrived and, after an hour's bitter street fighting, took the village. It was at this critical stage that the total failure of the Free French to advance and complete their share of the plan wrecked the success of the whole enterprise, for the Vichy forces in Damascus were able to concentrate their whole attention on Mezze. Although a Rajputana company broke through to the gorge, turned back a train and set fire to a petrol dump, they were forced to withdraw on to the main body of the battalion in the village, which was now working feverishly to consolidate and fortify it against the imminent attack. With the forts on the ridge still in enemy hands, with neither artillery nor armour available, the only salvation lay in a delaying action. Brigade headquarters and both battalion headquarters were established in Mezze House, 'a large square edifice surrounded by a high thick wall', and a 'keep' defence had been organized. The infantry companies were disposed round the perimeter of the village.

> Mezze House provided certain advantages for a force which aimed at making a 'backs-to-the-wall' resistance. From three sides it could only be approached by steep gullies, and its garden, thick with trees and dense under growth, was enclosed by a high stone wall. The previous occupant of the house, whoever he may have been, had kept a good cellar. Now the riches of Burgundy, Bordeaux and Moselle were poured away so that the bottles might be filled with petrol and converted into 'Molotov cocktails' with which to meet the coming assault. (14)

The Vichy attack, strongly supported by tanks, began soon after nine o'clock in the morning and the tanks were the deciding factor. Slowly but inevitably through the day the outlying companies were driven in, and the survivors rallied in Mezze House. But there by nightfall the situation was desperate. Ammunition was running low, medical supplies were exhausted. The manor house sheets had been torn up for bandages; under heavy fire the trees in the orchard had been stripped of fruit to eke out the scanty rations. At dusk Lieutenant-Colonel Jones selected three officers to run the gauntlet to Brigadier Lloyd at Syrian Force headquarters. 'After an adventurous night in which they crawled through gardens, crept over roofs, swam streams and burst through cactus *zarebas*, they arrived at 0500 hours and reported the critical situation.' (21)

Although the success signals sent up from Mezze had for some reason not been observed, the brigade commander had already scraped together his few remaining reserves and sent them off as a column with instructions to reach Mezze at all costs. They met stiff opposition but by the evening were in touch with two rifle companies who were lying in gardens below the ridge. As fate would have it, it was decided to deal with the forts above them before attempting to break into Mezze. The assault was to be made early next morning.

During the night the enemy had been tightening the ring round Mezze House.

The dawn assault was particularly severe. The assailants closed to bombing range; every door and window became a target. Field-guns over open sights systematically began to batter down the house. A top corner collapsed, burying many wounded including Lieut.-Colonel Great-wood (of the Punjab Regiment), who later died of his injuries. The building caught fire and it became necessary to take the wounded outside; from the hillside the tanks continued to rake the grounds, so that men were struck again and again. In the forenoon the defenders saw shells bursting around the forts on the ridge and knew that help was near. With ammunition exhausted it was decided to ask for a truce to move the wounded to safety; it was hoped the relief columns would arrive during the armistice. At the sight of the white flag the enemy came rushing from all sides. . . . The defence of Mezze House had ended. (21)

99

Captain Chatterjee, medical officer of The Rajputana Rifles, describes the surrender:

> The enemy rushed in, shouting, snatching arms and field-glasses from the officers and men. They were absolutely mad, threatening to shoot an officer and keeping him covered with their guns. A party of the enemy were ordered to carry the wounded to hospital. The officers and men were marched away while the wounded were being helped out. They were behaving very ruthlessly towards our wounded and paying no attention to their wounds and pain. One man with a gunshot wound in the abdomen was simply being dragged along. I could not stand the sight so I carried him on my shoulders for a distance of two miles. (21)

The relief column failed to save Mezze House by three hours and when they reached the village all was silent and deserted. 'The battered garden walls and damaged houses, the burnt-out tanks and the dead bodies were eloquent testimony to the terrific fight.'

That evening the Australians arrived and pushed through to the Barada gorge, while the Free French, reinforced, and that would seem to be the operative word, by a company from an Australian machine-gun battalion, began their tardy advance from Jebel Kelb and reached the outskirts of the city on the south-east. The heart had gone out of the Vichy Army and next morning the Free French and Australian commanders received the surrender of the city. They were 'conducted into Damascus and entertained at luncheon; later Colonel Collet and his Circassians arrived. General Legentilhomme made his formal entry at 4 p.m.'

Fighting without air support, let down by their allies, and, through a tragic blunder, without the transport carrying the defensive stores which might have enabled them to hold out, the two battalions lost 738 officers and men; the reader must judge for himself where the laurels for the capture of Damascus justly lie.

The Australian official history records that 'the advance to

Mezze had an influence on the conduct of the campaign that was out of proportion to the local gains or its immediate effect on the defence of Damascus'.*

The fall of Damascus by no means ended the struggle for Syria. With the arrival of the headquarters of 6th Division from Egypt, an attempt was made to force a passage between the Anti-Lebanon and Mount Hermon and to open the road to Beirut, but when the armistice was signed our troops were still held up on Jebel Mazar, only twenty miles west of Damascus. To the north, the Free French succeeded in advancing half way to Homs. On the coast, the Australians had taken Sidon on the fifteenth, but it was not until the twenty-fourth that they recaptured Merjayun and were free to turn their whole attention to the direct advance on Beirut. They ran into a very strong position based on the river south of Damour, which they began to attack on 5 July, and on the ninth they took the town, only to meet, the following day, stiff opposition at Khalde, five miles south of Beirut. The fighting on the coast had been on a larger scale, and the resistance offered more severe, than anywhere else in the campaign; but, with the Australians almost on the outskirts of the city, General Dentz realized that further resistance was of no avail, and on the evening of 11 July he asked by radio that hostilities should end at midnight. On the following day his representatives came in to discuss terms.

There were two contributory factors which must have gone some way to convince him that the situation was hopeless. With the end of Battleaxe in the Western Desert, the R.A.F. had been able to divert aircraft to Syria, a number of Vichy machines had been destroyed on the ground, and harbours, airfields and railways were under constant attack. Also, as a result of the capture of Deir-ez-Zor by 10th Indian Division from Baghdad, the whole of north-east Syria was in our hands and a threat to Aleppo was developing which ruled out any possibility of his withdrawing to make a last stand in the north of the province.

---

* *Australia in the War of 1939–1945: Greece, Crete & Syria* (8).

CHAPTER SEVEN

North Africa

March–December 1941

When 4th Indian Division left for Keren after the battle of Sidi Barrani, their place was taken by 6th Australian Division, and there were no Indian formations in the Western Desert for about three months. Over the next two and a half years their numbers varied and their fortunes fluctuated, very much as did those of the army of which they formed a part.

The Australians captured Bardia and Tobruk, and in company with 7th Armoured Division pursued the demoralized Italians. Then, on 7 February, in the battle of Beda Fomm, sixty miles south of Benghazi, the Western Desert Force inflicted a final crushing defeat on the whole of the *10th Italian Army*. South of Beda Fomm, where the coast turns westwards along the Gulf of Sirte, there is a line, marked on no survey map nor yet on the ground, which defines the limit beyond which, in those days when transport was limited, we could not maintain troops in battle. There was, therefore, no prospect of exploiting our success and, indeed, there were demands for troops elsewhere which ruled any further advance out of court. The call came from Greece which had been attacked by Italy, though with such little success that there was every prospect that the Germans would come to her rescue. If they did, they would very quickly overrun the whole country unless there was some backing from outside.

General Wavell was faced with a most difficult decision: to stand any chance of success he had to send every man and every tank he could spare; on the other hand, he was obliged to keep enough troops to hold what he had won in Cyrenaica. Working on the quite reasonable assumption that the Benghazi front was safe till May—by which time he would have at any rate one division back from Keren—he decided that it was an acceptable risk to leave, south of Benghazi, no more than one fresh Australian division and 2nd Armoured Division, newly arrived from England. As events turned out he made two miscalculations: first of all, the Germans, under the newly arrived Rommel, attacked so very much earlier than had been expected that they had occupied El Agheila by 24 March; secondly, the mechanical condition of 2nd Division's tanks was so poor that they were unable to put up the resistance which might have been expected of them. Rommel had seized the initiative and he was not the man to let it go.

By 2 April, the strength of 3rd Armoured Brigade was reported at twenty-two cruisers and twenty-five light tanks, with a forecast, only too soon to be proved accurate, that further breakdowns would occur at the rate of one tank every ten miles. This really was the crux of the matter: if at this juncture the brigade had been in a state to deliver a sharp counter-attack, it is likely that the German advance would have been halted; as they could not do so, the whole position in Western Cyrenaica became untenable. 3 April was a gloomy day of order, counter-order and disorder, and saw the start of the demolitions at Benghazi. By the seventh, 9th Australian Division were back fifteen miles west of Tobruk, where two brigades of 7th Australian Division were working against time to prepare the defences.

On 3 April Brigadier Vaughan, commanding 3rd Indian Motor Brigade, was ordered to occupy Mechili as a base onto which 2nd Armoured Division could retire. The brigade arrived there the next afternoon, and that evening received an invitation from the enemy to surrender, an offer which they rightly interpreted as a bluff: the Germans needed the water supply, and were in a hurry to press on to Tobruk. The

Armoured Division was actually ordered to Mechili on 6 April, but due to fuel shortage and breakdowns it had by then virtually ceased to exist as a fighting formation, and all that arrived was the divisional headquarters, a battery of R.H.A. and some Australian anti-tank guns; they turned up at 10 p.m. Next day there were two more demands for surrender, the second of which, just in case there had been some misunderstanding, was signed by Rommel himself. Late that evening the brigade commander was ordered to escort the armoured divisional headquarters out next morning in a 'mobile box' to El Adem. The eastern side of the box, consisting of a squadron of 18th Cavalry carried in 15 cwt trucks, carried out their part of the plan and made a most gallant charge on the enemy guns in position; they broke through, but the operation as a whole did not succeed and both divisional and brigade commanders were taken prisoner. Early on the eighth enemy armour overran the brigade, but moving in small parties, and finding their own way across the desert, a number of men managed to escape, bringing, indeed, a number of prisoners with them.

Brigadier Vaughan, who wrote the regimental history of 2nd Lancers, one of the regiments of his brigade, concludes:

> For those officers who took part in the battle one final consolation remains—the staunch courage with which the Indian ranks, young and inexperienced, lacking full equipment and training, standing firm when others retired, so finely upheld the traditions of their race and the regiment. Where much else failed, their spirit did not.*

Once they were seriously attacked, there was of course nothing they could do: but it is worth considering just how much, for all their weakness, they did in fact achieve. Rommel's armour had reached Msus on the third; Mechili, only eighty miles to the east, defied him till the ninth; Tobruk was invested on the sixth, but until the armour arrived he could not mount a proper attack. Thus, it is likely that this

* *History of the 2nd Royal Lancers (Gardner's Horse) (42).*

gallant stand did buy, albeit at such a cost, the few precious days the Australians needed to settle themselves firmly for the siege. They were able to withstand the repeated attacks made towards the end of the month and, having held out for one month, they held out for seven months longer.

By mid-May Western Desert Force was back on a line running from Buq Buq to Sofafi and Halfaya Pass was in enemy hands, but the German position was by no means secure. Their attempts to take Tobruk had failed and administratively they were on the end of a string, much as we had been at El Agheila. So it was that, with the arrival from England of tanks to re-equip 7th Armoured Division, General Wavell decided he must attack Rommel before he had time to consolidate his gains. The operation was to be known as Battleaxe and was intended to defeat the enemy on the frontier, relieve Tobruk, and exploit towards Derna and Mechili; the garrison of Tobruk was to co-operate vigorously. The troops taking part were 7th Armoured Division, with two armoured brigades and a support group; the infantry consisted of 4th Indian Division, back from Keren with all its artillery and one of its own brigades, and 22nd Guards Brigade under command.

Certain 'disquietening facts' now came to light regarding the equipment of the armoured division. It was found that their armoured cars were outgunned and outpaced by those of the enemy; more seriously, the two armoured brigades were equipped with quite different types of tank, one having the cruiser, the other the more heavily armoured, but much slower, 'I' tank. These latter had fought decisively in support of the infantry at Sidi Barrani, the role for which they were designed, but they were not suited for battle between armoured forces; nor had the two brigades had time to train together and evolve tactics by which one might support the other. In consequence, before Battleaxe began General Wavell had revised his views; he felt confident that the first object would be secured, but was less happy about the other two.

The plan for the opening phase of Battleaxe was for 4th Indian Division to destroy the enemy forces in the area

Bardia–Sollum–Halfaya–Capuzzo, while 7th Armoured Division was to cover the left flank and co-operate in destroying the enemy in the frontier area. 4th Division had 4th Armoured Brigade, equipped with 'I' tanks, under its command. The divisional plan gave 11th Indian Infantry Brigade, supported by sixteen tanks, the task of a frontal attack on the Halfaya Pass, while the Guards Brigade with the rest of the armour moved to attack Capuzzo and Sollum from the south-west. This detour had been ordered at the last moment when air photographs revealed a tank obstacle on the more direct route, and it had the unfortunate result that the success achieved by the Guards Brigade was too remote to threaten the rear flank of the enemy holding out at Halfaya. The armoured division was to capture high ground six miles west of Capuzzo.

The action of 11th Brigade was dominated by the line of the escarpment, a geographical feature that was to affect the tactics of so much fighting in the Western Desert over the next eighteen months. The escarpment marks the dividing line between the plain at sea level and the plateau, perhaps 200 feet above it, which stretches away 100 miles to the south. It is mostly steep bare rock, but the rim of the plateau is not like the edge of a cliff. Gullies cut their way inland, so that the top of the ridge weaves in and out, and from below the whole presents the appearance of a steep, rugged range of hills, all of which are the same height. Vehicles, and indeed armour, can pass between plain and plateau only where the infrequent road or track exists. One of these is at Halfaya Pass, where the plain is less than two miles wide. The brigade plan was for 2nd Mahrattas and 1st Rajputana Rifles with six tanks in support to attack through the broken ground on the edge of the plain, and for the Camerons with twelve tanks to advance along the edge of the plateau.

At 6 a.m. the Camerons opened the attack, the screen of twelve tanks moving ahead of them, and as they approached the top of the Pass the Germans sprang one of the most significant tactical surprises of the war. They had fitted their long-barrelled 88 mm anti-aircraft gun with a horizontal mounting; with its flat trajectory and heavy high-velocity shell, it was to be the scourge of our armour right to the very end of the war. They would site the guns at effective killing range on the reverse slope of a low ridge, and on this morning of 15 June eleven of the supporting ranks were blazing wrecks in a matter of minutes: it was the turning point of the whole battle. The Camerons pressed on, the Indian battalions below on the plain fought their way forward in the broken ground, but with less than half the divisional artillery to support them, they had to fight bitterly for every yard of ground; by evening they were still 1,000 yards short of the Pass. The armoured division out on the left had been held up short of its objective, but the rest of 4th Armoured Brigade had captured Capuzzo and the Guards Brigade, passing through them, were pressing on towards Sollum. Possession of the Pass would very much simplify the co-ordination of the two halves of the division, so it was decided to press the attack that evening. Just before zero hour Colonel Skrine of Wellesley's, raising his head to exhort a party of his men to keep under cover, was killed instantly. 'This bitter blow failed to deter his men who swept to the assault in splendid style. Five hundred yards were gained; the coveted gap was almost in their grasp when unbearable fire beat them into the ground.'

The brigade clung to the ground they had gained but the tide elsewhere was running against us. The Guards Brigade had taken Sollum, but out in the desert the enemy had won the armoured battle and were reported to be coming in from the west to strike our flank south of Halfaya, thus threatening to cut off the whole of the division. In the circumstances there was no alternative but to order the withdrawal of the Guards Brigade. The divisional artillery fought off the tanks threatening from the west, 11th Brigade hung grimly on about the escarpment, and the whole force on the plateau got safely away. 11th Brigade withdrew during the night of 17–18 June and, thanks to a determined rearguard action fought by a company of the Mahrattas under their subedar-major, it was not seriously molested.

After the battle, on 6 July, the officers of 1st Battalion Rajputana Rifles were invited to dine with the officers of 2nd Battalion Queen's Own Cameron Highlanders when 'the tune

"With Wellesley's at Keren", composed by Corporal E. Berney, was played. The Camerons had composed this tune in honour of Lieut.-Colonel Skrine who was killed at Halfaya Pass and it was first played as his burial march'.*

In July General Auchinleck,† who had been commander-in-chief in India, changed commands with General Wavell and there was some reorganization in the Middle East. The old Western Desert Force became the Eighth Army, with two corps, the XIIIth and the XXXth. There was a lull after Battleaxe for five months during which no major operation was attempted by either side; both were too busy reorganizing, training and building up stocks forward for the attack that each planned to make. The Germans, before they could do anything at all, had to remove the threat that Tobruk imposed on their communications; we naturally hoped to forestall this operation, and to strike the enemy while his high command was still preoccupied with events in Russia. This latter factor, indeed, provided the Prime Minister with the necessary ammunition for urging General Auchinleck to start Crusader, as our operation was to be called, at the earliest possible moment. There was, however, the overriding factor that, if it was to succeed in its object of driving the enemy out of Cyrenaica, it must be mounted in strength. On this ground it was possible to resist the numerous suggestions that reinforcing formations should be used piecemeal as they arrived, to keep the enemy under pressure and so prevent him from building up his resources. Reviewing the course of the fighting that followed, the official history supports the view that the Eighth Army attack was made just as soon as the general state of readiness made it possible to do so.

The initial plan for Crusader was deceptively simple. XXXth Corps, together with all the armoured troops, was to move wide on the left flank in a north-westerly direction, seeking to bring the enemy armour to battle, destroy it, and open the way for a sortie by the Tobruk garrison; XIIIth Corps,

---

* *History of The Rajputana Rifles* (54).
† Field Marshal Sir Claude Auchinleck, G.C.B., G.C.I.E., C.S.I., D.S.O., O.B.E., LL.D.

consisting of New Zealand and 4th Indian Divisions, was to pin down and cut off the troops in the Omars, the large defended localities on the line of the frontier. Away to the south, 29th Brigade from 5th Indian Division was to seize the oasis of Jalo and secure a landing strip from which the R.A.F. could attack the enemy's communications.

Crusader has earned a book in its own right of over 450 pages and more than fifty maps and diagrams.* It was the first of the great desert battles in which large numbers of tanks, supported by lorry-borne infantry, were engaged, and it was fought over an expanse of desert perhaps a hundred miles long by fifty deep, where there was considerable freedom of movement for both tracks and wheels. It is not to be wondered at that the official historian, striving to unravel the tangled skein of the fighting, should record that at times the plot of movements resembled the 'scurrying of ants'.

It is obviously impossible here to attempt to describe the battle as a whole. 4th Indian Division, the only Indian Army formation engaged, was in the opening stages concerned with one small corner of it, the Omars, but its action there, and later at Bir el Gubi and Alem Hamza, was typical of the role of infantry in desert warfare, and its stand at the Omars had in fact a decisive effect at one stage of the fighting.

Armoured forces in the desert have been compared to fleets at sea: like fleets they are based on harbours, and when in harbour they are vulnerable; unlike fleets they need to harbour every night and it is the role of infantry to secure the harbours from which armoured forces operate. Harbours may well be sited in areas which must be held anyway; high ground, road and track centres, or where there is water; the enemy is then forced to attack them; equally, if the enemy has got there first, the infantry, closely supported by its armour, must fight for possession.

At dawn on 18 November, the great advance began; the New Zealand Division was on the right of XIIIth Corps, 4th Indian on the left, having with it only 7th Infantry Brigade. 11th Brigade was watching the enemy position at Halfaya Pass

---

* *Sidi Rezegh* by J. A. I. Agar-Hamilton and L. C. F. Turner.

and 5th Brigade, very short of transport, was back at Sidi
Barrani. The frontier defences with which the Indian division
was concerned were known as the Omars, three defended
localities astride the track from Sollum down to the oasis of
Jarabub. Omar Nuovo, and Libyan Omar two miles to the
west of it, were established around large humps, rising
slightly above the desert and offering excellent observation
over the surrounding plain; the third locality, Cova, five
miles away to the north-east, was less conspicuous, and did
not really come into the fighting. The enemy had had months
in which to complete the defences, which were hacked out of
the solid rock, well camouflaged and difficult to locate, and
covered by deep belts of wire and mines, except possibly on the
approaches from the north. The garrison consisted of the
Italian *Savoia Division* with a considerable German stiffening,
including a number of the deadly 88 mm guns.

The intention was that the capture of the frontier defences
should be deferred till the result of the armoured battle to the
west was known, and to start with 4th Division did no more
than move 7th Brigade into position in readiness for the attack.
It was, however, clear to General Messervy, commanding the
division, that so long as the Omars remained in enemy hands
he could not hope to prevent the garrisons taking part in the
battle if their armoured forces appeared in the neighbour-
hood, and he accordingly pressed the corps commander to be
allowed to attack. Permission was duly given and the morning
of 22 November saw The Royal Sussex going into action
against Omar Nuovo.

> The little carriers of the Royal Sussex led, followed by the
> tanks with their pennants flying. Immediately behind the
> tanks came the leading companies of the infantry in
> lorries. Behind them brigade headquarters. Then came
> the remainder of the Royal Sussex, and following, more
> tanks, lorries and carriers for the 4/16 Punjabi attack,
> until as far as the eye could reach the plain was filled with
> fighting machines speeding into battle. I had just said:
> 'Trafalgar must have been like this', when a whizz and a
> crash showed the enemy to be ranging on us. On the

horizon upright black streaks marked the telescopic ladders of his artillery observers.*

The carriers headed for a previously reconnoitred gap in the minefield, but it proved to be a trap and four tanks and three carriers were blown up; however, the infantry tumbled out of their lorries and attacked, and within two hours the main resistance had been broken and they had taken 1,500 prisoners.

The leading vehicles of the Punjabi attack fouled a minefield, and it was decided to change their start line to a position within Omar Nuovo but, just as they were debussing, the supporting tanks ran into trouble from concealed 88 mm guns and mines, and only five were left in action. The infantry attacked with great determination 'with platoons and sections methodically stalking enemy weapon pits and strong points, destroying post after post', but without armoured support progress was slow. By nightfall they had captured 500 prisoners and penetrated to a depth of some hundreds of yards, but it was clear that the capture of the whole of Libyan Omar—it was discovered later that the fanatical determination of a single German officer was responsible for the opposition they encountered—was going to be a long business. The Royal Sussex had lost eleven officers and 105 men, while the Punjabis had 147 casualties of all ranks.

4th Battalion The Sikh Regiment in the south had been demonstrating against Cova, which they found to be strongly held; to the north New Zealand Division had taken Capuzzo and were moving north-west. The divisional commander, his flank uncovered and with the probable need of a fresh battalion to complete the capture of Libyan Omar, ordered 5th Infantry Brigade forward to join him.

On 24 November he was preparing to continue the operation against the Omars when a considerable 'unorganized movement' of transport, heading eastwards, began to stream past his headquarters. Obviously, something had gone very wrong, and later in the day the headquarters of XXXth Corps arrived with the first authentic news of events. Rommel's

* *The Tiger Kills: Story of British and Indian Troops with the Eighth Army in North Africa* (16).

armour was loose and heading east; all soft-skinned transport was being withdrawn. At nightfall hundreds of vehicles were heading into the south-east for safety. 'Some lorries had never travelled so fast before.' 7th Indian Brigade supply echelons drew into closer leaguer, and 'refused to be infected by the motoring craze'.

During the past two days the enemy armour had had very much the better of it, a South African infantry brigade had been overrun and, by the evening of the twenty-fourth, the balance of tanks remaining fit for battle was in the German favour. The exact position cannot have been altogether clear to their high command but, whereas General Cruwell, commanding the *D.A.K.*,* was in favour of exploiting to the full his advantage in the area south of Sidi Rezegh by making a clean sweep of the remaining British armour, the more adventurous Rommel decided that a drive to the east would relieve the hard-pressed garrisons on the frontier and perhaps yield even more spectacular results.

The consequences of this decision became apparent to 7th Brigade at sunrise on the twenty-fifth when an armoured car drove in to the Sikhs and 1st Field Regiment, still some ten miles south of Cova, with a warning that twenty-five tanks were approaching from the south. The field regiment moved into position covering the infantry and the transport, but there was no time to dig gun positions, and there was no cover except slit trenches dug in case of air attack. Twenty-eight tanks appeared advancing from the south, 3,000 yards away.

At 2,000 yards they opened fire on the field-guns, halting to fire their cannon and maintaining machine-gun fire while in movement.

They closed from the south-east and concentrated on 52 Battery on the left of 1st Field Regiment's position. The gunners, lying beside their pieces and waiting for the word, suffered heavily. The tanks crept closer and closer, one gun after another was struck. When the panzers

* *Deutsches Afrika Korps. 15th* and *21st Panzer Divisions* and *90th Light Division.*

were only 800 yards away and the final rush imminent, the gunners sprang into action. For ten minutes in close deadly encounter, the adversaries swapped punches. The tanks flinched first, broke away and lumbered to the west for 400 yards, where a low dune afforded hull-down protection. Ten tanks in line, the battle continued. When artillery fire grew unbearable the panzers charged 52 battery head on. Among the strewn bodies of their comrades the gunners, working like mad, held the enemy armour from the close. At 300 yards the panzer line broke and scrambled away to the south-east. . . .

The discipline and courage of the artillerymen halted the panzer foray before it could reach the supply routes to the north of the Omars. (21)

A medium battery was also present, and it was the first and only time of the whole war that 6 in howitzers firing point-blank took on enemy tanks, 'with wonderful results'.

The gunners deserve all the more credit for their action in that the direct engagement of armour is not the role of field artillery but of the anti-tank regiments who, at that time, were still equipped with the 2 pdr, a gun which was ineffective against German armour. There was another similar battle that same afternoon, but by next day *5th Panzer Regiment* had given up the attempt and made off to the north.

The whole situation to the west had been so uncertain on the twenty-fourth that it was only on the personal intervention of General Auchinleck that the decision to continue the offensive was taken: 'The operations of the XIIIth Corps at Tobruk were to continue; the 4th Indian Division was to stand fast.' It was fortunate indeed for the Eighth Army that it did so.

Two days later 3/1st Punjab arrived from 5th Brigade and the final assault on the Omars was made. The battalion contained a number of young soldiers, replacing the casualties it had suffered at Mezze, but in company with 4/16th Punjab Regiment they attacked with great spirit.

A wounded sepoy, Sepoy Mohammed Ayub Khan,

insisted on crawling after his company despite his wounds. He saw his comrades held up by an enemy machine-gun post, crawled painfully up to it and blasted the foe out with hand grenades. He was killed attacking another post. (16)

While all this was going on the Central India Horse were watching a twenty-mile stretch of desert to the north. In considering the exploits of this regiment, as it roamed far and wide across this tank-infested battlefield, it is well to remember that the only armoured vehicles they had were a handful of carriers for the close protection of regimental headquarters, and a lone armoured car they had captured from the enemy. Otherwise they were carried in unarmoured 15 cwt Chevrolet trucks, and that they achieved so much and lived to tell the tale is a tribute alike to their wits and to their courage.

First light 25th November was the start of a period of intense action; every day—a twenty-four-hour day—food was snatched and generally left unfinished, beards sprouted, washing forgotten, even if there had been time —hours were so packed with incident following each other so rapidly that they were forgotten in the plether of the whole. (41)

On 3 December they were reconnoitring twelve miles ahead of a small column of all arms when they came across eight tanks in line abreast 'steaming towards them'. The main column was warned.

By this time stuff was flying about and it was time to be off, and back we went along the track to lead the tanks on to our 25-pdrs. Bullets and shells were now whistling around us, but going into the dustiest part of the track we soon created a screen between us and the tanks. (41)

The ruse was completely successful and the enemy lost

three tanks and suffered casualties to an M.T. column that was accompanying them. A few miles to the north two other squadrons of the regiment were repeating the manœuvre in co-operation with the New Zealanders.

> We heard later that the Maoris had withheld their fire until the enemy were within 400 yards—killing many before they could get out of their vehicles. "A" (squadron) also joined in the hunt, firing from the escarpment on to the road below reporting very good 'shikar'! (41)

The general progress of the battle was now sufficiently favourable for a fresh attempt to secure the initiative, and on 3 December 11th Infantry Brigade was ordered to attack El Gubi, the southernmost of the pivots of manœuvre which the Germans had established in the desert south of Tobruk.

Just before nightfall, 11th Brigade, with 31st Field Regiment and six Valentine tanks under command, formed up twelve miles to the south-east of El Gubi. The plan of battle called for an attack from the north-west after an encircling night march. 'The columns moved off for thirty miles by compass bearing over unreconnoitred ground. The approach was carried out with exceptional skill and at 0400 hrs 11th Brigade was astride the Trigh El Abd, three miles in rear of the El Gubi encampment.' (21)

The Camerons and the Mahrattas attacked but, although they fought all day, they achieved only a partial success. The attempt was renewed next morning, reinforced at noon by 1st Rajputana Rifles, who by evening had lost another commanding officer. Just before dark there was a counter-attack by some fifty panzers, but after a determined stand by a Mahratta company they managed to rally round brigade headquarters.

During the night the brigade received orders to withdraw to the south where the rest of the division was concentrating. The withdrawal through a screen of 22nd Guards Brigade was a hazardous business, and for the next three days there was much confused local fighting. However, it was becoming apparent that Rommel was moving back. XIIIth Corps was given the task of pursuit and took under its command 7th Armoured Division, which had only one armoured brigade left, and 4th Indian Division. The first obstacle to be overcome was the enemy position running from Gazala south-west to Alem Hamza. In the south 4th Indian Division was to make a direct attack while 4th Armoured Brigade moved wide to the flank and came in some twenty miles to the rear. The brigade was equipped with the Stuart tank which had only a restricted radius of action and, in the event, the distance to be covered proved beyond their capacity and they did not succeed in influencing the course of the main operation.

The army was leaving the desert behind them now and entering the belt of broken land, 'cut by innumerable watercourses', which led up to the Jebel Akhdar ahead. The Alem Hamza position, on high ground blocking the trails to the west, could not be by-passed, and on 13 December 4th Battalion Rajputana Rifles and 1st Battalion The Buffs opened the attack. The Rajputana Rifles on the right made some progress but then ran into the most determined opposition; The Buffs, through what seemed to have been a mistake by the Germans, gained their objective unopposed. 7th Brigade, on the left, were then sent forward to Sidi Breghisc but, as they were about to debus, a report came in of an approaching enemy force of forty tanks supported by artillery and lorried infantry. Once again the Royal Artillery saved the day; supported by 31st Field Regiment and 65th Anti-Tank Regiment from the north, 25th Field Regiment beat off a direct assault. When the lorry-borne infantry at last wheeled and drew off to the north, the tanks followed, leaving a dozen wrecks behind them. Seven officers and fifty-eight men of the regiment had fallen around their guns.

The position was obviously held in such strength that it was decided to mount a full-scale divisional attack the next day, but before this could be done news came in that 4th Armoured Brigade was still thirty miles short of its rendezvous to the west from which it was supposed to attack the enemy's rear. The effect of this information was being debated when a bombardment of terrific intensity on the Alem Hamza area heralded an enemy attack.

Under the devastating bombardment the panzers began to creep forward. Simultaneously three battalions of *115 Lorried Infantry Regiment* advanced, two swinging to the flank accompanied by self-propelled guns. 31 Field Regiment, under heavy pressure from in front, could not prevent the approach of these forces, which debussed within machine-gun range, mounted their weapons and pelted the unprotected gunners with a sleet of steel. The gun crews thinned till single men fired on. When no one was left, from all sides the enemy closed for the kill. The tanks crashed into the Buffs' position with tommy gunners riding outside and infantry swarming behind. The Buffs passed gloriously, meeting the Germans with a blaze of fire, and fighting bitterly in small, grim groups until the flood closed over them. (21)

The enemy paid heavily and a wireless intercept from the commander of *115 Infantry Regiment* revealed that he had suffered such casualties that he was unable to exploit his success. The next day the Polish brigade broke through south of Gazala, and that night *D.A.K.*, keeping well into the desert and eluding the clutches of 4th Armoured Brigade, was heading for Antelat, leaving Italian *21st Corps* to fight its way back along the coastal roads. 4th Indian Division was given the task of pursuing them.

Starting at Tmimi, and up to just short of Benghazi, the coastal road passes through a land dominated by the Jebel Akhdar to the south.

It forms a cloud and wind barrier, yielding plentiful rains. So the Jebel is a green and fruitful expanse, carpeted with grasses, gay with flowers in spring and summer; its stony ridges clad with bright shrubs and bushes and, in the deep wadis and canyons, with tall and lovely trees.

The last greenness dies fifteen miles east of Benghazi, where the coastal plain squeezes off the Dehar Al Ahmar ridges. Thence to the south a steep escarpment marks the edge of the desert plateau for nearly one hundred miles, until it dies away in the broken country round Antelat. (21)

But, as W. S. Gilbert has told us, 'the flowers that bloom in the spring have nothing to do with the case'. It is not the Jebel, with its 'neat chequerboard fields and rolling pasturelands', nor yet the road as it zigzags down a cliff in 'a series of cleverly constructed switchbacks', that sets the pattern for the battle for western Cyrenaica; it is the desert tracks running along the chord of the Jebel arc, west to Charruba, Msus and Antelat, where mobile forces can manœuvre with all the freedom they have been used to further east. The battle for Benghazi is won or lost in the desert a hundred miles from the town. It was a point that the chiefs of staff did not succeed in bringing home to the War Cabinet.

There are links between the two routes where desert tracks from Mechili and Charruba cut north into the coastal roads and, if Eighth Army had not been so convinced that the enemy would stand to fight rearguard actions at Tmimi and Derna, the Indian division might have been directed more boldly to block the roads well behind the retreating Italians, when they would most certainly have cut off many of the infantry who managed to escape. Immense quantities of war material were captured, but in the main it was a stern chase and the prisoners taken were mostly the administrative troops manning the dumps and airfields along the route. The divisional cavalry regiment, the C.I.H., were of course in their element, though to their lasting chagrin they entered Benghazi at 6 p.m. on Christmas Eve, three hours behind the King's Dragoon Guards who had come up from the south.

7th Armoured Division, consisting in effect of its support group and 22nd Guards Brigade, was pursuing the enemy across the desert roads. It was not till the twenty-second that the reconstituted 22nd Armoured Brigade was ready at Mechili to move in their support. On the twenty-second and again on the twenty-eighth, *D.A.K.*, which had received a timely reinforcement of twenty-two tanks from a ship which unloaded at Benghazi on the nineteenth in the very nick of time, gave evidence that the speed and extent of their withdrawal were no index to their readiness for battle. On both days they hit back sharply at advanced guards who had placed themselves in vulnerable positions, and on the latter date drove back 22nd Armoured Brigade with the loss of thirty-seven tanks.

The New Year found 4th Indian Division strung out along the coast of North Africa. 11th Brigade, which had suffered 500 casualties at Bir El Gubi, was in Tobruk; 5th Brigade, The Buffs gone and both Indian battalions under strength after heavy losses at Alem Hamza, was in the central Jebel protecting the Italian colonists from the local population. 7th Brigade, which had suffered considerably at the Omars, was in Benghazi, while the C.I.H. were on the line Ghemimes–Soluch, forty miles to the south.

In the six weeks since Crusader began, the division had taken 6,000 prisoners, destroyed in action fifty-one German tanks, and shot down twenty-seven aircraft. The losses had been heavy, the gunner regiments had all suffered as badly as the infantry, but they had proved that they could meet on equal terms the picked troops of the *D.A.K.*

CHAPTER EIGHT

The Far East: Hong Kong and Malaya

The student of military history will thumb the pages in vain if he is looking for a story of troops committed to battle with such slender hopes of success as the army that faced the Japanese in the Far East in December 1941.

There are two common causes of failure in the early days of campaigns fought by the British Army. One is lack of money in peace time to provide modern arms and equipment; the other is failure to foresee the course of operations dictated by the country and by the enemy, and to train our troops accordingly. In Singapore millions of pounds were spent on the naval base, but the project as a whole was not kept properly under review as the years went by. The Navy got the lion's share and, with so little to spare for the other two services, there was pretty brisk competition between the army and the Air Force; the feud went on and it never seemed to be anyone's business to resolve it. By the time we were at war with Germany it was too late; by then the things that Singapore needed were wanted elsewhere, and we found that plans had been based on aircraft, weapons and equipment that were not available.

It is difficult also to account for the wishful thinking, for that is what it was, that blinded so many people to the enemy's intentions, and to his formidable fighting strength. The record was there for all to read. In 1915 Japan presented

her 'Twenty-One Demands' to China. These, if complied
with, would have given her virtual dominion over her neighbour and were so blatant that she was forced to modify them
in the face of protests from Britain and America. However,
she had given a clear pointer as to the size of her ambitions. In
return for her part in the war, the occupation of the ex-
German concessions in China was recognized, and she was
given the mandate for the far-away islands in the Pacific that
she had taken from the Germans.

This kept her quiet for a bit. Then, one after the other, came
the Japanese aggression in Manchuria in 1931, the Shanghai
incident in 1932, and her departure from the League of
Nations in 1933—also the year in which her forces crossed the
Great Wall and entered north China. In 1936 she joined
Germany in the Anti-Comintern Pact; in 1937 she provoked
an incident near Peking which led to open war with China,
while at the same time her forces made a number of minor un-
provoked attacks directed at British and French interests. In
1938 she extended the war on the mainland to south China,
and the following year occupied the island of Hainan, 300
miles south of Hong Kong.

Japan may well have been encouraged by her easy successes
over China and Russia in the past, and to the lack of any
resolute opposition to the course she had now set herself, but
at rock bottom the cause of this aggressive policy was the need
to solve a very pressing economic problem: how to maintain
an excess of population in a few small islands that were far
from self-sufficient in food and raw materials. Expansion into
China was the obvious answer and, as the magnitude of the
problem became apparent, her ambitions grew. With each step
taken, it was, of course, all the harder to turn back. In the
quarter of the globe she hoped to dominate, a clash with our
interests was inevitable, but we comforted ourselves with the
thought that she would take no action which would bring the
United States into the war against her, because it was thought,
and correctly, that if this happened she must lose in the long
run. However, the day came when she decided—and she may
be excused for doing so—that the British Empire, at any rate in
the East, was a thing of the past; she felt that, if she could

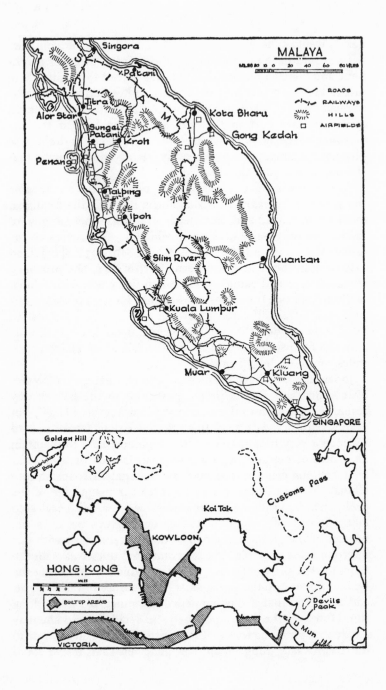

establish herself at one fell swoop so deep into the Pacific that she had a sufficient margin of loss, she could fight on against America till a compromise peace became acceptable to both sides.

We certainly underrated her and took refuge in the thought she would never take the plunge. In January 1940 the governor of the Straits Settlements was advising the home government that the threat of war had receded, a view which was supported by the Foreign Office who felt that, owing to internal conflict in Japan between the army and the moderates, the threat to Singapore could be regarded as remote; and it was a view which the Prime Minister himself found acceptable. Preparation for war cannot be made without the active support of the civil government: in the light of what has been said it is not surprising the Services found it well nigh impossible to convince anyone in government or business circles that there was any substance or urgency over matters which required their backing and co-operation.

HONG KONG

The British colony of that name consists of the island itself, ceded by China in 1840; the Kowloon peninsula, ceded in 1860; and the Leased Territories, with an area of 400 square miles, extending some sixteen miles to the north. The island is roughly eight miles by four and between the city of Victoria and Kowloon on the north shore lies one of the finest harbours in the world. The bulk of the population of one and three-quarter millions was contained in that densely inhabited area. Because of variable and uncertain rainfall, the water supply, depending on reservoirs fed by channels sited to catch the surface water, was always a matter for concern, and half the island's supply came from reservoirs sited on the mainland.

Up to 1921 Hong Kong was our only naval port in the Far East. As it was not possible to expand it to meet the requirements of the shift of naval power in the east, nor could it be defended against a major attack, Singapore was chosen as the site for the new base and it was decided that Hong Kong was an outpost that must hold out as long as possible. There was a small naval force consisting of a destroyer and about a dozen coastal craft; the R.A.F. had five obsolete machines used for target towing which, when war came, were destroyed on Kai Tak aerodrome; and there were a few anti-aircraft guns manned by detachments of the Hong Kong and Singapore Artillery, a regiment largely recruited from India. The garrison amounted to four infantry battalions, two British and two Indian.

It was foreseen that a demand for an increase might well be made, but it was decided at the highest level that this would be resisted. However, on a change of command in July 1941, the outgoing commander, himself a Canadian, travelled home via Ottawa, where he advised the chief of the Canadian general staff that if Canada could spare two battalions as reinforcements for Hong Kong it would considerably prolong the period of resistance. He repeated this advice when he reached England and, as a result of negotiations with the Canadian Government, two battalions were dispatched. They had been employed on garrison duty, and it seems to have been understood that this would be their role in Hong Kong; though just what this reservation was held to mean is not very clear. They arrived three weeks before the Japanese attacked; their carriers and transport were loaded in a separate ship which was caught in the tide of war and swept away to Australia.

Plans for the defence of Hong Kong were in two parts; the defence of the island itself, and the delaying action on the mainland designed to allow time for demolitions, mostly of the naval installations in the Kowloon area. Until the arrival of the two Canadian battalions, the covering position on the mainland was the responsibility of 2nd Battalion 14th Punjab Regiment, and no more than a twenty-four-hour delay was contemplated; but with extra troops available the plan was changed. Of the original garrison, one of the British battalions, The Middlesex, was a machine-gun battalion committed to manning the emplacements round the island which constituted the main defence against an enemy landing; the other battalion, 2nd Battalion The Royal Scots, together with 5th Battalion 7th Rajput Regiment, was now added to the mainland force, which was given a brigade headquarters to command it. With these reinforcements, the expected period of delay was stepped up to a week. The Punjabis retained the responsibility of covering the demolitions at the river crossings on the frontier, some fifteen miles to the north. The Royal Scots had been overseas for many years and had recently suffered a lot from malaria; both the Indian battalions carried a high proportion of reservists and young recruits, sent out to replace the trained officers and N.C.O.s taken from them for the raising of new battalions in India. For rather obvious reasons, the line the brigade was to occupy was the shortest that could be found, and ran from Gindrinkers Bay in front of Golden Hill, then back south-east to Customs Pass and on to the sea at Port Shelter. The position was about ten miles long and, for want of time and materials, was by no means complete when it was attacked. Each battalion had a troop of four mountain guns in support, and there was a medium battery firing over the whole front.

Against this small force the Japanese Goliath brought two good field divisions, with a reserve division behind them, supported by some seventy aircraft; and, in addition to outnumbering the defenders by perhaps four to one, they had the not inconsiderable advantage of knowing almost down to the last rifle the layout of the defences. That they had been able to collect this information was due to the difficulty, in the general apathy that prevailed, of enforcing proper security measures.

In the small hours of 8 December the senior intelligence officer at garrison headquarters tuned in to Tokyo Radio and heard an announcer informing Japanese nationals that their country was at war with the United States of America and Great Britain. The demolitions on the frontier bridges were duly blown and, after inflicting quite heavy casualties, the Punjabi company withdrew without loss into reserve behind its battalion in the centre sector of the line. On the left were The Royal Scots and on the right the Rajputs. At 8 p.m. came the attack on Kai Tak airfield which destroyed all five R.A.F. machines on the ground. By nightfall on the ninth the enemy were in contact with our defences along most of the front and during that night succeeded in capturing the Shing Mun redoubt in the left battalion sector, a position of great importance as it dominated the surrounding country and housed an artillery observation post. On the tenth they were able to launch an attack from that flank on a company of the Rajputs which had been put in to fill a vacant part of the line, but were beaten off with great loss and withdrew to the redoubt. However, the next morning, the eleventh, they penetrated the defences south of the redoubt, thereby threatening the safety of the whole position, and a withdrawal to the mainland was ordered to begin that evening. The Royal Scots and a company of the Winnipeg Grenadiers got away that night through Kowloon. The Indian battalions were to withdraw past Devil's Peak through a rearguard found by the Rajputs. Forced through lack of transport to hump their machine-guns and mortars, the two battalions were faced with a long and hazardous march over broken country; they had been fighting for four days, were desperately short of sleep, and the fact that they arrived at the embarkation point with men and weapons present and correct is a tribute to their discipline and training. After the Punjabis had left the mainland on the night of the twelfth, the Rajputs rearguard position was attacked throughout the following day and again, after bitter fighting, the Japanese were beaten off.

After a summons to surrender, under threat of severe aerial and artillery bombardment, had been refused, the island was attacked for four days and, after an attempt to cross the Lei U Men channel had failed with heavy loss, a second summons was made on the morning of the seventeenth. This also was rejected with contumely. The weight of the bombardment now increased and, on the night of the eighteenth, an attack by six battalions of completely fresh troops had landed on the island by midnight. The whole weight of the attack, on the north-east corner, fell on the Rajputs who inflicted heavy casualties, but after the loss of nearly all their officers, British and Indian, they were driven from their positions. During the next few days the enemy landed at further points along the north shore and split the island by the capture of the Wong Nei Chong Gap. The story of the week that followed the landings is one of numerous small actions fought with great gallantry by groups, British, Canadian and Indian, from the infantry garrison, and of all arms hastily formed to meet the emergency of the moment; men also of the Navy, and of the island Volunteer Corps. For the Indian Army it is adorned by a desperate but unsuccessful attack by the remnants of the Sikh company of the Punjabis, led in person by the battalion commander, Lieutenant-Colonel Kidd, who was killed. By Christmas morning the two sectors of the defence had been driven back, one to a line running north along the Aberdeen reservoirs, the other covering the approaches to the Stanley Peninsula. That afternoon the Fortress commander, on learning from the western sector that they could hold out no longer, gave orders to the garrison to cease fire and to surrender to the enemy as the opportunity presented itself. The brigade commander at Stanley asked for the order to be confirmed in writing, and did not give up till 2.30 the next morning.

There were voices at home that had the temerity to express surprise that the surrender had come so early; but what could anyone expect? We must face the fact that the garrison of Hong Kong was thrown to the wolf pack and, by the gesture, the Japanese were compelled to deploy against them two first-line infantry divisions and a considerable air force. Had these forces been available for use elsewhere, in the Philippines or in Burma, they might have speeded up the dates of victory in those places. What matters is the verdict of the official historian; that all the evidence examined shows that the high tribute paid by the Prime Minister to the sense of duty and gallantry of all concerned was well merited. The two Indian battalions took the first shock of the enemy attack, and thereafter they fought on for as long as it lay in their power to do so.

At the cost of over 3,000 casualties the garrison inflicted more than three times that number upon their enemy.

SINGAPORE

The decision to establish a major naval base on Singapore Island was made in 1922, and the site chosen was in the north-east on the Johore Strait. The progress of work suffered the inevitable vicissitudes, political and otherwise, but at least there was a coherent and generally accepted plan and when Japan entered the war the base itself was nearly complete. The seeds of the trouble that bedevilled the whole course of events were sown way back in 1925 when consideration was given to the defence against external attack of the base itself and of the adjacent airfield at Seletar. 'Considered military opinion' at that time, when the problem was reviewed by a committee headed by Lord Curzon, was that an approach from the mainland would present very considerable difficulties owing to the nature of the terrain. It was accordingly decided that attack, if it came, would come from the sea and, as the whole object of the base was to accommodate a considerable fleet, it was no doubt comforting to find something that everyone could agree about.

Heavy guns were installed as part of the main project of the base but it was accepted that air attack against enemy ships would be a supplementary part of the defences.

The Air Ministry now put forward the view that the heavy gun, up till then considered to be the basis of all coast defence, had been superseded by the aeroplane, which could not only do the same job but could do it while the enemy was still far out at sea, and had the added advantage of strategic mobility; it could be kept elsewhere until needed, and flown in when danger threatened. It was an attractive but specious argument, and the fallacy was exposed in 1941 when of course no aircraft could be spared for the purpose. A fresh review of the possibility of an approach to the island from the mainland was made in 1938 and this time it was concluded that such an attack was quite feasible. In 1940, when it seemed doubtful if there would in fact be very much of a fleet to use the base, the primary responsibility for the defence of Singapore passed to the R.A.F., although they were as short of aircraft as the Navy was of ships.

The army had always questioned the validity of the claim that enemy landings would be impossible in the face of air attack. However, the R.A.F. went ahead on their own and sited a number of aerodromes up and down the peninsula, a decision which had a far-reaching effect on the whole course of operations. Not only were the sites individually indefensible, in terms of local tactics, but their general location and the need for defending them resulted in an overall strategic plan which was fundamentally unsound.

It is easy to be wise after the event but the suggestion cannot be resisted that when, after the fall of France, a pro-Vichy regime was firmly established in Indo-China, there came an opportunity that could have been a turning point in the whole approach to the campaign that followed. Two things now stood out like sore thumbs. Japan had a base within calculable striking distance of Malaya; and with the loss of the French navy and air force in Europe there was not the slightest hope, at any rate for a couple of years, of sea or air reinforcements reaching Singapore in time to be of any use. The conclusion was inescapable; the army was now the major partner and should have provided a high-powered commander-in-chief: abandoning all pre-conceived ideas, if he had been instructed to plan for the retention of sufficient depth in the peninsula to ensure the safety of the naval base, there would have been ample room for the deployment of other forces when the situation improved sufficiently for them to be sent out; he should have had authority to jettison all work outside the scope of that requirement; and he should have been given the executive powers to enable him to get on with it. A commander-in-chief was indeed appointed in October 1940, but he was a distinguished officer of the R.A.F., recalled from retirement, and the inevitable implication was that it was with his service that the major responsibility still rested; finally, the powers given him very much restricted what he was able to do.

The Malay peninsula is roughly 400 miles from north to south, 200 miles across at the bulge in the middle, tapering to sixty miles at the two ends. The island of Singapore, very like the Isle of Wight in shape, size and its relation to the mainland, lies at the southern end. A range of mountains, densely covered in primeval jungle, and varying in height from 3,000 feet to 7,000 feet, runs like a backbone almost the whole length of the peninsula. The beaches on the eastern coast, exposed to the north-east monsoon, are sandy, and there are considerable stretches where troops can be put ashore from landing craft with little or no difficulty; on the west coast there are dense mangrove swamps which are a very real obstacle except at selected places and for small parties. The plains are heavily cultivated; palms, pineapples, rice, and, best known of all, rubber. This last is worth a word in passing: life in a closely planted rubber plantation is all gloom and dampness, silence and isolation, and the effect of months spent in these depressing surroundings was to lower appreciably the morale of the troops. There were also the tin mines, making an invaluable contribution both to our war supplies and our dollar resources. Following the general pattern of commercial development, the main road ran down the west coast; good roads crossed the mountains at three points, but otherwise there was no east-west communication.

The population of Malaya numbered about five millions, and included Malays, Chinese and Indians. There was also a small Japanese element who owned rubber plantations and mines, almost always located, curiously enough, at points of tactical importance. Furthermore, a number were employed, no doubt profitably for the collection of intelligence, as fishermen, hairdressers and photographers. The polyglot nature of the population and the difficulty of enforcing security regulations made it almost impossible to check their activities. There was a small British colony of government servants and those employed on plantations and in commerce.

The government was a complete checker-board; the perfect pattern, surely, of the Better Land to which all good bureaucrats aspire to go, as there were no fewer than eleven authorities whose agreement had to be secured before any measure affecting all Malaya could be put into effect. Couple this difficulty with the fact that the rubber and tin interests, backed by the governor, were completely convinced, and not unreasonably so, that they were going flat out to win the war, and it is small wonder that military requests for the embodiment of Volunteer units, or the recruitment of plantation labour for the construction of defences, did not receive the attention they deserved.

What, then, was the overall military situation in Malaya at midnight on 7-8 December 1941?

For the R.A.F., the predominant partner, the chiefs of staff had accepted that 336 modern aircraft was the minimum needed, while in October 1940 the three service commanders on the spot made out a case for an increase to 582. All they had present were fifteen squadrons, several of them much under strength, with a total of 158 obsolescent aircraft of a performance inferior to the enemy's machines.

The Japanese made a bee-line for the target presented by our air forces and after seventy-two hours' fighting were in possession of three good airfields in North Malaya; they had by then also destroyed many aircraft on the ground and a lot more in battle.

During the next two months small fighter reinforcements reached the island from time to time, but although there was no lack of examples of great gallantry by individual pilots, they were numerically too small to be effective, and the enemy held undisputed air superiority throughout the campaign, a fact that had a decisive influence on the course of the fighting.

On 2 December His Majesty's ships *Prince of Wales* and *Repulse* berthed at Singapore. On 8 December, on receipt of the news of Japanese landings at Singora and Kota Bharu, the decision was taken to send them with their escorting destroyers to engage and destroy the enemy transports and the warships protecting them. It was a calculated risk; if surprise could be effected, and if the R.A.F. could provide fighter cover, there was thought to be a good chance of success. In the event it was found that the Japanese had been expecting the move and had made plans to meet it; and the fighter cover came too late. On the morning of the tenth both ships were sunk by attacks made by torpedo-bomber aircraft. It was a shattering blow; in the space of a morning, command of the sea had passed to the enemy. A small force, the Perak Flotilla, was formed to deal with enemy outflanking movements by sea along the west coast and fought valiantly until dispersed and destroyed by air attacks.

The peace-time garrison of Singapore consisted of three British battalions and one Indian, disposed for the local defence of the naval base. In August 1939 when the first Indian brigade left for the Middle East, 12th Indian Infantry Brigade sailed for Malaya. In November 1940 India sent a divisional headquarters and two more infantry brigades; in March 1941 she found a similar reinforcement. The record shows that during that same period India had sent two divisions to the Middle East and three to Iraq. More than once troops earmarked for one theatre of war found themselves diverted elsewhere; the change, on occasion, being made after they had actually embarked. One more brigade arrived in September 1941. All these formations consisted of regular peace-time battalions, but they were pale shadows of their former selves. Once, twice, and perhaps three times they had been 'milked', as the saying went—'bled' would be a better word—to find officers, V.C.O.s and N.C.O.s for the new battalions being raised in India. A colonel might think himself lucky if he had two pre-war officers besides himself; and of the new entry one or two would still be wrestling with the language their men spoke; half the V.C.O.s and N.C.O.s would be recently promoted; and more than half the men would be recruits with less than a year's service. Headquarters and one brigade of 8th Australian Division arrived in February 1941, followed seven months later by a second brigade. Two further Indian Infantry brigades arrived in January 1942, composed of war-raised battalions who, two months earlier, had been training to go to the Caucasus. When war with Japan began, 18th British Division was rounding the Cape *en route* for the Middle East. One brigade was diverted to Singapore where it arrived on 14 January, the others went first to Bombay, and then to Singapore. Loaded for an orderly disembarkation at Suez, short of its artillery and much of its essential transport, the men unfit after a long sea voyage and completely untrained for jungle warfare, they arrived eighteen days before the garrison surrendered on 15 February.

There were no tanks, whereas the enemy had a group with a total of nearly two hundred, light and medium; and there was no mobile anti-aircraft artillery to cover the troops fighting on the mainland.

The tactical conditions in Malaya were totally different from those on the North-West Frontier, to which the units of the Indian Army were accustomed; and the enclosed nature of the country placed limitations on the effectiveness of artillery and machine-gun fire, the backbone of the defence in open warfare. It should have been clear, therefore, that the first thing the army needed was some guidance as to how they were to set about fighting the battles that lay ahead of them, and that guidance should have come to them from command headquarters. That done, they should have been exercised in these tactics in situations on the ground where they might expect to fight. But before that could be attempted all battalions badly needed a shake-down period in which to adjust themselves to the loss of so many of their key men; the more so because in the close country that prevailed the junior leader, from the company commander downwards, was going to be the key man; and these leaders were young and lacked experience. When we examine what actually happened, there seems to have been a complete lack of any guidance from above, and battalions were unable even to get on with their own training, as best they might, because three-quarters of the time available was taken up on the construction of fixed defences; work that should have been done by the local labour that the civil government failed to recruit.

There was no lack of information about the enemy, the incredible thing is that it was so completely misleading. Intelligence reports from the War Office, and the advice of at any rate one officer at command headquarters who had first-hand knowledge of the Japanese Army, made it clear that they were well trained and tough. The local oracle, the Far Eastern Intelligence Board, controlled by the Admiralty, spoke otherwise; our troops were told they would find their enemy stereotyped, unable to fight off roads or to fight or fly by night, and that his airmen by reason of defective vision could not make low-flying attacks. It was not so much that the truth came as an unpleasant surprise, it was rather that it had been no one's business to train the army for battle against the Japanese.

A glance at the map shows how the airfields, scattered like confetti over the peninsula, confronted the army with an almost insoluble problem; for defend them they must, if only to prevent the enemy from using them. As if that were not grief enough, the higher command took upon itself a further burden, entirely of its own devising. Operation Matador had as its object the forestalling of the enemy by the occupation of

Singora, some fifty miles across the border in Siam. Singora had the only rail-served harbour of any significance on the whole east coast, and there were airfields in the vicinity. The advantages of seizing it were great, so great that they seem to have blinded the planners to the attendant difficulties. To start with, this was to be no tip-and-run affair; not only had we to get there, we had to be able to stay there. The prize was equally tempting to the enemy, who could be counted on to make the most determined attempt to forestall us, or to drive us out if we arrived first. To a straightforward calculation of the time both sides would need to reach Singora, we had to add a margin of say three days to get dug in to resist attack, and it was plainly touch and go. But there was another factor, the Queensberry rules; Singora was in Siam, a neutral country, and on no account must we provoke Japan by an act of aggression: the word 'go' must therefore come from London, and the time-consuming implications of this restriction need not be underlined. Next comes the apparently simple question; were the land and air resources needed for the job in fact available? But it was not quite so simple. Matador bore a strong resemblance to a move carried out by the British Expeditionary Force in the Low Countries in May 1940, when at the first sign of German aggression they forsook the defences they had been preparing all the winter and advanced to the Brussels area to fight a war of manœuvre in which, owing to their inferiority in armour, they were at a great disadvantage; and they had no secure base behind them from which to operate. If that lesson had been learnt, it should have been clear that any force used for Matador must be over and above what was needed to hold a secure position in north Malaya, a position on which to withdraw if the venture fell short of complete success.

The truth is that not only were the forces, ground and air, short of the minimum calculated to be necessary, but they were those same troops, using some of the same materials, who should have been securing the position that was to hold up the enemy advance. Matador was persisted in to the very last futile moment; on 28 November, 11th Division was placed at six hours' notice; on 6 December this was cut to half an hour, and the operation was not called off at command level till the morning of the eighth; by the time orders reached the troops—who had been standing by to advance—to occupy their defensive positions, the enemy had a flying start of thirteen hours. It was all and more than he needed. The Japanese troops who made the landings consisted of battle-tried formations, equipped for the campaign, who had spent the last three months carrying out exhaustive training on Hainan Island where the terrain resembled Malaya, and in executing landing operations on the south China coast.

The picture then on 8 December is of three crack Japanese divisions, a force calculated to a nicety as to size and composition for the task in hand, trained to a hair, and equipped to the last gaiter button, matched against an army which was inferior in numbers and equipment and less well trained: caught, moreover, off-balance and on the wrong foot, in a moment of fatal indecision. Nor is that all. To have any chance of success, they needed the close and effective support of both Navy and Air Force; but, after forty-eight hours, the army was to all intents and purposes left alone in the ring.

The defence of the northern part of the peninsula rested with IIIrd Indian Corps, commanded by General Heath,* who had commanded a division with distinction in Eritrea. 9th Indian Division (Major-General Barstow) had 8th Brigade at Kota Bharu and 22nd Brigade back guarding the airfield at Kuantan. 11th Indian Division, consisting of 6th and 15th Brigades (Major-General Murray-Lyon), had been standing by for Matador, and when it was cancelled occupied the defensive position at Jitra covering the Alor Star airfield. 28th Indian Infanty Brigade was in corps reserve at Ipoh, earmarked to reinforce 11th Division; 12th Indian Infantry Brigade, which had been the first Indian formation to reach Malaya in August 1939, was in command reserve near Singapore.

The first Japanese landings at midnight 7–8 December were carried out by three regiments of *5th Division* at Singora and

* The late Lieutenant-General Sir Lewis Heath, K.B.E., C.B., C.I.E., D.S.O., M.C.

135

Patani, in Siam, and by *56th Infantry Regiment* of *18th Division* at Kota Bharu.

It is obvious how the need to protect the airfield layout dictated the dispositions of IIIrd Corps. In north-east Malaya, with its vast tract of mountainous jungle, there was nothing except Kota Bharu airfield that need be defended north of the cross-road Kuantan–Raub, and the protection of that again would have been easier but for the actual siting of the Kuantan airfield.

8th Brigade at Kota Bharu had been in the area for over a year, but orders that nothing must be done that might interfere with the daily lives of the inhabitants very much hampered the preparation of the defences. Only at the final weekend were they allowed to lay mines and clear fields of fire, and under such conditions there could be no security.

> No restrictions could be put on the free movement of the many Japanese in the country and free access to even beach defences had to be allowed as the closing of these areas would have put a stop to fishing. The attackers eventually landed with ready prepared maps showing the brigade defences down to the last detail.*

The brigade had two battalions on the beaches, and 3rd Battalion The Dogra Regiment, on whom the attack fell, were holding a front of close on ten miles. There were two battalions in reserve, one having been lent by 22nd Brigade. The first landings came soon after midnight and, in spite of determined resistance, the Dogras in the section posts were killed to a man. By dawn, the Japanese had obtained a foothold in the centre of their front. One Japanese troop carrier was sunk and two damaged by gunfire and air attack based on Kota Bharu; further aircraft were sent up at dawn from Singapore to renew the attack, but the ships had withdrawn northward. It was while the bombers were refuelling on the forward airfields that they were caught on the ground by Japanese

* *History of the Frontier Force Regiment* (57).

attacks based on Indo-China, made with the express purpose
of neutralizing all air support over the battle area. Kota Bharu
airfield was bombed and machine-gunned throughout the day
with consequent casualties and damage to aircraft, and though
it had afforded valuable support in the very early stages, it then
became a serious liability to the army. It was located only two
miles inland and, since it was important to prevent it falling
into enemy hands, a very difficult counter-attack across the
line of numerous creeks and rivers had to be made to prevent
this happening. The attack did not succeed. At 4 p.m., after a
rumour that the enemy had reached the perimeter defences,
the ground staff departed without destroying the runways or
the stocks of petrol and bombs. The next day the brigade was
ordered to withdraw. It was extricated with great skill and,
after ten days of well-conducted rearguards, entrained at
Kuala Krai. On 20 December it rejoined 9th Division in good
heart at Kuala Lipis. The Japanese afterwards erected on the
beach at Kota Bharu two stone memorials as witness to the
first and also the toughest battle of the whole campaign. They
lost over 3,000 men.

Difficult though the task of 8th Brigade was, they did at least
know what it was they were trying to do. 11th Indian Division
on the west coast was less fortunate, for it was not till 1.30 p.m.
on 8 December that they received the order that Matador had
been cancelled and that they were to occupy the defensive
position at Jitra. A vast amount of time and care had been devoted to planning for Matador—for example, the divisional
engineers had been standing by, in drenching rain, since the
afternoon of the sixth, their lorries loaded with bridging
material calculated and marked for every bridge the whole
way to Singora. Quite apart from the fact that this work had
been done at the expense of work on the Jitra defences, it was
obviously not possible to switch from attack to defence without
considerable delay and reorganization; to say nothing of the
effect on the morale and temper of the troops.
   Apart from its tactical weakness, the position was strategically unsound as it lay many miles north of where the road
from Patani via Kroh cut into the trunk road behind it. To

cover this line of approach, a force, Krohcol, under Lieutenant-Colonel Moorhead of 3/16th Punjab Regiment, was standing by to advance into Siam to seize The Ledge, where there was a good delaying position. The order to move was unaccountably delayed and when at 3 p.m., still short of its second battalion, the force at last crossed the frontier, it at once ran into opposition from what may or may not have been Siamese constabulary. In consequence, it did not reach The Ledge before the enemy. There followed three days of stubborn withdrawal, in which the battalion lost over 300 men, before it was forced back across the frontier where it handed over to 12th Indian Infantry Brigade which had come up from Singapore to relieve it. Despite these early losses, 3/16th Punjab Regiment fought on and never broke throughout the long weeks of the campaign.

The incomplete defences of the Jitra line were in such poor order after the heavy rain that it was decided the troops must have a clear forty-eight hours to work on them. 1st Battalion 14th Punjab Regiment was sent forward to impose delay and was reinforced by 2nd Battalion 1st Gurkha Rifles of 28th Brigade which had joined the division. It was pouring with rain when, on 11 December, Japanese tanks blitzed down the road and caught 1/14th Punjabis withdrawing in open file to occupy a position in rear of 1st Gurkhas.

> Suddenly at the height of the storm and without any warning the Japanese armed blitz burst through, straight on down the road through the rest of the battalion. In the van of the blitz were twelve medium tanks with cannon and machine-guns blazing hard. Behind them came twenty-four light tanks in groups along a column of lorried infantry nearly a battalion strong. Subedar Budhilal Gurung described how seven Japanese tanks swept over their position, impenetrable to Bren fire, and then drove on.*

Both forward battalions were overrun, and the enemy were

* *History of 1st K.G.O. Gurkha Rifles* (61).

in contact with the main position by nightfall when they were held by a section of 80th Anti-Tank Regiment and 1st Battalion The Leicestershire Regiment. At that critical moment they were, according to their own account, misled by an over-optimistic report from one of their patrols as to the weakness of our defences, and pressed recklessly on, whereas, on their own admission, they would ordinarily have paused to mount a full-scale divisional attack. However, fortune favoured the brave and they penetrated our defences east of the road, despite gallant resistance by 2nd Jats and 1st Battalion 8th Punjab Regiment, to an extent that disorganized the whole divisional plan, and led to its withdrawal the following night down a single road in pouring rain to a position fifteen miles behind.

It was a calamitous start to the campaign and it is worth analysing the reasons which, collectively, were responsible. First of all, the position was a bad one, but had to be occupied to protect the Alor Star airfield, which on the evidence of their eyes and ears the troops knew was out of action before their battle even began. Secondly, the layout of the position was weak in that, instead of being concentrated in depth down the road, it was spread out in an attempt to block every possible line of approach. Thirdly, any spare time left after the demands of Matador had been devoted to the actual construction of the defensive position at Jitra, so the troops had not been trained or rehearsed in the role they were supposed to be carrying out. Finally, the belated cancellation of Matador, for which they had been prepared, followed by three days of non-stop work on the defences in drenching rain, combined to lower the morale of battalions that were full of young and partially trained men.

For the next fortnight 11th Division continued the withdrawal, imposing as much delay as possible but, towards the end of the month, an outside factor arose which affected the operations of both 9th and 11th Divisions: a convoy with reinforcements was expected and, to protect it as far as possible from air attack, it was decided that the airfields at Kuantan, Kuala Lumpur and Port Swettenham must be denied to the enemy for as long as possible, the date for the two latter being placed as late as 14 January.

At Kuantan there was some confusion as to just what the priorities were. The corps commander, apparently misunderstanding the intention of the army commander, had decided that, rather than allow the brigade to become involved in fighting for the retention of an airfield which the R.A.F. was no longer using, it was better to keep it intact, withdraw it across the east to west lateral road, and possibly inflict a flank attack on the Japanese on the west coast. Orders in this sense were accordingly given to the brigade commander.

On 30 December, 2nd Battalion The Royal Garwhal Rifles, who were occupying an extended coast-watching position to the north of Kuantan, were heavily attacked from the north. They were eventually withdrawn to a position covering the ferry:

> Had a close outpost position on these lines been occupied on the 29th December, when the Japanese intention to attack Kuantan from the north became clear, the battle forward of the town would have been fought on more even terms. As it was, the long telephone communications broke down, largely as the result of cut wires, and once the enemy got well into the area even despatch riders could not get through to company headquarters.*

In two days' fighting the battalion lost two British officers and over 250 Garwhali ranks. The brigade now became involved in an attempt to prevent the enemy capturing the airfield, located some nine miles inland from the town, but to conform with the position on the west coast it was ordered to withdraw, 2nd Battalion The Frontier Force Regiment acting as rearguard as they left the airfield. The battalion was commanded by Lieutenant-Colonel Arthur Cumming† who, after he had been twice wounded during an attack on his headquarters, left his subedar-major to conduct the withdrawal

---

* *Historical Record of The Royal Garwhal Rifles* (59).
† Brigadier A. E. Cumming, V.C., O.B.E., M.C.

while he went forward in his carrier to give orders to the rear-most company. Although wounded again three times on the last return journey, he ordered his carrier driver to charge a tree blocking a cutting, ran the gauntlet of the enemy lining the banks, and reached brigade headquarters with his driver also badly wounded. He was the first British officer of the Indian Army to win the V.C. in the Second World War.

It was three weeks since the disaster at Jitra when on 4 January 11th Division, fighting a continuous delaying action and having had no rest, occupied what was known as the Slim River position, disposing itself in depth down the road with 12th Brigade in contact with the enemy; behind them 28th Brigade had been told by the divisional commander, who was rightly anxious to give his troops a rest where possible, that having reconnoitred their positions they need not occupy them for forty-eight hours. Although the enemy were of course known to be using tanks, only two anti-tank guns and a few mines were allotted to the forward battalion, on whose front there was, moreover, a disused loop road which by-passed the main road block. When he attacked, the enemy once again used his tanks with great boldness in a concentrated drive down the main road.

> The mines had been planted in a cutting and our men had taken position on the high banks on either side of the road. The leading tank struck the first mine and blew up. The din which followed was beyond description. The Japanese tanks were nose to tail—their engines roaring, their crews yelling—their machine-guns spitting tracer, their mortar and cannon firing all out. The platoons astride the road hurled grenades on the tanks below them and the solitary anti-tank rifle disabled at least one tank, while another brewed up on the mines. It was complete chaos. For want of other weapons a few men tried their hands with Molotov cocktails but the fuses were damp. They spluttered and went out. (61)

The enemy discovered the loop road and by-passed the

main block and, for all its gallant stand, the battalion checked the enemy advance for only a few hours. The regimental history attributes the result to

> the utter weariness of officers and men. For days they had been fighting and moving day and night with practically no rest, and they had received no reinforcements. By the time the 5/2nd was called on to fight its last battle its fighting strength had been depleted by more than 250. The number of casualties suffered at Slim will never be known with accuracy but many of the 244 who had to be reported as untraced found an end to their unendurable weariness in this battle. No men could have fought with greater gallantry.*

There was an almost complete failure of signal communications so that the news of the break-through did not reach the battalions behind, or even brigade or divisional headquarters. The reserve battalion of 12th Brigade was caught moving forward; the enemy tanks went straight through 2/2nd and 2/9th Gurkhas who had just got into position—and who stood fast—but caught the rear battalion, 2/1st Gurkhas, on the line of march.

> I was marching in the centre of the battalion which was in open file along the sides of the road. We had marched about a mile when I sensed a feeling of unease behind me. I couldn't understand it. True, the sound of battle sounded a bit close, but we were nearly twelve miles from the front and there were no hostile aircraft about. The men behind me were looking back and hurrying. The next thing I knew was a gun and machine-gun blazing in my ear, a bullet grazed my leg and I dived into a ditch as a tank bore down on me. It had passed through half my battalion without my realising anything was amiss.
>
> The tanks, about a dozen of them, stopped for ten minutes firing into the rubber groves before they moved on. It was a terrifying experience. (61)

* *The Golden Galley: History of 2nd Punjab Regiment* (52).

Employed on troop carrying was 2/3rd Australian Reserve M.T. Company, described in the story of 11th Division as 'a hard-swearing set of tough old soldiers, most of them veterans of the First World War. None of them had a field-marshal's baton in his knapsack but most of them had a 'Dimpled Haig' under the seat. They were full of guts, extremely unpunctual, and invariably good on the job'.

The enemy had repeated his tactics of the Jitra position, and had attacked with a powerful force of tanks, infantry and engineers straight down the road; thanks to the gallantry of two of his young officers who, under heavy fire, cut the fuses leading to the demolition charges, two important bridges fell into his hands intact. But the fact remains that in a space of some ten hours he had again defeated 11th Division; it was to recover to fight with great determination the last battle of all, but for the moment it was not fit for action.

At this juncture, General Wavell on his way to Java to take over the new command for the whole of South East Asia, visited Singapore, and saw for himself the state of the brigades who had been in contact with the enemy. He at once ordered IIIrd Corps to be withdrawn to Johore State to rest, and for 8th Australian Division, which had not been in action but watching the east coast in Johore State, to send one brigade forward to relieve it. His immediate problem was to gain time; for the defences in the north of Singapore Island, which had not even been reconnoitred, to be constructed, and for the arrival of 18th Division which was still on the high seas.

The Australian division signalized their entry to the fray by a most successful ambush on the Japanese which inflicted heavy casualties. Their key position was astride the main road which here ran some sixteen miles inland; 9th Indian Division was covering its right, while 45th Indian Infantry Brigade, which was under the Australian command, was ordered to hold the enemy on the crossings of the Muar River and so cover the left flank. The enemy opposing this brigade was the *Imperial Guards Division* who were fresh, having taken no part in the fighting to date.

Under orders from the divisional commander, 45th Brigade

was disposed with two battalions forward, covering between them a frontage of twenty-four miles, each with two companies across the river. The enemy attacked the left-hand battalion with a full regiment of three battalions, and in addition to this frontal attack, he was also landing from the sea as much as twenty miles in rear of the Muar line, a threat which put an end to 11th Division's period of rest after only one day.

Before considering the course of the battle, a word must be said as to the fitness for war of this brigade which had disembarked at Singapore ten days earlier. They had been part of 17th Division and until Japan came into the war had been training to go to the Middle East. The ancillary units of the brigade had been raised from scratch, while the signal section was not completed until just before sailing.

The three battalions were all just over a year old. On raising, two thirds of their men had been recruits or reservists and, during the six months since June 1941, they had actually parted with 250 men to help raise other new battalions; furthermore, on the point of embarkation, each had sent to its training centres a party of forty-five officers and N.C.O.s. There were perhaps three pre-war officers in a battalion, the rest holding emergency commissions and having at most a year's experience of Indian troops, their customs and their language.

In the accepted sense of the word, the brigade never fought as such, partly because the role given them made it very difficult, partly because they were completely untrained to do so. What they did, or tried to do, emerges from the story of one of their battalions, 5th Royal Garwhal Rifles.

Communications, as so often happened, had broken down, and the battalion which was in brigade reserve was surprised by the speed with which the enemy broke through the forward positions. The commanding officer was killed in the early hours of the battle which opened on 15 January and, three days later, out of fifteen officers only three were left.

The men appeared dazed by the individual suicide tactics of the Japanese Imperial Guards Division, whose snipers concealed themselves in trees and picked off the officers. That the sniper himself had always been shot down was no compensation for the loss of an officer.

Heavy firing broke out from time to time from both the front and the flanks, but the medium machine-gunners, who throughout the action maintained admirable steadiness and coolness, kept the enemy on the high ground to the west in check. There was no sign of panic among the young riflemen, they were evidently bewildered by the situation, and their firing at times became rather wild. Captain Rodgers however did a great deal to keep them in good heart by going round the position, pointing out good targets and joking with the men. (59)

Although small parties of the brigade fought on under their own leaders, there was no organized resistance and 2/19th and 2/29th Australian Battalions were sent across to attempt to check the enemy's advance. They both fought with outstanding gallantry, and one battalion commander, Lieutenant-Colonel Anderson, was awarded the V.C., but the thrust of the Japanese *Guards Division* was overwhelming and they were not able materially to improve the position. During the final withdrawal on the twentieth, the commander of 45th Brigade himself led a counter-attack with the bayonet. A note written by one of the Australian commanders records:

Brigadier Duncan was killed in the counter-attack. I always feel very honoured to have been associated with this able and gallant gentleman. He had the complete confidence of his troops and his presence had a most stimulating effect on his men. He loved his brigade and I had the deepest sympathy for him that it was their unfortunate lot to be used at Muar.

Other Australian officers testified that after the men had recovered from the initial shock the Garwhalis were with difficulty held back when they had someone to lead them. On several occasions the men carried out local kukri attacks in their desire to get even with the Japanese.

The leading brigade of 18th British Division, 53rd, was rushed forward three days after disembarkation to join 11th Division twenty miles south of Muar. They were lucky to escape the fate of 45th Indian Brigade, although in the confused fighting that followed they lost over 500 men. The loss of the Muar position uncovered the main road and the Australian division and 9th Indian Division were ordered to withdraw. For their part, the Japanese claim that this was the decisive battle for the mainland; nothing could now stop them reaching Singapore Island.

Immediately before this withdrawal, 5th Battalion The Sikh Regiment was holding a position forward of Kluang. It was patent that they would have to withdraw before the day was out, but in the meantime, no orders had come through from brigade and the gunner forward observation officer and his staff had been knocked out.

It was obvious that unless the enemy could be dissuaded from following up the withdrawal would be a desperate business, and further that if we secured the high ground in front our movements would be screened from observation. It was decided to attack and give the enemy a blow from which it would take him some time to recover and further make him believe that we intended to advance.

Five minutes before the attack was due, the artillery support was called off because of an accident back at the battery position.

All 3″ mortars were now turned on the artillery tasks with very good effect and at 1100 hrs 'A' Coy swept forward, Havildar Lehna Singh's platoon well to the fore. They were met by a somewhat ragged fire and some half-dozen men were seen to fall; the rest with loud shouts of 'Sath Siri Akal' charged up the crest. The Japs hastily left their position and some of them threw away their arms in an effort to escape, the rest were bayonetted. From the number of Japs concentrated in a small space it looked as if he had been about to attack and had been forestalled.*

In the very last stages of the withdrawal, touch was lost with 22nd Indian Infantry Brigade which had been protecting the Australian right flank, and it was left behind when on 31 January all other troops crossed The Causeway, which was then blown up. The 600 mile retreat which had begun at Kota Bharu and Jitra seven weeks before had ended.

Fifteen days later Singapore fell. Virtually no defences had been constructed on the north of the island, the enemy had almost complete supremacy over sea and air, and with the exception of the newly arrived 18th Division all brigades had lost heavily in the fighting on the mainland.

The Indian troops now consisted of 11th Division, with 8th and 28th Brigades; 15th Brigade in corps reserve; 12th Brigade, down to 1,000 men, in command reserve; and 44th Brigade, newly arrived and of similar composition to 45th, under command of the Australian division.

Disposed to defend the island were 18th British Division on the east coast; 11th Indian Division covering the naval base; and the Australian division on The Causeway and round the west coast. It was on their left-hand brigade, 22nd, that the whole weight of the attack fell on the night of 8 February. They inflicted very heavy casualties on the enemy but there were no reserves placed to take advantage of this temporary success, and they were forced to withdraw. Their 27th Brigade moved back in conformity, exposing the flank of 11th Division, which at once restored the situation by a counter-attack; and when ordered to retire to the final perimeter round the city, withdrew in perfect order, and was facing the *Imperial Guards Division* at the time of capitulation.

5th Battalion The Sikh Regiment kept a diary of their action in Malaya and it closes with the proud boast:

The short campaign was over and for reasons beyond our control had ended in defeat. The battalion when given an

* *The Sikh Regiment in the Second World War* (55).

objective to take, took it; when given a position to hold, held it; in no instance did the battalion withdraw from any position till ordered to. (55)

There were plenty, British, Australian, Indian and Gurkha, whose endurance and will to fight never faltered. There were many, indeed, who fought all the better when they had settled down to the business; and if there were some who, in the stress of this or that battle, fell short of this high ideal, the reader, before he passes judgement, must ask himself two questions: Did they have a fair chance? Had I been there, would I have done any better?

CHAPTER NINE

Burma

January 1940–May 1942

The small force that opposed the Japanese invasion of Burma were little better off than their comrades fighting 700 miles away to the south in Malaya.

Until just before the war Burma was a province, administered by the Government of India, its military affairs controlled from Army Headquarters. The Government of Burma Act which came into force in April 1937 separated the two countries and Burma became a territory under the Crown in its own right. Throughout the negotiations leading up to separation successive commanders-in-chief in India had seen only too clearly that the defence of Burma was indissolubly bound up with that of India, and had urged that the responsibility should remain with them; but considerations of national prestige ranked higher than common sense, their advice was not accepted, and Burma became responsible to the chiefs of staff for her own defence.

In August 1940 India once more raised the matter, but she was told that she should be looking west, not east; and when in the following November a unified headquarters was set up for the Far East in Singapore, operational responsibility for Burma passed to that command.

A year later, when the entry of Japan into the war was clearly only a matter of time, General Wavell once more returned to the charge, and he was the fourth of his line to do so;

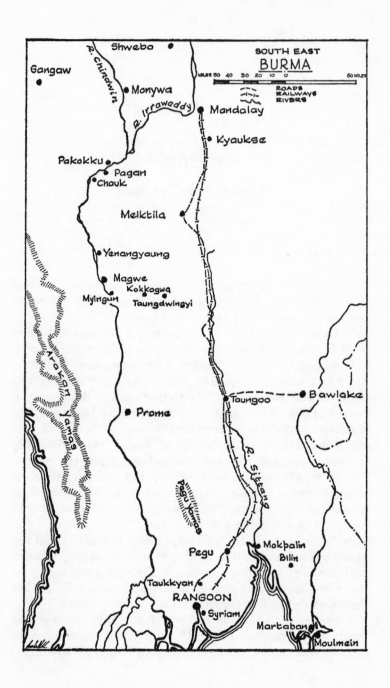

the arguments in favour of the defence of Burma passing to his hands were becoming more cogent as the weeks sped past, but they seem to have fallen on deaf ears. For all that, just one month later, and only four days after the Japanese attack on Malaya, operational control for Burma was passed like a hot brick to the commander-in-chief, India.

In January the new South West Pacific Command, known as Abdacom, was formed, with its headquarters in Java, and General Wavell, who was appointed to command it, found that he was to take his newly assumed responsibility with him. Before leaving Delhi he recommended that the existing arrangement, which had already resulted in considerable improvement, should not be disturbed, but once again political considerations prevailed. Whatever the reasons for the transfer, in practice the new arrangement just did not work; to visit Burma, and he managed to do so twice, General Wavell had to fly 2,000 miles, and as there was no direct signal link all messages had to be routed via Delhi. Who can wonder that information was out of date by the time it reached Java, or that orders were often impossible of fulfilment by the time they reached Burma. On the dissolution of Abdacom at the end of February Burma passed back to India, the fifth change of responsibility in less than eighteen months.

On the map of Asia, Burma is apt to be dwarfed between India on the west, and on the east the great block of countries that merge into China itself. For all that Burma is as large as France and Belgium put together, has a coastline on the east of the Bay of Bengal of 1,200 miles, and at that time occupied a corner of great strategic importance. The Burma Road, running forward from railhead at Lashio, was the sole remaining line of supply for warlike stores to maintain the Chinese armies who were successfully containing very considerable Japanese forces in the field. Moreover, all these stores had to pass through the port of Rangoon. The possession of Burma also secured the eastern frontier of India and the industrial areas around Calcutta from invasion and air attack; and the chain of airfields on the Imperial reinforcement route to Malaya ran down the Tenasserim coast to its southern tip at Victoria Point.

The central plain of Burma and the Tenasserim seaboard are separated from China on the east, and India on the west, by the dwindling off-shoots of the Himalayas, densely wooded hills that are as high as 7,000 feet on the northern frontiers. Between Calcutta and Rangoon, communication by sea was so convenient and so well-established that, although from time to time consideration had been given to the idea of a land link between India and Burma, by rail or road, the cost and the difficulties were so great that nothing was done, and all that existed was a cart track forward from Imphal to Palel. Perhaps the outstanding feature of the country's geography were the three rivers running from north to south which were to influence so greatly the course of events. The Irrawaddy, with its tributary, the Chindwin, had the great port of Rangoon situated on its delta, and was navigable by a regular service of steamers for 1,000 miles from its mouth. About 250 miles north of Rangoon were the oilfields of Yenangyaung, connected by pipeline to the refineries at Syriam, which supplied India with something like one third of her oil. The other two rivers, the Sittang and the Salween, flowed into the sea at Mokpalin and Moulmein respectively.

The Burmese were an easy-going and unwarlike people who inhabited the central plateau. In the hill tracts there lived, starting on the west and going round clockwise, the Nagas, the Chins, the Kachins and the Karens, and from these tribes were recruited the men of the Burma Army. There were in Burma about 300,000 Chinese mostly engaged in trade; and about one million Indians, business men, public servants and un-skilled workers in industry or on estates. It was the deter-mination of the Indians to return to their country when Burma was threatened by air and land that gave rise to a refugee problem that very much complicated the withdrawal.

The peace-time army of Burma consisted of two battalions of British infantry, four battalions of The Burma Rifles, and one mountain battery and one company of Sappers and Miners on loan from India. There were also the Burma Military Police, recruited very largely in India, which had been converted into the Burmese Frontier Force. Army Head-quarters, Burma, with such an inconsiderable army to look after, was very small and quite unable to meet the demands that were to be placed upon it. For the first twelve months of the war, the one thing that everyone was able to agree about was that there would never be a land attack on Burma; indeed, only two months before the Japanese attacked, Mr Duff Cooper, the Resident Minister in the Far East, could commiserate with the officers at the Bush Warfare school, Maymyo, that they were serving in a backwater that would never see any fighting.

A Far East Defence Committee sitting in Singapore in November 1940 had recommended that Burma should receive reinforcement of seven battalions of infantry with a suitable proportion of artillery, engineers, and a company of light tanks. As they had nothing to contribute towards the proposal the chiefs of staff not unnaturally considered this to be a complete over-estimate, but they did suggest that India might contribute an infantry brigade, which with commendable promptitude was sent in February 1941. In July, as a brigade had already been formed from battalions of The Burma Rifles, the headquarters of 1st Burma Division was established in Toungoo. The commander was sent from India, but otherwise everything was found locally and, as may be imagined, there were many shortages—staff, artillery, engineers and signals, supply, transport and other administrative services. In August, the commander-in-chief Far East recommended that a second infantry brigade was necessary. India once again answered the call and, when Japan entered the war, 16th Indian Infantry Brigade was just completing disembarkation at Rangoon.

When responsibility passed to India an immediate reinforcement of officers was sent to strengthen the staffs and services of Army Headquarters, Burma. The chiefs of staff informed General Wavell that he could retain for use in Burma 17th Indian Division, then forming and intended for Iraq, and that 18th (British) Division, then at sea and destined for the Middle East, would be diverted to Bombay and placed at his disposal. These were fair promises for, of course, the whole of the British division and two brigades of 17th Indian Division were snatched back and sent to Singapore. In the end, all that reached Burma during January were the headquarters and the remaining brigade of 17th Division, a fourth brigade at the end of the month, and a fifth and last just before Rangoon fell. Three unbrigaded battalions of British infantry arrived from India at the end of January and 7th Armoured Brigade, consisting of 7th Hussars, 2nd Battalion The Royal Tank Regiment, one battery of Royal Horse Artillery, and 1st Battalion The Cameronians reached Rangoon on 24 February. It was a reinforcement of incalculable value, a decisive factor in a number of engagements on the long withdrawal to India after the fall of Rangoon.

The Air Ministry had agreed that a force of six fighter squadrons, seven bomber, and two army co-operation squadrons was needed for Burma. Had these materialized, we should still have been well short of the total of 200 fighters and bombers which in the opening stages the Japanese had within range of Rangoon. The actual strength was little more than half what had been promised, and we were fortunate to have one squadron of the American Volunteer Group, flying P40 fighters. This was a force of highly skilled pilots recruited in America for the general protection of Chinese interests and, in view of the importance of Rangoon as a port, Chiang Kai-Shek had agreed to allot one squadron to reinforce its defences. Together with the three R.A.F. fighter squadrons they gave invaluable support to the army in the first seven weeks of the campaign, and were instrumental in breaking the Japanese bid for air supremacy at the end of January.

General Wavell visited Rangoon just before Christmas. He had been told by the chiefs of staff that he need not expect an attack on Burma till after the Japanese had completed the conquest of Malaya and the Philippines and, with the feeling that the first and most urgent necessity was to get the basic organization of staff and services on a proper war footing, he appointed his own chief of the general staff from India, General Hutton,* as commander-in-chief. What he did not do, no doubt because he felt there would be time for it later on, was to set up a corps headquarters for the conduct of operations in the field.

---

* Lieutenant-General Sir Thomas Hutton, K.C.I.E., C.B., M.C.

On the day Japan declared war, Generalissimo Chiang Kai-Shek, through the British Ambassador in Chungking, placed the whole of China's resources at the disposal of the British and United States Governments for the prosecution of the war against the common enemy, expressing the wish that in particular employment might be found for them in Burma. From Rangoon General Wavell flew to Chungking to discuss how this should be done. He found that the Generalissimo was insisting on certain provisos for the employment of these forces, which consisted of the Vth and VIth Armies. They were to be given a separate operational role under their own commander, and the British were to be responsible for rationing them, for which purpose a separate line of supply would have to be arranged. The Chinese armies were at that time somewhat scattered and would have to be regrouped before they could be used; moreover, until reorganization in Burma had made some progress, there was little hope of accepting any responsibility for looking after them. Whatever his reasons, and he may well have felt there was no great urgency to decide, General Wavell did not accept the offer in quite the unreserved spirit in which it was made and a certain coolness resulted, perhaps accentuated by the fact that the Generalissimo, who had a penchant for grand strategy, was disappointed to find that General Wavell was not empowered, and perhaps not even too keen, to discuss at the very highest level the proper prosecution of the war.

In reviewing the various plans made, it must be remembered that Army Headquarters, Burma, suffered throughout under two crippling handicaps. Owing to the frequent change of masters there never was a clear-cut policy to work on and, as there had been in peace no properly organized intelligence staff or service, there was no time to set one up after war broke out. To all intents and purposes, for information of what was going on over the mountains in Siam, Burma was dependent on Far East Command. The view they took was that, in the early stages, the most that could be expected was a series of raids directed at the Tenasserim airfields, which were in fact all they were worried about. There was the possibility that there might later be an attack directed on Meiktila. In the summer of 1941, when 1st Burma Division was formed at Toungoo, one brigade of the Burma Army was moved there together with the brigade that had already arrived from India. The other Burma brigade was dispersed in Tenasserim. These dispositions conformed with the instructions received from Far East Command, which were to ensure the retention of the chain of reinforcing airfields, and to protect the Burma Road and the communications with China. It was realized that an attack could be made from Raheng, directed on Moulmein, which would threaten not only the airfields but Rangoon as well, and of course this is exactly what the Japanese did; but there was a stretch of twenty miles of road through the mountains of exceptional difficulty, and it was felt that the threat to the north was the one most to be feared.

On 10 January, General Hutton reviewed the problem confronting him. Deducing that until he received considerable reinforcements the only possible role for him was the defensive, he felt he must consider the possibility of invasion on three routes: from Raheng directed on Moulmein and Rangoon; from Chiengrai directed on Toungoo; and one further north directed at Meiktila. Had his intelligence services been better organized, they could have told him how very busy the enemy were across the frontier in Siam, improving the road forward from Raheng and concentrating two whole divisions for a drive on Rangoon, divisions which never moved a mile further north than was necessary to outflank the positions we took up to oppose the crossing of the Salween and Sittang rivers. In consequence a considerable portion of General Hutton's small force remained covering lines of approach that were never used.

It is difficult to present a coherent picture of the strategy on which the defensive battle for Burma was fought for the good reason that, with the troops available, Napoleon and all his marshals would have been at a loss to devise a plan that even began to carry out the tasks laid down by H.Q. Far East Command; these involved watching 700 miles of frontier, and at the same time trying to protect a line of airfields scattered down the coast from Moulmein to Victoria Point. If 17th Indian Division had been at full strength, trained and tested in battle, it would still have been too small. As it was, the divisional commander assumed control of operations no more than three days before the enemy attacked; short of artillery, engineers and signals, and with brigades he had never seen before joining him after the battle had started, the initiative was inevitably and always with the enemy.

What perhaps throws as much light as anything on the course of events is a consideration of the points of view of the three senior commanders concerned. There was no more fervent believer in the virtue of the offensive than General Wavell, and his successes against the Italians only a year before can have done nothing to make him change his views. On his own admission, he rated the Japanese very little higher than the enemy who had given him so little trouble at Sidi Barrani whereas, taking them all round for the campaign they were about to fight, they were probably the finest troops that could have been found anywhere in the world; and it may well be that he did not realize that his own brigades fell far short of the seasoned veterans of 4th and 5th Indian Divisions who had served him so well in Africa. Couple these considerations with the fact that his headquarters in Java were 2,000 miles away from Rangoon, and it is not surprising to find he took a more optimistic view of affairs than was justified by the hard facts of the situation.

General Hutton, the commander-in-chief in Burma, was intolerably overworked. He was liable to receive encouraging and sometimes contradictory advice from both General Wavell in Java and the chiefs of staff in London, and he had to keep close touch with G.H.Q. India. He had to deal with the Governor of Burma on all the hundred and one matters with which the civil government was concerned, and to maintain liaison with Chiang Kai-Shek, involving long and sometimes perilous air journeys. He was also responsible for co-ordination with the Navy and the Air Force. So it was inevitable that he was able to give very much less attention than was necessary to the conduct of operations. So long as the port of Rangoon remained open it was always possible for reinforcements from outside to reach him: once it had gone, and the advantages it offered had passed to the enemy, there would be nothing to do but fight what must be a losing battle, maintained by the hopelessly inadequate lines of communication over the hills from India. Time, therefore, was a major factor in his strategy, and he felt that he must force the enemy to fight for the possession of every tactical feature on which it was possible to delay him.

A withdrawal is perhaps the most difficult of all operations of war, and places a severe strain on the morale even of seasoned troops, a strain that may increase to breaking point unless there are sufficient forces available to rest those who have been in contact with the enemy. In this particular withdrawal, all the possible delaying positions ran along the lines of the rivers, rivers over which there was never more than one bridge, if indeed there was a bridge at all. The divisional commander who actually had to fight the battle not unnaturally felt that the more often he stopped to engage the enemy, the more often he ran the risk of losing a brigade in doing so. He therefore favoured making a clean break back to a position where, given time for reconnaissance and the construction of proper defences, he could fight with his whole division concentrated and some chance of retaining a degree of local initiative and inflicting on the enemy a blow which might really check his advance. It was a conflict between strategic and tactical considerations: strategy won the day.

At the beginning of December 1941, 1st Burma Division had 1st Burma Brigade and 13th Indian Brigade disposed in the Mandalay area, with 2nd Burma Brigade in Tenasserim watching more than 300 miles of frontier and charged with the protection of four airfields spaced 150 miles apart on the reinforcement route to Malaya. Three days after declaring war, the Japanese crossed into the southern tip of Burma and obligingly relieved them of the responsibility of the southernmost airfield at Victoria Point. H.Q. 17th Indian Division arrived early in January with its 46th Brigade, which was in the same state as 44th and 45th which had gone to Malaya, and was joined by 16th Indian Infantry Brigade.

The Japanese, at the same time as their landings at Singora and Kota Bharu, had put their *55th Division* ashore further north along the east coast of Siam; by mid January both that division and *33rd* were concentrated at Raheng and, with the active co-operation of the Siamese, improvement of the road forward over the Kawkareik Pass was pretty well complete.

On 10 January 1942 they captured Tavoy airfield. By then 17th Division had 16th Brigade at the Kawkareik Pass, 2nd Burma Brigade at Moulmein, and 46th Brigade in reserve at Bilin. On 20 January the enemy attacked and surrounded a company of the leading battalion of 16th Brigade on the frontier and, as their orders were not to become involved, they withdrew to Martaban, though because of the sinking of a ferry boat they lost much of their transport. Moulmein was the next to go. The perimeter round the town stretched for over 8,000 yards, but the four battalions of the Burma brigade there put up a very brave defence and were withdrawn in good order by river steamers to Martaban in the small hours of the thirty-first.

17th Division now had an enormous front to watch; eighty miles along the Salween, forty miles west to the Sittang, and a further eighty miles of coastline north from Martaban. Ten days earlier the divisional commander had advocated abandoning Moulmein and concentrating at the vital Sittang crossing on a position where he could fight a divisional battle and hope to strike back at the enemy. He had been overruled; and his proposal now to withdraw from the Martaban salient was also turned down because of the need to impose the maximum delay and keep open the port of Rangoon for the reinforcements which were on the way.

The vulnerability of the exposed sea flank to turning movements was quickly apparent and, when on 9 February it was found that the enemy had landed west of Martaban and was moving on the town from the north-west, the small garrison was withdrawn. On the eleventh there were patrol clashes east of Kuzeik, held by 7th Battalion The Baluch Regiment, a young battalion of 46th Brigade which covered itself with glory in the action that followed. An attempt was made to reinforce them from Duyinzeik but, for various reasons, help came too late and the Baluchis were left to fight it out alone all through the night against the assaults of a complete Japanese regiment. Their colonel and six other officers were killed, and it was only when three companies had been practically annihilated that the enemy was able to occupy Kuzeik. They had won twenty-four precious hours, but the delay in coming to their assistance was unfortunate as the enemy were now across the Salween and in a position to attack the crossings of the Bilin and the Sittang.

The Japanese had by now made their final plans for the advance on Rangoon. Accepting, as was their custom, considerable administrative risks, both *33rd* and *55th Divisions* were ordered to press on without waiting for their rear echelons. After crossing the Sittang, *55th Division* was to move on Toungoo and destroy any Chinese forces they came in contact with, and *33rd Division* was to capture Rangoon and establish a base with as much elbow room as possible for subsequent operations in central and northern Burma.

The commander 17th Division now decided, and General Hutton was not too pleased at the decision, to withdraw the remaining scattered battalions of 46th Brigade to the line of the Bilin, where he was trying to organize a stand. It was not, in fact, a very good position; there was something like a ten-mile front with the right flank exposed to the sea, and only one brigade, the newly arrived 48th, was fresh and in good order; but with the pressure from above to contest every yard of the way he could have done no better. Both Japanese divisions were put into the attack, *55th* making a wide sweep to come in from the south. The enemy had little difficulty in crossing the river and, in spite of counter attacks by 4th Frontier Force Regiment and 5th Gurkhas, broke into the position. However, he had been forced to deploy nearly all his strength, the momentum of his advance was checked, four valuable days were gained, and it was clear that 7th Armoured Brigade would have landed and would be in action west of the Sittang by the time the enemy got there. The imperative necessity was to get the whole of 17th Division behind the river, which was a really effective obstacle, so that infantry and armour could fight a concerted battle to contest the crossing.

The withdrawal was timed to begin on the night of the nineteenth. Unluckily, a message ordering it went out in clear and was intercepted by the enemy, so that as the division, hampered by its long transport columns, began its move back along the road, a Japanese regiment was moving at top speed across country direct on the Sittang bridge to cut them off.

During the withdrawal, owing to a most unfortunate error in defining a bomb line, east of which they were free to attack anything they saw, both R.A.F. and A.V.G. fighters made repeated low flying attacks on our own troops, causing much confusion and a most unfortunate lowering of morale.

Road and railway run alongside each other in the approach to the Sittang bridge, but as the railway turns west to straighten out through a cutting, the road carries on for a short way before it also turns, enclosing in the loop between the two a ridge, with Pagoda Hill at its western end. The bridge is just over 500 yards long and had been decked over to take road traffic. The river is deep and fast-moving and widens to 1,000 yards both below and above the bridge. Initially, the only troops guarding it were a company of the Duke of Wellington's Regiment and a weak battalion of The Burma Regiment. On 21 February they were reinforced by 4th Frontier Force Regiment, and the Malerkotla Field Squadron sent to complete the work on the demolitions; the next day, after a warning that parachute troops might try to capture the bridge, 1/4th Gurkhas also arrived, to be greeted by a Japanese attack from the north-east. The cross-country column had arrived. However, The Frontier Force Regiment counter-attacked and restored the situation for the time being.

By the morning of the twenty-second, the leading battalions, 5th and 3rd Gurkhas of 48th Brigade, were still short of the ridge blocking the final approach to the river. At that moment a heavy enemy attack came in from the north and though both battalions fought with great tenacity they failed to clear the way, partly because, in the confused situation, it was not known that the bridgehead troops were also attacking Pagoda Hill from the far end. At the same time, a gap had occurred between 16th and 46th Brigades further to the rear, and the Japanese attacked and established a block between them. The brigade commander of the bridgehead defences found himself in a most unenviable position. With little more than two battalions available, he could not hope to beat off indefinitely the enemy attacks which were becoming heavier as the day went on; such news as he could get of what was happening down the road to the east came from stragglers and indicated that there was not much hope of organized help from that direction; furthermore, if the enemy captured the bridge intact, the road to Rangoon was wide open. Owing to a shortage of fuse, the demolitions had to be carried out from sites on the bridge itself, and as the crossing was under fire this meant that, to make certain of success, the order to blow must be given before dawn. The brigade commander referred the decision to the divisional commander, and at 5.30 a.m. on the twenty-third a great explosion was heard, 'all firing ceased, and for a brief period complete silence reigned'.

The defensive perimeter formed by 16th Brigade east of the river on the previous night held out during the twenty-third and undoubtedly slackened the pressure on the bridge itself and allowed many men to get across by swimming.

> The remnants of 17th Division withdrew to the Pegu area. As a fighting force the division had, for the time being, almost ceased to exist; it had lost some guns, most of its transport and the greater part of its equipment. On the 24th February the infantry of the division mustered only 80 officers and 3,404 other ranks, of whom only 1,420 still had their rifles. At Pegu the troops, most of whom were without boots and possessed nothing but what they stood up in, were reclothed partly re-equipped and rearmed.*

It was fortunate that the enemy were for the moment at the end of their administrative tether. They had advanced over 150 miles from the frontier in thirty-four days, which included a number of days' hard fighting, largely on what they carried or could obtain from the countryside, and now had to wait until they had completed a motor road to Moulmein and could bring forward the material to repair the Sittang bridge. On the twenty-fifth and twenty-sixth they made a determined attempt to secure air superiority over Rangoon, but they were decisively

* *History of the Second World War: The War against Japan*, Vol. II (6).

defeated by the R.A.F. and A.V.G. and abandoned the attempt. This victory contributed materially to the events of the following fortnight, during which 63rd Infantry Brigade and 1st Indian Field Regiment arrived and ensured that the withdrawal from Rangoon was carried out virtually without interference from the air.

On the day that the Sittang bridge was blown, 7th Armoured Brigade arrived in Rangoon and twenty-seven hours later the leading squadron reached Pegu. The rest of the brigade moved forward to an area north-west of Pegu covering the reorganization of 17th Division, and 1st Burma Division with two weak brigades moved down the Sittang with its southernmost battalion at Nyaungbelin; but there were thirty-five miles between the two. Appreciating the difficulty of closing this gap, and of being able to delay the enemy for more than a few days longer, General Hutton indicated that his intention was for 1st Burma Division to withdraw northwards on Toungoo to cover deployment of VIth Chinese Army, while 17th Division and the armoured brigade were to cover Rangoon for as long as possible and then withdraw on Prome. By the twenty-seventh clashes were occurring west of the Sittang with strong Japanese patrols and renegade Burmans of the Burma Independent Army, and that night General Hutton signalled Army Headquarters, India, that unless he received instructions to the contrary the following day he proposed to carry out the demolitions in Rangoon and abandon the city. He was told to wait and on 1 March was visited by General Wavell who had resumed his appointment as commander-in-chief, India. It was decided that in the battle for Burma still to be fought there would be a need for every man who could be landed, and that Rangoon must be kept open to allow the arrival of 63rd Indian Infantry Brigade and 1st Indian Field Regiment who were still on the high seas. Orders were accordingly given to the armoured brigade to check their withdrawal and to reoccupy Waw, but for the moment they were unable to do so. On 3 March, General Alexander,* who had

---

* Field Marshal Earl Alexander, K.G., P.C., G.C.B., G.C.M.G., C.S.I., D.S.O., M.C.

flown out to relieve General Hutton, met General Wavell at Calcutta and was briefed by him, but by the fifth, when he reached Rangoon, the situation had deteriorated somewhat faster than he probably realized. He saw that he must either close the gap or withdraw, and ordered one last attempt to save the situation. It was only partially successful, and he gave orders for the evacuation of Rangoon, the final demolitions to begin at 2 p.m. the next day.

1st Burma Division was ordered to withdraw on Toungoo; 17th Division, with the armoured brigade under its command, to keep the Taukkyan cross-roads clear till the column comprising the city garrison was clear, and thereafter to act as rearguard. The leading troops of the division had already cleared these cross-roads and moved on towards Tharawaddy, but when the column from Rangoon arrived they found the Japanese had established a road block which they could not break. A concerted brigade attack was then laid on for early next morning but during the night the fog of war descended thickly about the cross-roads. To the south, General Alexander was being prevented from joining the army he had come out to command; to the north, troops of the advanced guard, who had turned back when they heard of the block, found large numbers of Japanese moving westwards across the main road; the battalion out to the west reported enemy moving wide of their flank and south towards Rangoon; and when at daylight an armoured squadron reconnoitred the road block they found it was no longer held.

The explanation of these moves and counter-moves lay in the Japanese plan. *55th Division* had been ordered to move north from Pegu to engage the Chinese about Toungoo, *33rd Division* to capture Rangoon and destroy any of our troops round the city. Being, perhaps, a shade too clever, the commander decided to march across and attack the city from the north-west; the road block was the stop he placed temporarily on the road to protect his flank, and withdrew when his troops were across the road. He reached Rangoon to find to his surprise that it was empty.

The troops now available were 7th Armoured Brigade, 17th Indian Division (Major-General Cowan*) and 1st Burma Division (Major-General J. B. Scott†).

The two latter were much below strength. For all practical purposes as far as the arrival of reinforcements or the delivery of supplies and stores went, this force was cut off from India, but had stocks to last a few months which had been back-loaded from Rangoon to Mandalay. Moving south down the Sittang valley was Vth Chinese Army, worth about two weak divisions. The Japanese were now well based on the port of Rangoon, through which they were able to bring in reinforcements for the divisions that had been fighting and, also, over the next few weeks, two fresh divisions, *18th* and *56th*.

General Alexander's plan was to concentrate the British force by bringing 1st Burma Division across into the Irrawaddy valley, and to leave the Sittang valley to the Chinese; the British were to hold Prome, the Chinese, Toungoo. Feeling that with such extended responsibilities he could not also effectively command his own army, he asked, as indeed General Hutton had done, for a corps commander. A small headquarters, Burcorps, which throughout remained very short of equipment and signals, was formed and on 19 March General Slim‡ flew in from India to command it. Almost as soon as he arrived the situation got worse. On 21 March and succeeding days, reacting sharply to a raid that the R.A.F. had made on Mingaladon, the Japanese air force attacked our airfields at Magwe and Akyab in overwhelming strength and by the twenty-third had driven us from the skies: from then on Burcorps was without air support of any kind, no reconnaissance, no cover, no bombing: nothing. On 24 March, the Japanese *55th Division*, supported by elements of *56th* which had begun to arrive, attacked the Chinese 200th Division at Toungoo. It was perhaps their best division and it fought valiantly, and inflicted heavy casualties, but reinforcements arriving to support it refused to attack to restore the loss of the

---

* Major-General D. T. Cowan, C.B., C.B.E., D.S.O., M.C.
† Major-General J. Bruce Scott, C.B., D.S.O., M.C.
‡ Field Marshal Viscount Slim, K.G., G.C.B., G.C.M.G., G.C.V.O., G.B.E., D.S.O., M.C.

airfield to the north of the town, and two further divisions supposed to be coming down from the south flatly disobeyed General Stilwell's order to move. 200th Division was forced to withdraw, but unfortunately failed before doing so to blow the bridge over the Sittang carrying the Mawchi–Bawlake road, thus leaving wide open the road to Lashio and the whole of our left flank.

As a rather desperate gesture of allied solidarity, 17th Division, at some cost to itself, attacked south from Prome in the vain hope of relieving pressure in the Sittang valley, but once Toungoo had fallen there was no longer any chance of holding Prome. In a last attempt to prevent the great oilfields at Yenangyaung falling to the enemy, Burcorps was to be disposed covering the east-west road Taungdwingyi–Kokkogwa–Magwe and, to relieve the strain on the corps of covering so great a front, it was agreed that a Chinese division should take over Taungdwingyi. The corps would then have been able to hold two infantry brigades in reserve, and had a chance to counter-attack the enemy when he arrived. Unfortunately, the Chinese did not appear, and Burcorps had to keep all its brigades in the line, and to abandon its carefully laid plans for a counter-attack.

On the night of the 11–12 April, the Japanese launched a heavy attack on 48th Brigade in position about Kokkogwa. After 2/5th Gurkhas had repulsed one assault, on a night when a terrific thunderstorm was raging,

> there were signs of another impending attack. The enemy could be heard moving about and the clinking of metal indicated the mounting of mortars. A moment later a blinding flash proved the correctness of the deduction. A Bren gun opened fire on the flash and a combination of good marksmanship and good luck was decisive for in the morning the complete mortar crew was found dead beside their mortar. Shortly after this the Japanese very helpfully announced their intention to attack by the fixing of bayonets. The attack when it came was met by such intensity of fire that it withered and broke.*

* History of 5th Royal Gurkha Rifles (Frontier Force) (65).

166

The brigade commander, Brigadier R. T. Cameron, considered that the action

> gave birth to the real soul of the brigade. The tired troops of 48th Brigade had endured a major enemy attack. Each had supported the other. The spirit of Kokkogwa was the pervading influence to the end of the Burma campaign.

In spite of this quite considerable local success our defences were so strung out that there was nothing to stop the Japanese working through the gaps and pushing north in a direct threat to the oilfields.

It was at this juncture that the Chinese made amends for some of their past shortcomings by sending us their 38th Division under General Sun Li-Jen, who lived up to his reputation as being one of the most competent of the Chinese generals. His division fought skilfully in the battles of the next few days, remained in touch with Burcorps to the very end, and later withdrew to India for training before it returned, via the Ledo Road, to take part in the final campaign that drove the Japanese out of Burma.

While the destruction of the oilfields was going on, the enemy cut through in the centre and the portion of 1st Burma Division on the right of our line was cut off by a road block established behind them.

> The Burma Division had begun in real earnest the Battle of the Oilfields. And a brutal battle it was. The temperature that day was 114 degrees; the battle-field was the arid, hideous, blackened shale of the oilfield, littered with wrecked derricks, flames roaring from the tanks, and shattered machinery and burning buildings everywhere. Over it all hung that huge pall of smoke. And there was no water.*

General Bruce Scott tried in vain to tie the Chinese 38th Division down to a time for a joint attempt to break the block,

* *Defeat into Victory* (71).

167

NORTH WEST
BURMA

MILES 50 40 30 20 10 0   50 MILES

--- ROADS
~~~ RIVERS

Dimapur
Kohima
R. Chindwin
Kanglatongbi
Silchar
Ukhrul
Imphal
Bishenpur
Palel
Shenam
Tamu
Sittaung
R. Myitta
Tiddim
Kennedy Peak
Fort White
Kalemyo
Kalewa
Shwegyin
Yeu
Chittagong
Gangaw
R. Kaladan
ARAKAN
Monywa
R. Irrawaddy
Pakokku
Myingyan
Pagan
Bawli Bazaar
Taung Bazaar
Buthidaung
Maungdaw
R. Mayu
Foul Point
Akyab
Yenangyaung
Myebon
Magwe

but time meant very little to our ally, and Burma Division had
to attack alone and were not successful. Eventually piling as
many wounded as possible on the tanks, he gave the order

> to fight a way out on foot across the Pin Chaung. This the
> men did, some in formed bodies, some in small groups,
> and on the other side they met the Chinese. At the sight
> of the water in Chaung the mules that had come with them
> went mad, and the men flung themselves face downwards
> into it. The haggard, red-eyed British, Indian and Burmese
> soldiers who staggered up the bank were a terrible sight,
> but every man I saw was still carrying a rifle. (71)

In the meantime, matters had been going badly for the
Chinese, as the capture of the bridge over the Sittang at
Toungoo had enabled the Japanese to move wide to the flank
and they were now in a position to close in and threaten
Mandalay from the north-east. Recognizing that any stand on
the line of the Irrawaddy could only be temporary, the final
plan for the withdrawal to India took shape: 1st Burma
Division was to cross the river by ferry at Sameikkon, 17th
Division by the Ava bridge after covering across any Chinese
detachments which might wish to use it.

The 48th Brigade had been left holding a final covering
position at Kyaukse where their action was considered a
'really brilliant example of rearguard work'. 1/7th Gurkhas
were in the thick of it:

> One hour later the two enemy companies emerged from
> the jungle into the cleared area on the left of the road.
> There was bright moonlight and 'D' Coy's positions
> allowed the Japanese to approach within 100 yards and
> then let them have it. They ran back in confusion shout-
> ing and screaming.

Later on:

> At dawn the tanks following a practice that had proved
> effective at Kokkogwa, swept the front and found the

village area in front of 'C' Coy still occupied. Williams ordered 'B' Coy under Gribble to make a counter-attack. There was no holding the men. They burst through the village and the banana grove killing Japs right and left and driving others before them. The night's work cost the Japanese over 100 killed. Our casualties being one man killed and three wounded. In Kokkogwa we had mastered a difficult situation, in Kyaukse we were masters of the situation from the start.*

Once across the river, the final arrangements were that the Burma division should withdraw up the Chindwin from Monywa, with a strong detachment in the Myittha Valley to prevent the enemy forestalling us at Kalemyo; while 17th Division with the armoured brigade moved via Yeu on Kalewa. Largely owing to the lack of air reconnaissance, it was not appreciated that the Japanese had reached Monywa in strength before us. There was in the town itself no more than a small garrison and the headquarters of 1st Burma Division, when an enemy force totalling nearly a thousand appeared on the far bank of the river and were ferried across in large naval launches. A full-scale attack succeeded in restoring the situation, but the Burma division, instead of withdrawing up the Chindwin, now had to move to Yeu and along the jungle track to Shwegyin and Kalewa, adding considerably to the congestion and confusion in the last stages of the withdrawal across the river. The last 120 miles of this road were

no more, and often less, than an unbridged, earth cart-track with frequent sharp bends, steep gradients, and narrow cuttings. Long stretches, sometimes as much as thirty miles, were completely without water. It crossed several wide stream-beds of soft sand, difficult enough now for vehicles, and, when rain came, likely to be un-fordable rivers. When Shwegyin was reached, the track ended and there was a six-mile river journey upstream to Kalewa. Then came the long trek up the malaria-infested

* *History of 7th Gurkha Rifles* (67).

Kabaw valley, through dense jungle to Tamu to reach the unmetalled road we hoped was being built from Imphal in Assam. (71)

It was along this track that 2,300 casualties were evacuated, in addition to the many thousand refugees who were fed by the army and, where possible, given lifts in military vehicles.

A further hazard was that as far as Shwebo the army had been withdrawing up its lines of communications and drawing on supplies backloaded from Rangoon, but the route Yeu–Shwegyin had to be stocked from bases in the Mandalay area, and there was anxiety as to whether sufficient stocks could be put in for the extra troops now using the road. The corps commander had two more preoccupations: whether his force would be clear before the monsoon broke and immobilized his mechanical transport; and whether the enemy pressing up the Chindwin valley would reach Kalewa before him. On both counts he scraped home by a short head.

Shwegyin was one huge bottle-neck. There had been originally six river steamers, each of which would take five or six hundred men packed tight, but not more than one lorry, two or three guns, and a couple of jeeps. Steamers leaving Shwegyin had to proceed six miles up-stream to Kalewa, unload, and return, a round trip of several hours.

The road to the pier ran for about the last fifteen hundred yards in the 'Basin'. This was a horseshoe-shaped, flat space about a thousand yards wide, mostly open but with small clumps of jungle, surrounded on three sides by a steep two-hundred-foot escarpment, almost precipitous on the inside. From the edge of the escarpment the whole of the 'Basin' was displayed at one's feet. Looking down one felt it could be a death-trap, and now it was literally full of soldiers, refugees, animals, motor-vehicles, guns and tanks. (71)

On the morning of 10 May the Japanese began to attack from the south and for two whole days 48th Brigade, once again the rearguard, fought them off. Finally, the steamer crews were refusing to come down to Shwegyin, and the last parties of 7th Armoured and 48th Brigades were faced with a gruelling march along an extremely rough hill track to Kaing, opposite Kalewa, where the steamers took them across. Progress was incredibly slow owing to the congestion, and it was fortunate that the enemy did not follow up.

A last desperate attempt by 7th Gurkhas to drive the enemy off a hill commanding The Basin had been the final action of the campaign, and 7th Hussars record that it was a sore disappointment that the country was impossible for close co-operation between tanks and infantry, and that they had to stand off and could only use their guns at long range.

> This was the last the regiment was to see of the splendid Gurkha Brigade, with which it had been operating almost continuously since the battle of the oilfields. Nothing could depress them and their high spirits were obvious— and infectious—as they formed up amongst the tanks for the last attack on Shwegyin. They were always ready to grin and always ready to cheer. At Shwegyin they stood up and shouted 'Shahbash'—a little derisively—when a solitary Wellington bomber flew over, the first British aircraft they had seen since leaving the Tenasserim strip. They had earned the greatest affection, admiration and confidence of the 7th Hussars, who would have asked for nothing better than to serve alongside them for the rest of the war.*

A special raft had been built for vehicles but the first tank to cross had taken six hours to load and had nearly split the raft in the process, so there was no question of getting any more over. By one means or another they were all destroyed or rendered useless. For 7th Hussars, and the whole of 7th Armoured Brigade it was a bitter ending.

This formation with its mobility and fire power was able

---

* *The Seventh and Three Enemies* (30).

to give depth to the defence, provide support without delay in a crisis and break the ubiquitous road-block; was able to transport infantry units quickly to threatened points and bring in casualties who would otherwise have had to be abandoned. There is no doubt that the armoured brigade played a leading part in the campaign after the fall of Rangoon, and that without it .Burcorps might well have collapsed. It was sad that the brigade had to come out of Burma without its tanks. It deserved to have marched proudly with them into India at the head of Burcorps. (6)

It is clear that the troops in contact with the enemy maintained their fighting spirit to the very end. A battalion commander whose casualties were lighter than most attributed this to

very rigorous discipline. Insisting on digging in, proper dispersal against air and shelling at all times; not allowing people to halt behind obvious cover but pushing them on; strict water discipline; no falling out was allowed, and a little foresight in evacuating lame ducks; cooking meals ahead so that the men were not hungry when others were; these were the sort of things that kept down casualties.*

What does not emerge is any idea of the continued strain and hardship all through the days when there was no fighting. The Indian mountain batteries, who with their mules never got a lift, however lucky the infantry may have been, knew all about this side of the picture.

On one occasion 23rd Battery was given the fittest mules of another battery and sent to support the Chinese 38th Division.

This entailed a long march back the way the column had come, and the attack was not pushed home after all. On return to the place where it had left the division, the battery found that a further retirement had been made,

* *A History of 4th P.W.O. Gurkha Rifles* (64).

lorries having become available for the infantry. The starving mules had therefore to cover eighty-three miles in fifty-six hours to catch up, and the Derajat Battery received their mules back in very poor condition. (34)

The Sikh section of 12th (Poonch) Battery was in support of 48th Brigade at the Kyaukse rearguard action.

It was still fighting and marching; it recorded a march of eighty-seven miles by night and day with nothing more than tea for sustenance.

Although the enemy did his utmost to cut off Burcorps from the crossing, they were outmarched by our men— worn out, hungry, ragged, bootless in some cases, able to carry only their rifles and ammunition, but refusing to abandon their sick and wounded to a savage enemy. (34)

During the last stages before Imphal the mules were no longer able to carry the guns up the steep slopes and guns and gunners were glad to have lorries provided for them. Then:

Within two marches of Imphal, when our drivers had marched and fought over 360 miles in seventeen days in tattered clothes and broken boots, and when rain, wind and mud made marching an agony and halting a misery, we sent for the now rested gunners to take the mules and so allow the drivers to finish in lorries. But of the drivers whose mules still lived, not one man would hand his animal over. We were not beaten. (34)

In a withdrawal the whole army takes the strain, and the weakest links are the administrative units on the lines of communication. They are not trained or armed, officered or organized, to do much more than what the book lays down for them. Interrupt the sheltered routine of their lives and they are apt to disintegrate, and then it is a case of the devil—be he Jap or German—take the hindmost. Unfortunately, these units are the ones to catch the eye of the casual observer, they make the best news stories, and the army is condemned by the standard they set; it would be as reasonable to judge the Air Force by their ground staffs, or the Navy by its dockyard maties. The army in Burma in 1942 was set an impossible task, indeed it did not even know what it was being asked to do, but the fighting units did all and more than their commander expected of them:

> On the last day of the nine-hundred-mile retreat I stood on a bank beside the road and watched the rearguard march into India. All of them, British, Indian, and Gurkha, were gaunt and ragged as scarecrows. Yet, as they trudged behind their surviving officers in groups pitifully small, they still carried their arms and kept their ranks, they were still recognisable as fighting units. They might look like scarecrows, but they looked like soldiers too. (71)

CHAPTER TEN

India as a Base

Up to December 1941 the physical impact of war came no closer to India than the brief campaign in Iran, but to the war as a whole she had given generously and without stint. She had sent overseas one armoured and five infantry divisions, a total, with reinforcements and other troops, of 300,000 men. She had parted with some of her coastal shipping to Iraq, thereby increasing the load on her railways, and from those railways she had made considerable gifts of engines and rolling stock to Iraq and the Middle East. Furthermore, such thought as had been taken for her own defence had resulted only in the improvement of the layout for the deployment of troops to meet a threat on the North-West Frontier.

The entry of Japan into the war completely revolutionized India's position, in the most literal sense of the word. The country was now on a war footing and destined to become the base for a considerable network of operations against the Japanese by land, air and sea, and by the Americans as well as by ourselves. To make it all a thousand times more difficult, this had to be done on the north-east frontier, a direction from which, up till then, no right-minded man had ever supposed a threat to India would come. It meant starting from scratch. Communications consisted of a single road, and a metre-gauge railway of low capacity which wound its peripatetic way through the tea-gardens of Assam. There was not

176

even a bridge over that mighty river, the Brahmaputra. There
were no airfields, no camps, depots, hospitals or military installations of any sort. Figures are tiresome things, but three may
be quoted: over 200 airfields had to be built; hundreds of miles
of oil pipelines were laid; and the capacity of the railway was
increased eightfold, thanks almost entirely to efforts of
American engineers who took the system over lock, stock and
barrel. The strain on the whole economy was immense, and it
must be remembered that, in a comparatively undeveloped
country, it was frequently the case that if the army wanted a
job done the army had to do it. The army was also liable to be
called on to help in essentially civil matters, as during the
famine in Bengal in the autumn of 1943 when military help on
a large scale was given in the distribution of grain and the
organization of medical and other relief measures.

On more recognizably military matters, also, G.H.Q., India
had plenty to worry about. For nearly the whole of the first
two years of the war against Japan they were responsible for
operations in Burma, and for dealing with the chiefs of staff
on all problems of long-range strategy. It was eventually recognized that the burden was too much but it was not till
mid-November 1943 that Admiral Lord Louis Mountbatten*
assumed the duties of supreme commander of the newly
created South East Asia Command.

The defence of India proper naturally caused some concern
during 1942, when Japan seemed to be riding on the crest of
the wave; troops were deployed along the eastern and north-
eastern coasts to meet a possible invasion, and there were also
Indian troops in Ceylon. There were air raids on Calcutta in
December 1942, the nuisance value of which was considerable
as large numbers of the citizens took to the countryside, including all the dock workers and those responsible for the
municipal services.

Thanks to the steady hand in the North-West Frontier
Province of an outstanding governor, Sir George Cunningham
—'he was worth a couple of divisions' was the estimate of the

---

* Admiral of the Fleet Earl Mountbatten of Burma, K.G., P.C., G.C.S.I.,
G.C.I.E., G.C.V.O., D.S.O.

commander-in-chief—that frontier remained unusually quiet throughout the war. In July 1942 there was a small outbreak instigated by the notorious Fakir of Ipi, but it was put down with such commendable firmness that the occasion served as a salutary warning to those who might think they could turn to good account our preoccupation with the war against Japan.

The most serious demand made on the army was to suppress the civil disobedience campaign that followed the abortive conclusion of the Cripps Mission in 1942. In August the All-Indian Congress Committee passed a resolution sanctioning a mass struggle on non-violent lines on the widest possible scale. 'Non-violent' in this context is a term purely of convenience, and three days later there were concerted and planned outbreaks of mob violence, arson, murder and sabotage directed against railway, postal and telegraph communications and against the police. What was worse was that the areas affected were of major strategic importance. No fewer than fifty-seven battalions, mostly Indian, had to be used to restore order over a period of six weeks, and there were consequent delays of a month or more in a wide variety of projects, including the training of brigades which had had to be diverted to internal security duties.

More directly connected with the theme of this book is the story of the training of the great waves of recruits that poured into the regiments and depots, some of pre-war standing, others newly raised and with teething troubles of their own.

Up to the end of 1941 the problems were formidable but comparatively straightforward. Men were being trained to fight a European enemy over terrain to which the army was accustomed, and the divisions overseas were either tried in war, or had time to absorb and give the final touches to the training of reinforcements.

There were perhaps four major difficulties to overcome.

The first was the bewilderment of the new recruit, fresh from his village where life had not changed for a thousand years, speaking some outlandish dialect, and far from clear just what was expected of him.

The first week of the recruit's service was critical. A state of shock best describes the condition of many of these youngsters on arrival. They had to be inducted very gently. None of the shock tactics to which most army recruits had been subjected over the centuries were used.

The N.C.O. who was their father and mother throughout their training was the key man in a very complex organization. He got his recruits out of bed in the dark of the early morning and saw them to bed in the evening. In between he ensured that they were in the right place at the right time, and if possible in their right mind.

The second, of greater importance in the newly raised depots, was the creation of *esprit de corps*, the definition of a sense of purpose; this was met by such expedients as raising a pipe band, the introduction of small touches of ceremonial.

The third was the woeful shortage of equipment which in modern times is crucial.

The last affected not only the training units but the whole system of reinforcement. The commandant of a mechanical transport training battalion puts it with great clarity.

Alas for so much high endeavour and enthusiasm! The confident young soldier driver found himself posted to a holding unit where he remained for perhaps three months with very little driving experience. By the time he was posted to an active unit he was no longer a competent driver. Experience has shown that constant repetition of manual skills is necessary if standards are to be maintained.

Above all imagination and a fresh outlook were needed; experience of the leisurely methods of peace-time was perhaps worse than useless, indeed one training centre commander attributes his success to the fact that his officers were not handicapped by any knowledge of pre-war routine. He ran one of the best centres in India, where the object was to ensure that the man should not encounter on service any horror he had not been subjected to on training. In a home-built swimming bath every man had to swim a length in full battle order;

and, as the supreme test, he was made to lie down six feet in front of a crack shot with a loaded rifle, down whose barrel he could stare. Thunder flashes were then let off and if the recruit moved perceptibly the instructor put a bullet past his ear.

This training centre was asked to make a film of their activities for recruiting purposes. The film was made but never shown as it was felt that no mother would ever allow her son to enlist in a unit which did such things to him.

After a year of war against Japan, having lost the infantry of two divisions in Malaya, India had four divisions in action on the north-east frontier and in the Arakan, and four more under training. There were still five divisions in the Middle East, and for the rest of the war three of them were going to need a steady flow of reinforcements of a high standard for the enemy was now the German rather than the Italian. There was also the task of raising the huge numbers of units needed for the lines of communication in Burma and Assam, with the added complication that all units on that front, combatant or non-combatant, were liable to heavy casualties from sickness.

It is possible that the vastness of the problems obscured the fact that, numbers apart, the training of the army needed a completely new slant. In jungle warfare infantry was once more the queen of the battlefield; the infantryman must be trained to higher standards, which of course took longer; a completely separate organization was needed for the task as there was generally speaking no jungle country available close to the pre-war training establishments. It took the failure of the Arakan operations to bring these points home and in May 1943 the Infantry Committee was appointed. Its conclusions are worth quoting:

That failure arose from a number of factors which could not be attributed to any fault of the infantry soldier himself. These were: the lack of adequate basic training and of experienced leadership; the absence before operations of any collective training of the formations; prolonged periods in contact with the enemy, which included much hard fighting without relief or replacement of casualties;

the high incidence of malaria; and the inability of exhausted, under-strength and battle-weary units to absorb inadequately trained recruits in large numbers. The accumulated effect of all these factors led inevitably to a drop in both fighting efficiency and morale.*

The various recommendations of the committee were accepted and put into effect at once. Two divisions that had been withdrawn from operations to rest and train, 14th and 39th, were converted *en bloc* for training purposes. They were already located in the jungle and all reinforcements for Fourteenth Army, of whatever arm or service, spent two months with them before going up to join their units. During those two months, all too short for the task, they worked nine hours a day, six days a week, with night work in addition on three nights a week. The reader of today may wonder what on earth there was for the men to learn, but a final survey of their work written by 14th Division throws some light on the matter.

The qualities required in a soldier trained to fight in the jungle are:
Confidence in himself and his weapons.
Initiative and ability to operate alone by day or night.
A very high standard of observation and a suspicious mind.
Ability to move and carry out all functions in absolute silence.
Ability to react instinctively and immediately to surprise.
Quickness on the draw.
Ability to freeze and fade to a recognisable R.V.
Ability to find his way in the jungle.
Familiarity with the jungle and especially jungle noises by night.
Knowledge of how to live on the jungle in emergency.
The use of materials indigenous to jungles for water-crossing, for obstacles, for shelter and for cooking.
The habit of leaving no trace for the enemy.

* *History of the Second World War: The War against Japan*, Vol. III (7).

Ability to climb trees, scale cliffs, cut his way through
dense growth and cross water obstacles.
Team work.
Ambushes, how to avoid them and how to lay them.
A very high standard of fieldcraft and patrolling.
Cunning.

There is some account in Chapter 15 of the complementary
measures put in hand at the same time by the commander of
Fourteenth Army. It says a very great deal for the intrinsic
qualities of the Indian soldier that, once he was given a fair
chance, it took him only just over six months to retrieve his
failures and turn the tables on his enemy.

This new awareness of the rightful place of training in the
order of priorities, and the improvement in the equipment
field, led to higher standards all round. Particularly welcome
was the establishment of a tank driving and gunnery school
for the Indian Armoured Corps, whose brigades were to
fight in support of the Indian infantryman on the plains of
central Burma.

The war in Burma was the Indian Army's war, and everyone
who served in India can take his share of the credit for winning
it.

CHAPTER ELEVEN

North Africa

January–July 1942

On 8 December 1941, while the Crusader battles were still raging, Japan had entered the war. There was at once some diversion of troops and air force squadrons to the Far East, all at the expense of the Middle East, but by the end of the year joint commanders-in-chief in Cairo expressed the view that what they had lost would not affect the outcome of Crusader, nor would it prejudice the chances of Acrobat. Acrobat had been on the drawing board for some months, and was the name for the operation that was to exploit Crusader and capture Tripoli, thus removing once and for all the threat to Libya and Egypt. By mid-January Rommel had successfully withdrawn his forces after his defeat in the closing stages of Crusader, and patrols of the opposing armies were in touch around El Agheila, the invisible line beyond which it was for the moment impossible for us to maintain a force of any size. In the forward positions there was the equivalent of two infantry brigade groups, and back at Antelat in support there was an armoured brigade, which was somewhat below par in the state of its equipment and training. Feeling that he was a bit thin on the ground the commander of 1st Armoured Division asked that 4th Indian Division, which with 7th Indian Infantry Brigade was in the Benghazi area, should be moved forward to Agedabia, but the request was refused for the good reason that it was administratively impossible to maintain them

183

there. The advanced base was still at Tobruk and, far from making any start on building up reserves for Acrobat, the total deliveries there were falling short by 250 tons a day. General Auchinleck had already had to weigh up the rival claims of tactics and administration: there was much to be said for maintaining contact with the enemy as far west as possible, and accepting the risk of the forward troops being driven in; but on administrative grounds it would have been wiser to give up 150 miles of desert and hold the line Benghazi–Msus, on which a larger force could have been maintained and the accumulation of reserves begun earlier. The decision to stay forward was, as the official history remarks, very nearly the right one. It was a bluff, and against a less shrewd and adventurous enemy than Rommel it might have succeeded.

About the middle of January Rommel was told by his intelligence staff that he held a fleeting superiority in armour, at any rate in the battle area, and that a spoiling attack around Agedabia offered a good chance of success, though there was not much hope of exploiting it. Rommel eventually agreed and on 21 January began his advance. The general pattern of the fighting that followed very much resembled the events of the previous March: the infantry screen on an extended front was caught without support from the armour; an inexperienced armoured brigade was moved north to cover the supply dump at Msus, a role not well suited to an armoured force, and met a concentration of two Panzer divisions, being reduced after four days to an effective strength of forty-one tanks. Orders were given to concentrate the whole of 4th Indian Division forward at Benghazi, though in the event the one reinforcement which really counted was the arrival of troop-carrying transport to lift 7th Brigade, which had been forward the whole time. Reflecting no doubt the stream of orders and encouragement pouring into Middle East Headquarters from the Prime Minister and chiefs of staff, the division received a string of conflicting orders: to hold a position south of Benghazi; to evacuate the town; to return and establish a line in the desert sixty miles to the south—with uncertainty the whole time as to the whereabouts and strength of the armoured brigade between Msus and Charruba. So long as they were still there, covering the flank above the escarpment, 7th Brigade could continue to harass and oppose the enemy columns now coming up from the south. But Rommel, in spite of his success in the Msus area, seems to have felt that it was altogether too risky to press on towards Mechili, and decided that he would turn north-west to converge on Benghazi, joining the Italian division which was moving north below the escarpment. Unluckily, Eighth Army misread his intention and sent the armoured brigade eastwards in pursuit of an imaginary enemy.

4th Indian Division and its 7th Brigade were now in an impossible position—two armoured columns were advancing from the south, and the German Panzer division was about to cut in behind its left flank. The saving factor was that the brigade was already operating in three columns, roughly self-supporting, which were ideally suited to the one course that offered any hope of escaping from the net. Brigadier Briggs,* the brigade commander, found himself in an awkward predicament as, in the pelting rain, he sat in his staff car at the airfield on the Jedabaya road.

> Thunderous blasts shook the town as the demolition engineers worked on. To the east along the escarpment, the leaguer flares of the Germans rose constantly as more men and guns closed round the doomed port. Only to the south the darkness was unbroken. He was cut off, surrounded and in the greatest peril. As he studied his map the desert called with no uncertain voice. It was the only way out. If the enemy could be dodged in the coastal corridor his brigade might escape.
>
> The pelting rain drove the enemy into close leaguer and blurred the sentries' eyes. The darkness was a dense curtain, though later there would be a moon. If dawn broke with the columns beyond the Jedabaya–Antelat trails, the danger would be over. That meant seventy-five miles across rough country. Could it be done? (16)

* The late Lieutenant-General Sir Harold Briggs, K.C.I.E., K.B.E., C.B., D.S.O.

By 8 p.m. all plans had been laid. Messages were sent to two small columns that were co-operating, asking them to find their own way to safety; to his own Gold and Silver groups the brigade commander sent this model order.

Road cut. Groups must make their own way over desert. Carry only personnel and weapons. Conserve petrol by destroying surplus vehicles. Good luck, everyone.

Lorries and trucks over and above the number for which petrol for the 300 miles' journey was available were rendered useless; codes and maps were destroyed; private kit and everything else except food, water, fuel and ammunition were ruthlessly cast away. Before midnight all three columns were under way. Their stories differ only in detail, and extracts from the news letter of C.I.H., whose headquarters moved with the brigade commander's column, give a vivid picture of the hazards they encountered.

Our own night march was uneventful, though with Benghazi, an inferno of fires and flares, behind us, lights in Magrun and Solluch on our right and left, the enemy position at Antelat to be passed in the morning, tension ran high and it was in no way lessened by the act of some driver, who, abandoning his lorry well within sight of Magrun, set it on fire throwing into sharp relief all the vehicles of the column as they passed by.

Halting soon after it was light to check our position we found we were not so far south as we had hoped to be.

They began to run into various small convoys of enemy vehicles and enemy aircraft flew overhead.

After watching the enemy lorries for a few minutes the brigade commander went back to his car with the order 'Get on, cross the road behind those two convoys' and we set off on what all looked on as the critical phase of our journey. Nearing the road we could see three tanks about 800 yards away with men working on them, a motor cyclist passed 200 yards ahead of the leading truck, and a staff car coming from the opposite direction halted for a few minutes by the tanks and then went on, while, as I crossed, two big lorries which had been moving towards us halted, apparently somewhat suspicious, near the tanks. There was rather an ugly rush up the slope on the far side of the road, the final step from the coastal plain to the desert, but though most of us did not know it till later there was some excuse for hurrying on the part of the rear vehicles. Having at last realised our identity the enemy had attacked the tail of the column with tanks and lorried infantry and had unluckily captured two or three of our lorries. Five German prisoners who were in one of our vehicles were effectively prevented from trying to give the alarm to their friends as they passed by the guards standing over them with pickaxes.

Though at no time had there been any sign of depression spirits were noticeably higher when we halted some eight miles further on to reorganize our ranks.

Driving all day in a shallow depression of the desert with a run of high ground extending many miles round the horizon we might have expected to be observed from many of the numerous viewpoints, but neither on this day nor the next did we see any further sign of enemy movement. (41)

On the second of two sleepless nights, between which was sandwiched a long day's driving, tiredness began to produce hallucinations.

In the slanting rays of a low moon the play of shadows on the mass of vehicles moving over the flat horizonless desert produced visions of mosques and houses, palm trees, pools of water and even leafy English lanes down which one appeared to be driving, and keeping awake called for a strong mental effort. (41)

Halting when the moon went down they were able in the morning to light fires and make tea; breaking wireless silence they were relieved to hear that Mechili, for which they were heading, was still in our hands. A check from one of our own armoured car patrols showed that the column navigating officer had done a remarkable job of work throughout; after 'a final ten miles of the most atrocious going it had ever been my misfortune to meet', they arrived at Mechili late in the afternoon.

The report adds:

> So far as our own party is concerned the honours of this march undoubtedly go to 'Birdie'.* Under the trying conditions which have been described he brought through with him two ambulances carrying eight of our wounded on whom he was in constant attendance, and got them safely into hospital. (41)

> The balance sheet revealed the striking success of the operation. Headquarters Group lost a platoon of Punjabis and two anti-tank guns. Gold group had lost none. Silver group had incurred 38 casualties during a series of air attacks. On the credit side the Royal Sussex carriers had cost the enemy 14 dead and 35 prisoners. The missing platoon of Royal Sussex and the troops of 25-pdrs made their way across the desert unescorted and arrived at Tobruk on February 1st. (21)

> High resolve was allied to good practical management, and every man responded with a supreme effort. General Auchinleck made courage the keynote of his short stirring speech on March 7th, when he reviewed the refitted 7th Brigade. 'You got through because you were bold. Always be bold.' (16)

The remainder of the division, travelling by the coast route, fought a sustained rearguard action on two roads, the desert flank always open to the enemy.

In the middle of February, 4th Indian Division was relieved

* The regimental medical officer.

and moved back to the area of the frontier. But they had one parting smack at the enemy in the form of a raid on Martuba airfield from which the new 109F fighters were operating to harass the R.A.F. It meant a desert circuit of over a hundred miles for the small party which was entrusted with the task.

> On the night of February 22nd Captain Oldham with ten riflemen (from 2/5th Mahrattas) and two sappers set out in two trucks. Without incident this party navigated on a compass bearing to within a few miles of their objective. It was found impossible to attack during the night of February 23rd; all next day the raiders lay in cover within sight of the airfield. When darkness fell they crawled across the landing ground. Only one plane occupied the strip; the Mahrattas therefore returned to hiding for another day. Next evening three new fighters were found pegged down for the night. Having fixed charges the raiding party scurried away; in a series of heavy crashes the planes and an adjacent bomb dump went up. At the rendezvous Havildar Babu Jadhao and Sapper Ram Chandra Ghag were missing. Food and water were left behind and the remainder of the detachment without incident returned to the British lines.
>
> Ten days later the missing men arrived back. En route they had picked up Sowar Deep Chand of Central India Horse, who had walked from Benghazi. They had traversed the entire distance without food and with only such water as they found in puddles. They turned up clean, shaven and smiling. (21)

The retreat of Eighth Army came to a halt about thirty miles west of Tobruk, and Rommel was no doubt most agreeably surprised with the result of his little foray which had won him the port of Benghazi, no mean advantage in his preparations for the next round. From our point of view we had lost not only Benghazi, but also the airfields in Western Cyrenaica without which we could not hope to maintain contact with Malta. During April and May the island was subjected to such sustained attack that it was for the time being out of action as a base from which the Navy could attack enemy convoys crossing to North Africa, and there was considerable pressure from the Prime Minister for an early renewal of active operations, if only to create a diversion that would permit a Malta convoy to get through.

Conversely, the case for delay while the army was being equipped with new weapons which were coming along was once again a very strong one; all the more so as the arrivals included the Lee tank, which was very much more powerful than anything we had had to date, and the new 6 pdr anti-tank gun to replace the ineffective 2 pdr. By May, when Rommel attacked, just over a hundred of these guns had arrived, no more than a small fraction of the total required.

There have been two criticisms of the choice of the Gazala position: the first that it was not effectively linked with the defences of Tobruk, on the security of which the whole battle depended; the second that it forced an unsatisfactory compromise on the defenders. A compact and secure position would be so limited in extent by the infantry available to hold it, that the enemy would be able to drive round the desert flank. On the other hand the layout adopted did extend far enough to the south to stretch the German supply line to a dangerous limit, but at the cost of leaving two considerable sectors covered only by mines, and not by fire. Had we succeeded in defeating the German Panzer divisions during the first few vulnerable days while they were out on an administrative limb, the battle would have been won. But we missed our chance; the enemy located the unguarded minefields, breached them, relieved his supply crisis, and attacked in turn the defended localities he had succeeded in isolating.

Running south from Gazala, XIIIth Corps, with 1st South African and 50th Northumbrian Divisions, occupied continuous defences extending for the first twenty miles; then there was a mined but unwatched sector of six miles down to 150th Infantry Brigade's position covering The Cauldron. At the end of a further gap of fifteen miles was Bir Hacheim, held by the Free French. There were subsidiary positions in rear of the size of a brigade group blocking tactical points or for use as pivots of manœuvre for the two armoured divisions of XXXth Corps who were located in areas from which they were to move to engage the enemy when he was disorganized by the effort of penetrating the defences.

The main position was properly dug, wired, mined, and held supplies for a week; but the ill-starred 3rd Indian Motor Brigade was ordered to occupy pt 171, a bare expanse of desert on which no work had been done, just forty-eight hours before the battle opened; and it was destined to take the first ball of the match.

5th Indian Division, which had relieved the 4th when they went back to Egypt to train and refit, was in army reserve, but in truth was well scattered. It had with it only one of its brigades, a second was in a hastily occupied position at El Gubi, the third was on loan to 2nd South African Division in corps reserve west of Tobruk.

Gazala battle began with an enemy feint against the main defences in the coastal area on the afternoon of 26 May, followed by the main attack led by Rommel in person, when the whole of the *D.A.K.*, *15th* and *21st Panzer Divisions* and *90th Light Division*, made a wide sweep and came in south of Bir Hacheim early the next morning. The Italian *Ariete Division*, which was on the inner flank of the wheel, came up against 3rd Indian Motor Brigade at pt 171. There was hard fighting between the armoured formations over the next three days, and both sides suffered considerable losses, but at the end of that time the enemy had failed to penetrate the minefields, his forces were well scattered inside our defences, and he had no direct supply route open to him. However, an important change was taking place. The Trigh Capuzzo and the Trigh el Abd passed north and south of the isolated brigade of 50th Division, and the Italians began to gap the minefields on either side at places where they were not covered by fire. When that had been done, 150th Infantry Brigade found itself attacked from both sides and by 1 June, after a most tenacious defence, it was overrun. There were two consequences. The enemy now had a direct supply route open to the *D.A.K.*, and Eighth Army mounted a rather hastily staged counter-offensive to restore the situation and provide a firm basis from which to attack the enemy armoured formations which were still surrounded. The operation failed, and on 9 June the enemy succeeded in compelling us to abandon Bir Hacheim after a prolonged and gallant fight by the Free French. He was now well placed for his battle of 11–13 June when he inflicted losses of nearly 150 tanks on the two armoured divisions. After this, there was little to stop him driving north to cut off the South African and 50th Divisions; so, accepting the inevitable, early on the fourteenth Eighth Army ordered them to withdraw to the frontier.

On 24 May the brigade commander had been ordered to occupy the locality at pt 171, 'as a pivot around which British armoured forces could operate in the event of the enemy moving to outflank the Gazala line'. He disposed his brigade, which was still carried in soft-skinned transport, in a square: 2nd Lancers to the south, 18th Cavalry on the west, 11th Cavalry (P.A.V.O.) on the north, with the eastern face held by Sappers and Miners with some anti-tank guns of 2nd Indian Field Regiment; a British troop of light anti-aircraft guns joined the brigade the day before they were attacked. Each cavalry regiment had four 2 pdr anti-tank guns, which meant that they deployed a total of sixty pieces of artillery, not one of them ranking as a top-class anti-tank weapon, to beat off an attack of a complete Italian armoured division reinforced by some German tanks. The regiments were without their carriers, and there had not been time to lay any mines.

At 6.40 a.m. the guns of 2nd Indian Field Regiment opened fire. They were the first Indian Field Regiment to reach the desert and this was the first time they had fired in anger.

At six o'clock that evening (25th), the regiment was told that the enemy was expected to attack with armour and in strength early next day. The next morning showed that our information was correct. The enemy armour equivalent to about two armoured divisions were in harbour about 3,000 yards from our own most forward line. The commanding officer ordered all batteries to engage them. This fire scattered the enemy's soft vehicles, but the armour formed up for the attack. The troops of the 3rd and 7th batteries engaged the armour at 300 yards and hit a few with their first shots. The enemy however came on in greater strength. The orders were to fight to the last man, the last round. The forward troops continued to fight at the tanks which never stopped coming. In the meanwhile enemy tanks came round the flanks and engaged the 4th battery and the rear troops. The enemy engaged one troop at a time and at first concentrated on 'C' troop of 7 Field Battery. This troop fought till the last tank that it stopped was only ten yards from No. 3 gun. The gun position officer and one No. 1, Havildar Moden Singh, were killed, and the other No. 1 was severely wounded. 'B' troop of 3 battery was another troop that put up a magnificent defence. In spite of one shell which landed in the gun pit and killed three of the detachment, the gun was soon put in action and this gun along with the remaining three of the troop knocked out five tanks. 'A' troop of the same battery knocked out seven tanks.

Lance Naik Jesu Dass accounted for 12 tanks, Naik Janannathan, who was killed, knocked out 8, Fitter Raju repaired a gun in the heat of the action. Major Kumara-mangalam was awarded the D.S.O.*

For forty-five minutes chaos reigned. The battlefield was a mass of wreckage, enemy tanks knocked out and on fire, anti-tank guns overrun and crippled, soft-skinned vehicles ablaze and disabled. Panzers crawled all over the positions. The three Indian Cavalry Regiments had ceased to exist. Given enough anti-tank guns and the whole course of the battle might have been altered. Every anti-tank gun had been knocked out.

While the battle was at its height a handful of carriers of the 18th Cavalry under Lieut. Gillingham, which had just reached the battlefield, charged to a certain death in a gallant but unavailing effort to rescue their comrades. In the centre of the tank attacks stood Admiral Sir

* *History of the Indian Regiment of Artillery* (35).

Walter Cowan, Bart, who was still naval liaison officer
with the 18th Cavalry, although many miles from the sea.
He had become a legendary figure in the Desert—a
symbol of valour and chivalry. Called upon by two
enemy tanks at a few yards to surrender, 'Dog' replied
the Admiral, 'I will NOT surrender!' He emptied his
revolver at the tanks and was unarmed when bodily
seized and carried into captivity. (16)

Nelson's Blood laced with a dash of cavalry spirit is a
potent brew.

In three hours of combat 3rd Indian Motor Brigade had
been destroyed. Eleven officers and more than 200 other
ranks had been killed while very many more had been
wounded. The enemy however had paid a price. Fifty-
two tanks were strewn over the brigade's battle position.
(16)

One of the imponderable advantages the Germans always
held in the fighting in North Africa arose from the flexibility
of their system of command. In mobile operations *ad hoc*
groupings are inevitable, but when the enemy resorted to
them there always seemed to be a responsible commander
able to weld his force into an effective whole. Largely because
we had failed to solve the problem of co-operation between
armour and infantry we were very much less successful, if
sometimes that was the word to use at all, and in the battle
of The Cauldron the price of scattering 5th Indian Division
round the desert was paid in full.

Operation Aberdeen, designed to restore the situation after
the loss of 150th Infantry Brigade, consisted of three separate
attacks, each under its own commander, with no co-ordination
below the level of Eighth Army, who, in fact, never intervened
once the fighting began. In the north XIIIth Corps was to
capture the ridge forming the north wall of the arena and then
exploit westwards; 5th Division, consisting of only 10th
Brigade with a battalion of 'I' tanks, was to attack on the right

of XXXth Corps to recapture ground to block the northern gap the enemy had made in the minefields; finally, 7th Armoured Division with 9th Indian Brigade, rightly belonging to 5th Division, was to re-establish the southern block, where-upon its armoured brigade, specifically absolved of any respon-sibility for co-operating with the infantry, swept north and north-east to destroy the enemy armour. In the event, the attack by 10th Brigade was initially successful, but largely so because, due to the lack of time for a proper reconnaissance of the task, the objectives set and actually captured were far short of the main centres of enemy resistance. The brigade was heavily counter-attacked and, the sweep of the armoured brigade of 7th Division lacking a firm pivot, was very roughly handled.

A selection of comments by commanders at divisional, brigade and battalion level illuminate the scene far more effectively than any attempt to follow the actual course of the battle.

General Briggs notes that he was not called on to take part in the battle at all until 150th Brigade had been overrun and Bir Hacheim was threatened. He was then asked if he would consider attacking Tmimi on the coast twenty miles beyond our main position.

It was held by a German parachute division and half of 15 Panzer Division, protected by unlocated minefields. I had to collect the division, plan, reconnoitre, and attack within thirty six hours. I never thought harder in my life. My answer was in the shape of an alternative. I suggested a desert move round the south of Bir Hacheim on to Tmimi and Rommel's L of C by use of surprise mobility, and in a place where there were no mines. This was agreed to by both Ritchie and Gott, and I thought everything was settled. It looked as though we should have a good open fight with the whole division together. Unfortunately the armour intervened. It had been arranged that they should protect my right flank. Now they said they needed a day to refit. In my absence the whole plan was changed to a frontal attack on Rommel in a prepared position. And we were not to be a complete division after all. (22)

The commander of 9th Indian Infantry Brigade, operating under orders of 7th Armoured Division:

If we examine this plan from the point of view of Nine Infantry Brigade, we find that battalions were expected to advance in the dark, over ground they did not know, to an assembly area, the centre of which was marked by a barrel; to do a further advance to a point 'east of B.100' where they were to be joined by a battery of a regiment they did not know (it had arrived from Iraq two days previously) and by a squadron of the 4th R.T.R. which had already been in action in the dark. The axis of advance was marked with lamps, some of which went out during the night. (22)

And the Highland Light Infantry when 10th Brigade, after its initial success, was counter-attacked by enemy armour:

The 74th was in fact in most evil case, with enemy armour on three sides and no help forthcoming from the British armour. It had been a very similar situation at Assaye where it had been cut to pieces under the noses of the British cavalry, which had charged too late to save more than a mere handful. Now at the Bir el Tamar the British armour would not charge, although appealed to by Colonel Thorburn and both brigade and divisional commanders. The Colonel climbed on the Squadron Commander's tank and shouted at him, but the only result was that he was wounded in the head.

1803: 'Now, Sir! Now is the time to save the 74th! Do, pray, order us to charge!'

1942: 'Look here! Can't you see we're getting it in the neck from the panzers? *Do* something can't you?'

Infantry, however, were still expected to be able to look after themselves. Cavalry, whether on horseback or in tanks, is a tactical weapon whose primary object is

certainly not to rescue infantry. Indeed, in the battle of
The Cauldron the British armour had been specially instructed not to bother about the infantry. This is all very
well, but co-operation between the two arms is nevertheless essential. (32)

The official history leaves us in no doubt as to the reasons
for failure:

> Of the courage and self-sacrifice of the troops there is no
> doubt, as the enemy noted with admiration. . . . The
> British system of command was too complicated to deal
> with the unexpected, and was no match for the strong
> personal control of the enemy commander. This caused
> an unfair burden to be laid on the divisional commanders
> and resulted in many fine troops being thrown away. (3)

In February the commanders-in-chief in the Middle East
had decided that there must not be a second Tobruk, in terms
of a beleaguered garrison holding out on the enemy's flank behind his main defences. The army could not afford to leave a
division bottled up, the Navy could not face the losses that
would be involved in maintaining the delivery of supplies by
sea, and the R.A.F. knew that they could not provide air support. Yet the tactical and administrative importance of Tobruk
to the Gazala position was so great that the corollary was,
surely, that Tobruk must be held at all costs, and the way to
hold it was to stand on the defences to the south of it, El Adem
and El Gubi; it would then only have been necessary to defend
the western perimeter, the least favourable approach for the
attacker. Once 1st South African and 50th Divisions had been
ordered back to the frontier, there was little hope for Tobruk.

The defence works had been allowed to deteriorate and in
many places had been denuded of mines and wire taken for
use on the Gazala position; there were also gaps made where
the garrison had broken out during the Crusader fighting. The
defence was in the hands of 2nd South African Division,
which lacked battle experience, and lacked also clear orders
as to just what they were being asked to do. They held the

perimeter with two of their own brigades, and 11th Indian Brigade of 4th Division; but whereas each brigade held mathematically an equal share of the front, 11th Brigade was extended over twelve miles on the south-east, where it was known the Germans had planned to attack before Crusader and where they now concentrated the whole weight of their assault. In reserve was 201st Guards Brigade with 32nd Army Tank Brigade—consisting of two weak regiments of 'I' tanks—but no proper arrangements were made to concert counter-attack plans between these two brigades, with the result that although such an attack was ordered it was never made.

The loss of their forward airfields had driven the R.A.F. out of fighter range, and the 150 German and Italian bombers of all types, who in the opening assault dropped close on 400 tons of bombs on the brigade front, lost three aircraft through flying accidents, but not one from action by the R.A.F. or our own anti-aircraft defence. This great weight of metal fell on the centre battalion, 2nd Mahrattas, and on the flank company of the Camerons on their right. There followed a heavy artillery bombardment and then the attack by 1,000 special assault troops backed by *Panzers* and infantry of *90th German Light Division*. By 7 a.m. German infantry was only 400 yards from the Mahratta battalion headquarters and, although a counter-attack by the reserve company checked the enemy, it could not hope to do more than hold the ring for the main counter-attack, which of course never came. The battalion was overrun and a gap made through which German tanks came to wheel and take the defences from behind. The garrison formally surrendered after twenty-four hours of fighting, but the Camerons and 2/7th Gurkhas fought on to the evening of the twenty-first; 25th Field Regiment remained in action till every gun was destroyed.

It was unfortunate that communication with the Gurkhas was broken so early, as their morale might have had a tonic effect on others:

The men were fairly bursting with confidence. Things were a bit chaotic, but it was war and it was fun. They

198

had knocked everything for a six that had come up against them and had received almost perfect battle inoculation. Their overwhelming sense of superiority did not leave them till the end. They met panic, the most devastating of battle influences, with steadfastness and watched streams of demoralised troops passing through their positions with amused tolerance. (21)

That was the conduct of a battalion that had not been in action before.

The Camerons, of course, were equally staunch. The garrison commander's order to surrender was 'received with derision'.

An organised attempt to escape was made, but few made more than the first miles. On June 23rd a column of prisoners drew up at the cage on Tobruk airfield. The column halted, came to attention; the skirl of the pipes arose and the Camerons with dauntless bearing played themselves into captivity. The German guard turned out to honour the gesture. (21)

Six of the Camerons escaped capture; four officers and sixty men of 25th Field Regiment walked 400 miles to safety; five Gurkhas came in at Alamein, one riding a camel he had hired from an Arab; six Mahrattas came in six weeks later.

The infantry divisions withdrawing from the Gazala position had been ordered back to the frontier, but there was in fact little prospect of holding the enemy there, if for no other reason than that there was no effective armoured force to cover the southern flank. The intention then became to fight a delaying action on the frontier, and to stand at Mersa Matruh, where at least rudimentary defences survived from the early desert battles; but, without an armoured force no stand could last very long and when, on 25 June, General Auchinleck assumed personal command of Eighth Army, he ordered a withdrawal back to the Alamein position where the desert flank was protected by the Qattara Depression.

The possibilities of this position had of course been known

for a long time and some preliminary work had been done, but with so many projects elsewhere claiming a higher priority for labour and materials, all that had been achieved when the day came was the digging of a position at Alamein itself which had been partly wired and mined; the digging of trenches, and no more than that, at Bab el Qattara about two-thirds of the way down; and the reconnoitring of a third area on the edge of the depression itself.

It became a desperate race between the two armies: Rommel flogging his willing but exhausted *D.A.K.* on to break through while it was still within their powers to do so: Auchinleck trying to reorganize and regroup his scattered formations; to dig, wire and mine defences in the intractable rock on the ridges; and to collect some sort of effective armoured reserve. As was at once apparent, and as the subsequent course of the fighting was to show, the Ruweisat Ridge is the backbone of the whole Alamein position and had it fallen into enemy hands in the early days of July the loss might have proved decisive. But the Ruweisat Ridge was nowhere near ready to resist attack, and to gain time it was decided to occupy Deir-es-Shein, a large shallow depression with a series of rocky ridges at one end, which covered the flank of the Ridge some four miles off to the north-west. The task was given to 18th Indian Infantry Brigade, newly arrived from Iraq, under the temporary command of Lieutenant-Colonel Grey of 2/3rd Gurkhas; his own battalion and 2/5th Essex had never been in action. The third battalion was 4th Sikh Regiment, one of the original battalions of 7th brigade. The men laboured for three days in the burning heat. By the time the attack came, they had managed to excavate section posts in the solid rock and had achieved a thin wire obstacle as well as the beginnings of a minefield. They had nine 'I' tanks of an early model, manned by scratch crews, their supporting artillery came from three different regiments and lacked signal equipment, and the whole brigade was short of ammunition. However, as the official history remarks, 'whatever else was lacking the garrison had courage and determination in good measure'. (3)

At 9 a.m. on 1 July the Germans called on the brigade to

surrender. Heavy shelling followed their refusal and by mid-day they had managed to gap the minefield in the north-east corner; five hours later there were some twenty enemy tanks inside the position, and our own tanks and most of the artillery were out of action. The brunt of the fighting had fallen on the Essex and the Sikhs.

In the afternoon heavy concentrations fell on Brigade H.Q. and it became obvious that the position would be overrun. The brigadier and Garland discussed the feasibility of a counter-attack. It was decided to postpone this till after dark, when it was hoped to impose delay on the enemy by getting into his tank lager with grenades and kukris. In the event Bde H.Q. was surrounded and captured by 2100 hrs and the opportunity for this counter-attack did not come. In the evening enemy tanks occupied a ridge to the north of Bn H.Q. and overran C Coy position. It became apparent that the whole battalion area would soon be deluged by heavy armour. All 'phone lines were cut and runners were sent out with orders to companies to load every vehicle to capacity and to withdraw eastwards. The company and remnants of the battalion finally left the box at 2200 hrs.*

The New Zealand official history leaves no room for doubt as to the extent to which this gallant stand helped to bring the German advance to a standstill.

Contemporary records do not do justice to 18 Brigade. Auchinleck mentions its 'stalwart resistance' and that 'the stand made by the brigade certainly gained valuable time for the organization of the Alamein line generally'. Post-war revelation of all the facts show that the brigade did much more than this. Tactically and administratively insecure though it was the brigade fought with a vigour that upset Rommel's plan. Just as the fighting in July marked the turn of the Allied fortunes in the Middle East

* *Regimental History of 3rd Q.A.O. Gurkha Rifles* (63).

so that action of 18th Brigade marked the turn of the battle on the Alamein line. Had Eighth Army been able to avail itself of the opportunity created by the brigade a crushing defeat might have been imposed on Rommel.*

By the evening of 3 July Rommel seems to have decided that he must abandon his offensive thrusts, which were getting him nowhere, and pause to reorganize and rest his troops. General Auchinleck, looking ahead to the day when the reinforcements in troops and equipment that had been promised, or had already begun to arrive, would enable his army to resume the offensive, had no intention of allowing him to do so unmolested; moreover, he reasoned that the Italians, if not the Germans, must be pretty well at the end of their tether, and it was at least possible that they might crack if put to the test. There were a series of attacks by Eighth Army during July.

The operation which was known as the first Ruweisat was fought on 15 and 16 July. It was launched at the west end of the ridge against a sector known to be held by the *Pavia* and *Brescia Divisions*, and the troops involved were New Zealand Division on the left and 5th Indian Infantry Brigade on the right. 4th Battalion Rajputana Rifles on the left ran into wire and minefields in the dark and did not reach their objective till the afternoon, but 3rd Baluch Regiment met with little opposition and by evening the two battalions between them had overrun two Italian battalions and taken over 1,000 prisoners. The New Zealanders had been equally successful, but next morning they were very heavily counter-attacked by tanks and, though they fought with such determination that they won two V.C.s in the day, without support from our own armour they were forced to withdraw. 5th Indian Brigade was now left holding a narrow salient pointing into the enemy's defences and on the evening of the next day was itself attacked. This time there had been due warning of the attack and the defences were organized to meet it. 2nd Armoured Brigade, reinforced by an extra regiment, was concealed behind and there were a number of 6 pdr guns in position. The Germans

* *Official History of New Zealand in the Second World War: Battle for Egypt* (10).

were beaten off with a total loss of twenty-four tanks, and thirty pieces of artillery of all natures were left as wrecks upon the field.

By the end of July General Auchinleck decided that his army needed a considerable period for rest and training and ordered his corps commanders to 'strengthen their defences, rehearse plans for meeting attack, and rest, reorganize and train their troops'.

Once they had managed to stabilize their airfield organization after the withdrawal, the R.A.F. had been giving the army the most magnificent support, which had gone a long way to swing the advantage to our side, and if the fighting by Eighth Army had been less conclusive than had been hoped, it had at least brought the Axis advance to a halt, checked the run of their successes, and shown that the initiative had not passed for all time into their keeping.

On the historical front the battle still rages: a sentence in a dispatch lost here, a comma gained there—the scribes fight on to establish just how much, or how little, the new commanders who were soon to take over owed to the efforts of their predecessors. Neither side is ever likely to admit defeat, and the bewildered reader might do worse than leave the verdict to the regimental soldier. Recording General Auchinleck's decision to assume personal command of Eighth Army, *Proud Heritage* remarks:

> Had he not done so, it seems more than likely that the defeat which the Army suffered would have been decisive; in which case the consequences would have been quite disastrous. Sir Claude Auchinleck frustrated the enemy at the eleventh hour, and sowed the seeds of victory. (32)

CHAPTER TWELVE

North Africa

August 1942–May 1943

In the middle of August General Alexander relieved General Auchinleck at Headquarters, Middle East Command, and General Montgomery* assumed the vacant command of Eighth Army. They inherited a superiority over the enemy in numbers, both infantry and tanks, but there was much to be done before they could launch the great offensive which was to drive the Germans out of North Africa. In the infantry divisions a brigade here and there was missing but, in the main, artillery, infantry and engineers were hard-bitten, with months of desert fighting behind them. The armoured brigades had lost more heavily, not only in material but also in confidence, the result of having fought so long in tanks inferior to those of the Germans. The greatest need of all perhaps was to restore the cohesion of the army and establish effective co-operation between infantry and armour. The new tank, the Sherman, promised to be a match for all but a handful of a new German design; there were to be small numbers of the very latest anti-tank gun, the 17 pdr, and pretty well a full establishment of the 6 pdr which, by releasing the 25 pdr field-gun for its proper role of general support, spelt the need for some fresh tactical ideas. Over and above all this flood of new equipment there were four new, untried divisions—two armoured and

* Field Marshal Viscount Montgomery, K.G., G.C.B., D.S.O.

two infantry. On perhaps half a dozen major points, therefore, the army needed a period of intensive training if it was to make the best use of the considerable material advantages it now possessed.

At the end of August Rommel made his last attack which came in to the south of the Ridge in an attempt to cut off the troops holding the main position in the north. With great recklessness he thrust into unreconnoitred ground that he knew must be heavily mined, and when his attack was halted he was confronted by over three armoured divisions. He had thrust his head into a formidable trap, and he was lucky to be allowed to cut his losses and withdraw.

Early in September 4th Indian Division relieved the 5th and, in the weeks of waiting that followed, that restless curiosity, that urge to experiment and improvise which was the hallmark of a good Indian division, found a number of outlets. With the three field artillery regiments once more available for their proper role, the almost forgotten technique of the use of survey for concentrated shoots was revived and improved. The divisional artillery was trained to accept, as the occasion arose, additional field or medium regiments from corps or army resources, and became 'a flexible instrument trained to engage individual objectives with devastating effect, to swing from target to target with unequalled speed and freedom'. (21) They perfected methods which were adopted not only in the Eighth, but in other Armies as well.

The great battle of Alamein started on the night of 23 October. The head-on attack against the strongest part of the enemy defences in the northern sector made less than the hoped-for progress, and there was a premature move forward of the armoured divisions. The enemy were in great depth, and it was not until the twenty-ninth that the determination of 9th Australian Division in pressing their attacks on the right of the whole line forced Rommel to commit his last reserve. On the night of 1–2 November, Supercharge was launched further south to punch the hole for the break-through of 7th Armoured Division. In the early stages 4th Division had a holding role with the object of preventing the move northwards of reinforcements to the main battle, and at the very

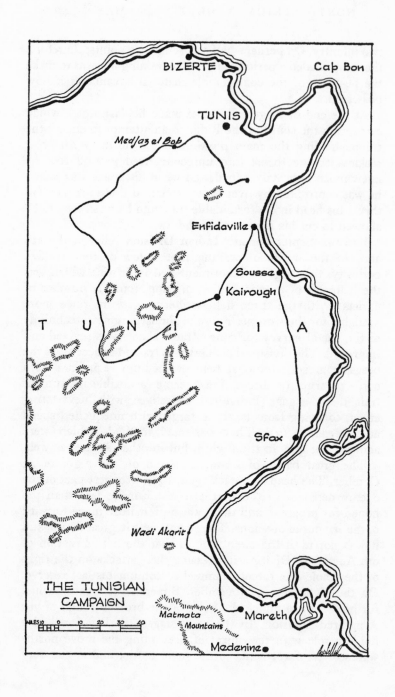

BIZERTE

Cap Bon

TUNIS

Medjaz el Bab

Enfidaville

Soussa

Kairough

T U N I S I A

Sfax

Wadi Akarit

THE TUNISIAN
CAMPAIGN

MILES 10   0   10   20   30   40

Matmata
Mountains

Mareth

Medenine

end it was 5th Infantry Brigade that launched the last decisive blow which went through to a depth of nearly five miles. The whole division was poised for the pursuit, and its commander claims* that, given the word, he could have reached Halfya Pass, 250 miles away, some eight hours ahead of the rain which, on the sixth, when the three leading armoured divisions were still east of Mersa Matruh, bogged down the whole pursuit.

Instead, the division's troop-carrying transport was handed over to the Greeks, and with 44th and 50th Divisions it was set to clearing up the battlefield. 'The men of the Red Eagle Division felt that the task of picking up scrap was something less than they deserved; so they gave vent to their feelings by turning in 1,500 tons daily of salvage—six times their assigned quota—in the hope of completing the job quickly and of catching up with the war.' (21)

But they were destined for a long winter of disappointment before they emerged from a welter of lines of communication tasks; then in early March, their commander reported at XXXth Corps Headquarters.

> He was advised that high level decisions militated against the operational employment of his division. It was about to be split up once more. 5th Brigade would go to XXX Corps, 7th Brigade would remain with X Corps, divisional headquarters would come under Army Headquarters. General Tuker stated that he could not accept this decision. He asked to be relieved of his command. Next day he was bidden to tea with the Army Commander. General Montgomery ended all uncertainty. Fourth Indian Division was to be concentrated for battle at once. (21)

Dragging the shackles of its administrative tail behind it, Eighth Army had been making its relentless way westwards, here and there fighting a German rearguard, and on 23 January it entered Tripoli. The port was extensively damaged

* *Approach to Battle* (72).

and it was not until the middle of February that stocks had been built up to support an attack on the Mareth Line, built before the war by the French as their defence against the Italians. It had been partially dismantled but the steel cupolas and massive concrete emplacements modelled on the Maginot Line were still there, and recently the whole system had been considerably reinforced with mines and wire: for a force supported by nothing heavier than medium artillery it was a formidable obstacle.

On 15 February the Germans launched a determined counter-attack against First Army advancing from the west, which met with considerable local success, and Eighth Army was ordered to hasten its attack on the Mareth Line and so relieve the pressure.

The Mareth defences extended for over twenty miles from the sea to the high buttress of the Matmata mountains, but stopped short of the Hallouf Pass; while a further twenty miles away to the north-west there was a switch line blocking the Tebaga Gap. Covering practically the whole of the main position ran the Wadi Zig Zaou with steep formidable sides, carrying sufficient water to render it impassable to tanks except at specially constructed crossing places. The whole mountain range extended inland for over a hundred miles, but reconnaissance by the Long Range Desert Group had reported that it would be possible to pass a force right round to the south to attack the Tebaga Gap; bad going and the length of the detour, over 200 miles, would limit its size to perhaps two divisions. The Eighth Army plan, accordingly, was for a frontal attack on the main position by a brigade of 50th Northumbrian Division, with 50th Royal Tank Regiment (Valentines) in support, while the New Zealand Division, with 8th Armoured Brigade, made the long detour to the south, breached the Tebaga Gap, and cut the road behind the Mareth Line. 51st Division, on the left of the 50th, was to make a supporting attack to cover its flank, and 4th Indian Division was behind waiting to go through and continue the battle in the plain beyond.

The Northumbrian division attacked on 20 March and fought with great gallantry, but after seventy-two hours they were back on their start line. Several things had gone wrong, perhaps the most important being that the tanks had run into trouble and, due to heavy rain, there had been continual hold-ups at the crossing places.

Until these had been repaired, no further attack could be made, and Sappers and Miners of 4th Indian Division were ordered up to help. Lieutenant-Colonel Blundell, the Royal Engineers' commander, decided to construct two temporary bridges of steel mesh stretched over fascines, and while these were being carried forward

> sections of sappers began to break down the eastern bank for approach ramps, while others dropped into the bed of the Wadi to work on the crossings. The enemy was alert. As the moon rose in the east the workmen on the eastern lip of the Wadi were silhouetted in plain view. From front and rear over the heads of the sappers tracer shell, mortars and sheets of machine gun fire streamed. In the wadi itself in the midst of an ear-splitting din and hail of bullets, the work proceeded calmly and steadily. Madrassi and Sikh Sappers and Miners lived up to the cool and imperturbable behaviour of their officers. Major W. J. A. Murray and Lieut. J. R. S. Baldwin of 4 Field Company, Major John Cameron and Subedar Sampangiraj of 12 Company supervised the tasks as calmly as though on exercises. (21)

Blundell, emphasizing to his men how safe it must be since a man of his height remained unscathed, had the peak of his hat shot off.

> Hour by hour the work continued. Small groups of men dashed forward a few yards at a time to deliver material to the workers in the cleft of the wadi. The ramps were cut, the fascines laid, the ballast spread to make firm crossings. At 0300 hours the shoot died away. Ninety minutes later enemy guns opened with extremely heavy concentrations which seemed to herald a counter-attack. Amid a torrent of shells the crossings received their

final touches. Wadi Zig Zaou had been bridged. It was now time to withdraw. The Sappers and Miners might have been pardoned had they scurried for safety. But along the wadi the infantry assault waited. Before withdrawal Lieut.-Colonel Blundell explained to his men that it might have an unfortunate effect on these troops if men were seen running to the rear. He therefore ordered that all should move back at a casual pace, chatting and joking as if on some ordinary occasion. The C.R.E. himself walked more slowly than the others, stopping often to speak to infantry groups, explaining the situation. On such occasions the Sappers and Miners halted round their officer moving only when he moved. This cool behaviour was not wasted. After the battle a number of units testified to the heartening effect of the calm and confident bearing of the Indian Sappers and Miners. (21)

It was now decided to slacken the pressure on the frontal position and to make the main thrust at the Tebaga gap; 1st Armoured Division was sent to reinforce the New Zealanders, and 4th Indian Division was ordered to execute a short hook through the Hallouf Pass. Some weeks earlier Eighth Army had held a sand-model exercise to consider the best method of attacking the Mareth Line, and the divisional representative had at the time advocated the seizure of the Pass as an essential preliminary to any attack near the coast. His solution was not adjudged to be correct, but on arrival in the area the divisional commander decided to investigate the possibilities, and from the study of air photographs and interrogation of local Frenchmen it seemed likely that the roads were much better than the maps showed them to be. The order therefore fell on willing ears, 'at long last a decisive and individual role had been allotted to the division'.

7th Brigade, moving by a smaller pass to the south, was quickly under way, but 5th Brigade, which was making the main divisional attack, was held up in Medenine to allow the armoured division through, en route for the Tebaga Gap. By the evening of the twenty-fourth 5th Brigade had reached the eastern entrance to the Hallouf Pass and twenty-four hours later was in contact with the outer flank of the main position; pressing on, it seized the heights overlooking the Al Hamma plain. Both brigades had been held up by minefields at the start, and later by considerable demolitions on the roads but, exploiting the mobility of good infantry in broken country, they refused to allow these obstacles to hold them up for long.

Next day they dropped down to the plain and sent patrols northward to make contact with the New Zealanders, only to learn that they too had broken through and that 1st Armoured Division was in pursuit of the enemy. The battle was over and 4th Indian Division, moving on the inner flank of the wheel, could claim to have done their share in turning the main position. Demonstrating their particular aptitude for mountain warfare, they had rendered the enemy's rearguard positions untenable.

And it was no bubble reputation. Less than ten days later they repeated their performance and proved once again that, given the chance before the battle gets bogged down elsewhere, first-class infantry, working in infantry country, can force a decision at a fraction of the cost that must be paid by more stereotyped tactics.

The thrust through onto the plain south of Gabès had come too late to trap more than a few of the enemy, and Eighth Army was now faced with another position in many respects similar to the Mareth Line. Twenty miles north of Gabès there is a gap of less than fifteen miles between the sea and the impassable Fedjadi salt marshes which extend 120 miles to the south. There was a stretch along the shore which was heavily defended and covered by the Wadi Akarit, every bit as formidable as the Wadi Zig Zaou. Then came a whale-back feature about 600 feet high, known as Roumana, which was connected by two miles of easy rolling country

to the fantastic pile of Fatnassa. This freakish and outlandish agglomeration of high ground is reminiscent of a Disney drawing. A series of transverse crests merge in a labyrinthine tangle of pinnacles, escarpments, counterescarpments, deep fjord-like chimneys and corridors. On the left of this wild tangle a ravine pierces the El

Meida feature, carrying a military road which connects the two plains. Beyond the road the high ground falls away in a series of cones and ridges until five miles to the south-west the barrier ends within a mile of the oozy shore of the salt marshes. (21)

As the division lay among the dunes some two miles short of the position the divisional commander reviewed the problem confronting him.

Across the road to the west of the Zouai, at the front of the enemy position, was a series of shallow razor-edged cliffs, a hundred or two feet high, and behind them the same sort of rolling, broken country as to the east. This whole area also, right out to the marshes, lay under the eye of the Zouai hills.

All this amounted to the one dominating factor, and it was that the Fatnassa–Zouai–El Meida features must be in our hands in order to throw the enemy out of position; in fact, that they must be in our hands before anyone attempted to cross the valley in front of the anti-tank ditch. But, once in our hands, the enemy was at our mercy; he would be completely commanded on the left to the western marshes, on the right to the eastern end of the low Roumana ridge, and way out behind his defences to the plain as far as Sfax.

Having determined this, we looked ahead. With these features in our hands we could hold with a few men against any counter-attack up the steeps and, best of all, swinging east we would turn the whole centre and render useless that anti-tank ditch and minefield. Then, if we could improvise a way round the west of it, the powerful X Corps could go through, its infantry turning sharp right on to and behind Roumana and its armour deploying and making out on to the plain and cutting off the whole Axis army where it stood. This was worth everything to achieve; it would be the end of the campaign. We set to work to find a way of bringing it about.

Patrols went out. We did not want identifications; in

fact, we wanted no fighting in front of or inside the massif. All we wanted to know was whether our men thought they could—on a starry, moonless night, perhaps using the odd flare, the Bofors direction shoots on selected points, and a very occasional artillery concentration at call to fix their position—whether they could scale those sheer cliffs and infiltrate right through to seize all the heights by daylight; and to know whether we could improvise a track for wheels and tanks at the west end of that ditch; and if there was any continuous wire or any mine-belts anywhere among those broken hills. The patrols were resolute and efficient. They satisfied us. (72)

When the Eighth Army plan was disclosed it was found that it involved an attack, at 4.30 a.m., behind a barrage straight at the enemy position—the Highland division on the right to seize the Roumana feature, the 4th Indian on the left to capture the low ground between the Roumana and Zouai-Fatnassa massif. It was clear that the Zouai hills were thought to be unassailable. After the conference called to explain the plan, the divisional commander, in company with his opposite number from the Highland division, went to put their views before the commander of XXXth Corps

virtually guaranteeing to him that the Indian Division would take the great massif by night before the Army attack started at 4.30 a.m. next morning, and pointing out that we must not fail because if any attack were made across the low ground facing the enemy's centre while he was still holding those heights, it would be swept away. No barrage could prevent that happening and the rocky hills could not be neutralised by artillery fire. In other words, any such attack as had been contemplated would fail, and bloodily. I asked that a third division, the 50th, should be brought up between the Highlanders and 4th Indian and that 4th Indian should side-step westwards so that it could take the Zouai hills. I stressed our confidence that we could quickly build a crossing for tracks and wheels at the west end of the tank ditch. (72)

213

Eighth Army conceded all these points, and rehearsals began. In reading the story of the battle it must be remembered that the division had no divisional motor regiment for reconnaissance and had only two brigades, instead of three; indeed, so short was it of infantry that most of the anti-tank gunners, for whom there was no task, acted as porters for infantry signal sets and ammunition, 'a vital, humble role they nobly fulfilled'.

The attack began:

A sentry was discovered asleep. As he died he gave the alarm. Shouting broke out and riflemen, kukri in hand, surged up the escarpment. Along its crest enemy outposts in stone sangars opened fire with automatic weapons and pelted the slopes with Italian hand grenades. Then as the assault closed there was borne through the night an eerie sound, an excited whimper as of hounds striking scent. It was the 'view halloo' as men of 'C' Coy, the need for concealment over, guided each other to the kill.*

At 0130 the first success went up, but wireless sets at both brigade and battalion headquarters had been destroyed by mortar fire, and it was some time before the extent of the success was known. From the all-important corridor between the escarpments into which 'D' Coy 1/2nd Gurkhas had disappeared came the crash and rattle of heavy exchanges.

Under the command of Subedar Lalbahadur Thapa, two sections of Gurkhas had moved forward to secure the only pathway which led over the escarpment at the upper end of the rocky chimney. This trail reached the top of the hill through a narrow cleft thickly studded with enemy posts. Anti-tank guns and machine guns covered every foot of the way, while across the canyon, where the cliffs rose steeply for some 200 feet, the crests were swarming with automatic gunners and mortar teams. Subedar Lalbahadur Thapa reached the first sangar without

---

* *History of 2nd K.E.O. Goorkhas* (62).

challenge. His section cut down its garrison with the kukri. Immediately every post along the twisty pathway opened fire. Without pause the intrepid subedar, with no room to manoeuvre, dashed forward at the head of his men through a sleet of machine gun fire, grenades and mortar bombs. He leapt inside a machine gun nest and killed four gunners single-handed, two with knife and two with pistol. Man after man of his sections were stricken until only two were left. Rushing on he clambered up the last few yards of the defile through which the pathway snaked over the crest of the escarpment. He flung himself single-handed on the garrison of the last sangar covering the pathway, striking two enemies dead with his kukri. This terrible foe was too much; the remainder of the detachment fled with wild screams for safety. The chimney between the escarpments was open, and with it the corridor through which 5 Brigade might pass. It is scarcely too much to say that the battle of Wadi Akarit had been won single-handed before the formal attack began. (21)

Subedar Lalbahadur Thapa was awarded the V.C.

Three battalions, Royal Sussex, 1/9th Gurkhas and 4th Rajputana Rifles went through on the right of 1/2nd and spread eastwards; the Essex came through at the western edge of the anti-tank ditch and covered the construction of the crossing; 4/16th Punjab Regiment had attacked and captured the feature west of the road. Dawn found a battle raging over a front of twelve miles. In spite of the success of 4th Indian Division, 50th had had some trouble in reaching their objective, while the Highland Division attacking Roumana met the most determined resistance. Persisting in their struggle to maintain their positions so as to cover the Indian division, 'deep behind the enemy's line', they finally won a victory described by *The Times* as one of the greatest heroic achievements of the war.

The Indian battalions ranged the hills through the day, mopping up and beating off the occasional counter-attack, but the crux of the battle had come at 8.45 in the morning

when 7th Brigade came through to report that the sappers had
the crossing over the tank ditch ready to take tracks and wheels,
and that Xth Corps could go through. 5th Brigade had reported
that 'all was clear, the enemy stunned, and that we were in
positions looking right out on to the plains behind him'. The
corps commander was at divisional headquarters, and after a
telephone discussion with the army commander announced
that his armour was going through at once. This is no place
to analyse what went wrong, but it is a sad fact that the armour
did not go through till the next morning. If only the division
had had its missing brigade, it could have pressed down and
attacked Roumana from the north and west, relieving the
pressure on the Highlanders, and bringing observed artillery
fire down on the main road behind the enemy.

The division's casualties had been under 400 in all. Their
commander sums it up:

> Officers and men of 4th Indian knew they had fought
> well and they knew that they had won a great battle. No-
> where was this more evident than in the field ambulances
> where Mollen, my chief doctor, and I were everywhere
> met with at least an attempt at a gay, friendly smile from
> even the most grievously hurt. Those that could, raised
> a hand of greeting to show that all was well with them.
> Always to meet the bravest of the brave makes one feel as
> if one's heart will burst from one's chest. I have never
> known why soldiers are so valiant, and so lighthearted in
> their greatness. Is there any other profession in which
> men give so much and ask so little? (72)

But that same evening the division suffered a grievous loss.
A shell had struck a group of engineer officers watching the
work in progress on the crossing over the tank obstacle.
Three, including an American liaison officer, were killed out-
right, and Lieutenant-Colonel John Blundell was mortally
wounded. The divisional commander wrote: 'He died yester-
day evening, mourned by thousands of humble Indian
soldiers.' (21)

On a lighter note, a patrol of 9th Gurkhas pressing down

into the plain had made contact with American troops of First Army.

The news-conscious North American continent was avid for details. One of the first jeeps to arrive from First Army bore an American correspondent, who ruefully displayed his editor's admonition: 'Whats-a matter. Your latest unnews. Shoot rapidest feature Indians. Pictures, knives, turbans, skedaddle.' (21)

The enemy was now driven back on the fronts of both armies into his last stronghold, of which the weakest point was in the centre about Medjez-el-Bab where the ground was favourable to our superiority in armour. Eighth Army were ordered to part with one armoured division and, in the final offensive, given the role of preventing any reinforcement of the centre by the German divisions that had escaped from the Wadi Akarit. The army was now but a shadow of its former self: the Highlanders had suffered terrible casualties, one battalion had lost fifty-one officers and over 500 men in the fighting since Alamein; New Zealand and 4th Indian Divisions were down to two not very strong brigades each; 7th Armoured Division was probably in best shape of all, but until the infantry broke through north of Enfidaville there was no ground suitable for their employment.

The hill features of Garci and Takrouna which barred the way presented difficulties even more formidable than Fatnassa; they were higher, the cliffs were steeper, there were less opportunities for infiltration, there was greater depth, with the consequent drain on infantry strengths to find carrying parties. In the circumstances any determined attack on the position, and that was what the plan envisaged, was an acceptable risk only if the ground was lightly held by the enemy, and there was a sharp difference of opinion as to just how strong they were. The leading divisions, New Zealand and 4th Indian, put the figure from their patrol reports at twenty-four battalions; the corps estimate was one quarter of that figure, but after forty-eight hours' fighting they had to concede that the divisions had been right.

The attack was made on the night of 19 April; New Zealanders, British, Indians, fought with unexampled dash and tenacity—Outram's Rifles won their second V.C. of the war—but, after three days, and the loss in each division of 600 casualties they could ill afford, it was only too clear that there were no prospects of success. On the night 22–23 April they were relieved by the Highland Division, whose role was to be no more than to hold on to such gains as still remained in our hands. At that stage it was apparently still a 'matter of high level policy' that the attempt to break through must go on, and the opening attack of a fresh plan was actually launched. When that too failed the views of the two attacking divisional commanders were at last accepted, and the whole operation was called off.

There are two aspects of the battle which merit a little more notice. The training that the divisional artillery had been carrying out to increase the flexibility of control of fire had paid a very handsome dividend. With ten additional regiments in support there is absolutely no doubt at all that the speed with which crippling concentrations of defensive fire were brought down was the decisive factor which enabled the battalions to hang on in exposed and unfavourable positions.

The other is the part played by the medical services.

> Scattered along the broken slopes in shallow wadis and in the lee of rocky ledges, regimental aid posts and advanced dressing stations endured the flailing enemy bombardments while the doctors and orderlies bandaged the wounded and eased their pain. Everywhere the stretcher-bearers followed the fighting; the greatly enduring infantry knew that they were not alone on this naked mountain but that their medical services stood near at hand to succour them. The courage of the doctors and the confidence reposed in them by the sepoys sustained morale at its highest pitch. (21)

The 2nd Gurkhas paid this tribute to their medical officer, Captain Christopher Arumainayagam, when he was drowned while bathing a few weeks later.

We shall always remember his unselfish gallantry in ministering to the wounded. Armed only with a hypodermic syringe and a fountain pen (to write the magical 'M' on the foreheads of those he had relieved from pain), he was usually found where the fire was hottest; indeed often in the most forward sections. (62)

And the scene at an advanced dressing station:

There had not been a minute's rest for twenty hours. Mazhar and I decided to run the night ADS so that Chaudhari and Willson could start again fresh in the morning. The stream of cases continued till midnight. Pictures come to mind of a constant stream of people. The medical corporal of the Essex scrounging tea and sugar; a boy Gurkha proudly displaying his blooded kukri; a wounded B.O.R. blasted into near coma; constant visitors asking news of friends. Stretcher-bearers arriving exhausted with hands bleeding; reliefs sent up, young Madrassis to prove themselves. (21)

Four hours after receipt of the message calling off the operation, 7th Armoured Division and 4th Indian Division had turned around and were off on the long road through Kairouan to join First Army at Medjaz-el-Bab. They arrived in what must have seemed to them a different world.

Here British First Army appeared. The contrast was extreme. With their new vehicles camouflaged in dark colours to blend with the trees and fields, this other Army might have belonged to another nation. Into its ordered scene swept the battered old trucks of Eighth Army, painted a light sandy grey, with never a windscreen, rarely a hood, with mudguards tied on with bits of wire; scratched, rusty veterans of an advance of two thousand miles. (21)

Almost as outlandish as their transport were the tactical ideas the newcomers brought with them. 'What! No barrage and no dawn attack! But surely . . . ' The operation for which the division had been brought trundling round from Enfidaville was to attack the gap in the high ground about ten miles east of Medjaz-el-Bab through which the road passed on its way to Tunis: 1st Division was on high ground on the left, 4th (British) Division further to the right, 4th Indian was to attack, in company with the latter, in between the two. 1st Division was to attack at dusk the evening before to clear a hill which gave observation over the whole battle.

The factors which influenced the divisional commander in his preference for a night attack with artillery concentrations, rather than a dawn attack behind a barrage, were that the infantry would have to pass through a considerable belt of high, tangled vegetation where they might well lose the barrage, and would then be advancing up a long open rising slope where the enemy automatic fire would sweep with devastating effect, not only on his own front but even more so on the British division on his right. Returning from the second corps conference at which he had again failed to win his point, he records that he met 'a petulant crew of brigade and battalion commanders' who had been examining the parts they would have to play under the scheme as it stood, and 'explained to me in an unenthusiastic way how at dawn they would march their men up the hill behind the barrage, if they ever caught it again after emerging from the bullrushes, and if they had any men left to go after it'. (72) However, after two more conferences with the corps commander, it was at last agreed that 4th Indian should go in at 3 a.m. with 4th British following later, which meant that the vital high ground to the left would be cleared before they started.

The Indian Army was well served by its Public Relations men, who put a strictly literal interpretation on the word 'eyewitness'.

Their representative on this occasion was

> the bird-like little fighting man from Coorg in southern India, Captain Unni Nayar. He marched with the leading battalion. If any man was hatched from a cannon-ball, it was he. He had only to hear there was a chance of a clash

for his eyes to light and for him to be hurrying round asking anyone, everyone to let him get into it. He was shot through the face at Akarit but never missed a battle. Once we refused to let him go out on a night patrol and his face went ash colour with vexation. Anyway, he tells us:

'We were only a mile from the first objective which we could see dimly across the cornfields. We were guided by a Bofors gun which fired three red tracer shells on a fixed line every five minutes. Our artillery bombardment now opened. The twenty-five pounders and the mediums deafened us with their roar. Thousands of shells streaked over our heads towards the enemy positions. From the German lines Verey lights went up. The enemy had obviously been surprised by the intensity of the bombardment.

'Wading through the ripening grain breast high, the aroma of crushed corn and wild thyme came to us mingled with the acrid smell of the cordite. About 0320 hours we heard the roar of tanks on our left and right. The Churchills were closing up. The apt timing of the attack enabled the assault troops to escape the enemy's defensive fire which fell well behind the 1/9 Gurkhas as they drew up to Ragoubet Souissi, a low ridge on the right flank of Fourth (Indian) Division's front. Three companies deployed and swept uphill. After a short, sharp encounter the success flares rose.' (72)

The whole attack which cost the division 140 casualties was a complete success. This had been on 6 May, and 11th Hussars won the race for Tunis, 'a well-earned entry in the game book of this great regiment', but there was still a patch of trouble in the block of mountains north of Enfidaville, and 4th Indian was called in to help. The enemy were crumbling fast, 'even the company cooks of 1/4 Essex brought in prisoners, taking care to fetch them in captured transport'. Early in the morning of 13 May, The Royal Sussex took the surrender of 3,000 men of a Panzer Grenadier Regiment, in the forenoon they picked up another 500; 'in the mountains around

Enfidaville 90 Light Division, doughtiest of enemies, had surrendered to the New Zealanders'.

And there was bigger game astir. To The Royal Sussex came a German staff car bearing a personal letter from General von Arnim, the Axis commander-in-chief, offering the surrender of himself, the commander of *5th Panzer Army*, and his head-quarters. The offer was at once passed to divisional head-quarters, and the corps commander was informed, but while the usual channels were busy the 1/2nd Gurkhas had been taking a hand. Their commanding officer, Lieutenant-Colonel James Showers had climbed a ridge to reconnoitre. In a nearby hollow he spotted a staff car with a German officer beside it waving a white flag. He had stumbled upon von Arnim's headquarters.

> I and my orderly got into the German staff car and drove up the road and up a side valley. Here hundreds of Huns had fallen in rows. We got out of the car and walked to von Arnim's caravan. I must have looked a grim sight, covered in dust and sweat, two days' beard, plaster on a cut over one eye, a captured Luger pistol and a kukri in my belt, my orderly with Tommy Gun at the ready, taking no chances. Real pirates we must have seemed to the neat German staff officers, but they were all most punctilious about saluting. (62)

In the meantime the corps commander, General Allfrey, had reached divisional headquarters and the two generals, with the German envoy in the car between them, set out for von Arnim's headquarters. He flatly refused to believe that 4th Indian Division were on that front, insisting that they were still at Enfidaville, and he was first inclined to be unco-operative. It did not actually prove necessary to threaten to hand him over to the safe keeping of the French African troops, a possibility that seemed to be on his mind, and in due course and with due ceremony he took leave of his staff and was driven away. If there was any small crumb of comfort left to him at that final interview, it was that while in the staff car Nolte had asked the name of 4th Divisional Commander, it had been written down for him in his notebook, and it was by that name that his captor had been introduced. General 'von Tucher'.

The following month His Majesty the King reviewed the division in Tripoli, decorating Subedar Lalbahadur Thapa with the V.C.

In August an even more unusual compliment was paid them. Led by the commanding officer of Outram's Rifles and a major of the Royal Artillery a party of thirty-three all ranks made a tour of Great Britain. A correspondent wrote: 'Not a section of the Indian Army had been left out; Sikhs, Pathans, Jats, Punjabi Mussalmans, Mahrattas, Dogras, Gurkhas; technicians from Madras, Bengal and Bombay. Among them were Britishers. It was perhaps that aspect of an Indian division—that Indians and British fight together—which left the deepest impression wherever the contingent went. They offered visual evidence that dangers and hazards shared make for great comradeship.' (21)

CHAPTER THIRTEEN

Italy: The Gustav Line

September 1943–May 1944

As early as January 1943 a Summit Conference in Casablanca had reviewed the course of the strategy to be followed after the end in Africa, which by then was something that could be expected in the foreseeable future. Geographically Italy was the obvious place to deploy the considerable number of British and American divisions in North Africa which would no longer be gainfully employed when First and Eighth Armies joined hands near Tunis; and there were considerable advantages to be gained from carrying the war across the Mediterranean, capturing Sicily, and advancing northwards to Naples and Rome. Italy, after only a little more hammering, could be expected to throw up the sponge, whereupon Germany would be faced with a whole string of further commitments: to oppose our advance in Italy, which would call for high-quality troops; to replace the Italian divisions that had been keeping the peace in the Balkans; and to guard the Mediterranean coast of France from invasion. From our own point of view it would be a great relief to have the Mediterranean cleared finally for the passage of shipping to the Far East.

British and American troops landed in Sicily on 10 July and the island was in our hands after just over five weeks' fighting. The Italians then did what was expected of them and on 15 August, through our embassy in Madrid, made overtures for an armistice, which after a rather regrettable delay, was signed on 3 September, the day of Eighth Army's landings across the straits of Messina. The news was kept secret until American Fifth Army landed at Salerno six days later.

A few Indian battalions were employed on beach-head duties at the landings on Sicily and the mainland, indeed an Indian state battalion, the Jodhpur Sardar Light Infantry, won a D.S.O. and five other awards working with the Americans at Salerno, but no Indian formation went into action until the arrival of 8th Division towards the end of September. Just four years earlier the Indian Army had been told that it would never be called on to fight German armies on the continent of Europe. If there was ever any justification for the verdict, it can only have been a doubt of their ability as fighters to stand up to the German soldier. The enemy who fled stumbling and screaming among the rocky hills of Tunisia from the kukri that stalked by night gave the lie to that story. There remained possibly a doubt as to the ability of the yeoman soldier, with something rather less than the rudiments of a modern education behind him, to master the technicalities of the modern weapons with which he would have to fight. Once again the Indian soldier surprised even his admirers by the ease with which he mastered these difficulties.

> The older *jawans*, now seasoned veterans, are few but unmistakable. They stand out like trained ponies in a ring of raw walers. They can cook, sew, drive, maintain, navigate; work wireless, rifle, tommy gun, anti-tank gun, mortar, machine gun, lay mines and drink beer. (41)

The selection of exploits to bring home the signal contribution the Indian Army made towards the eventual Allied victory in Italy has been peculiarly difficult to make. Although there were involved at the peak three divisions and a lorried brigade, they did not amount to more than a sixth of the total of the Allied forces, and divisions were constantly being switched from one corps to another, so for all their gallantry and resolution it is not always easy to pick on a battle and say: 'That is what they did, and it was decisive'. Another point was that

225

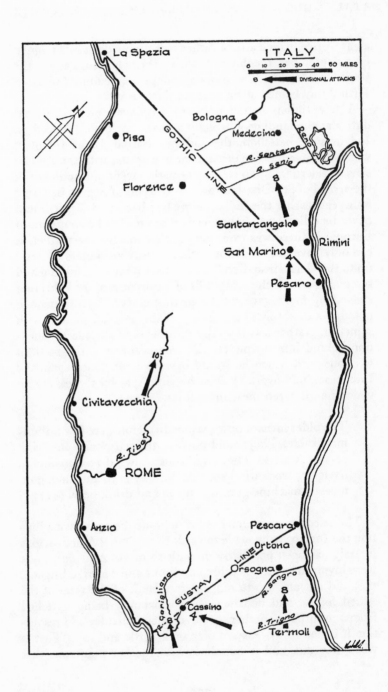

with the relentless determination of the enemy to contest every yard of ground the pattern of fighting was often the same for days, or even weeks, on end; and since one of the objects of this book is to portray the Indian soldier under the test of war, there is no great interest for the reader in details of fighting which differ only in the names of the rivers and villages and of the brigades involved.

The Germans stood and fought twice: on the Gustav Line in the south, which was under attack from September 1943 till the following May; and on the Gothic Line in the north where they held out from September 1944 until the final assault in April 1945. A chapter has been allotted to each line and, ruthlessly and regretfully, anything between the two has been ignored.

By the end of September both Fifth and Eighth Armies had secured their immediate objectives: the Fifth entered Naples on 1 October, and the Eighth had reached Foggia. These early successes encouraged the idea that the enemy would now do no more than leave rearguards to cover his withdrawal to his main stronghold in the mountains north of Florence, the Rimini–Pisa line, as it was somewhat vaguely known, and on 3 October, General Alexander, commanding the Army Group, was signalling the Prime Minister that he foresaw no difficulty in maintaining momentum and initiative at any rate until that line was reached. Only three days later sudden and quite unexpected evidence made him change his mind. The Germans had recovered with remarkable speed from the shock, if shock it was, occasioned by the loss of their ally: they had stabilized the position in the Balkans; taken over effective control of the transportation system in the north of the country; the Todt organization was busy conscripting civilian labour for work on the defence lines, and, on taking stock, they appreciated that the Allies were still 120 miles south of Rome, of which 'every mile lay in the shadow of the mountains'. They accordingly decided to hold at a point where the Italian peninsula is at its narrowest, what became known as the Winter or Gustav Line, based on the R. Sangro on the east, the R. Garigliano in the west, and anchored in the centre to the well-nigh impregnable Cassino position which was quite literally the hub of the whole position. In the eyes of the world the capture of Rome was the justification for the campaign; Highway 6, the road to Rome, ran through the town of Cassino and up the Liri valley; Monte Cassino dominated Highway 6.

By way of giving depth to the position, the enemy held, in the east, as far forward as the R. Trigno. In the face of ever-stiffening opposition, the Eighth Army crossed this river and captured Termoli. It was at this juncture that 8th Indian Division appeared on the battlefield. The division, which was commanded by Major-General Dudley Russell,* consisted of 17th, 19th and 21st Brigades, 18th Infantry Brigade having been lost at Deir-es-Shein. It landed at Taranto on 19 September after serving in Iraq and Syria and had undergone intensive training for combined operations and mountain warfare.

After the wide open spaces of the Western Desert the reader must adjust his vision to completely fresh surroundings:

> . . . north of Taranto the broken land begins, rolling ridges and valley bottoms succeed in monotonous procession. Where spurs from the central mountain spine approach the coast, the ridges are sharper and more irregular, the valleys narrower and more abrupt. Twenty miles west of the mouth of the R. Sangro the ridges are high, hog-backed and even razor-backed; the watercourses are deep-cut and steep-banked. The roads usually traverse the crests of the ridges in exposed positions. The countryside is intensively cultivated, even steep rocky hillsides being terraced for garden patches and vines; the ditches and terrace walls are lined with pollarded willows and larches.†

The combined onslaught of war and winter magnified the natural difficulties confronting the attacker:

Placid streams became brawling torrents overnight.

---

* Lieutenant-General Sir Dudley Russell, K.B.E., C.B., D.S.O., M.C.
† *The Tiger Triumphs: Story of Three Great Divisions in Italy* (17).

Sodden roads crumbled under the unaccustomed traffic, and retaining walls slid from under the steep hillsides. The fields and pastures churned into mud; all bridges had been systematically destroyed and the approaches to fords and to likely diversions had been heavily mined. Every resource of military science had been enlisted to impede advancing troops, to expose them to fire, and to shelter the defenders. Distances must be measured by hours rather than by miles. The countryside swarmed with civilians, homeless and vagrant, giving enemy agents cover for their activities. Surprise like speed of movement was impossible to attain. The battle therefore had to be fought the hard way. The enemy must be found and destroyed in his strength. (17)

These conditions persisted throughout the long, hard slog that lay ahead, and dictate the whole course of the fighting. The Italian peninsula offered immense possibilities for a sea power to exploit the advantage of being able to land behind the enemy and, if all available landing craft had not been allotted to the Normandy operations, there would have been quite a different story to tell; as it was we had no choice but to attack the enemy on ground of his choosing.

At the crossing of R. Trigno, 8th Division's introduction to battle in Italy, conditions were exactly those with which they would become only too familiar. With 78th (British) Division heavily engaged on their right flank towards the coast, the leading brigade had no great difficulty in forcing a passage over the R. Biferno, but the main operation over the Trigno was very much more formidable. The single stone bridge had of course been blown; the road down, destroyed in many places, ran through mountains towering steeply 1,500 feet above the stream; the stream itself was a raging torrent a hundred yards wide. For three days the troops waited in full view of the enemy while heavy rain hampered the preparations for the attack. 'Nevertheless officers of 6/13 Royal Frontier Force Rifles did carry out a daylight reconnaissance of the river. They spent the morning crawling down on their bellies and the afternoon crawling back again.'

The assault went in:

Frontier Force Rifles, though out of timing with the barrage, surged up the spur for nearly 2,000 yards, and by 0800 hours had mustered on their start line for the attack on Tufillo village. The Frontiersmen's assault was launched against a typical German 'Hedgehog' position. All approaches were mined and booby-trapped. A curtain of mortar bombs covered the minefield. Every house held a sniper. Attempts to close were met with a shower of grenades. Quick savage sallies were flung against any ground won. (17)

The convex slope of the spur prevented the battalion from helping The Essex who had run into difficulties on their left, and it was not until the third assault, three days later, that the brigade—whose third battalion, 3/8th Punjab Regiment, had also been deployed in the early stages—found that the German paratroopers opposing them had been withdrawn. Fighting in the hills for the first time, Indian troops found two of their own pack-mule companies available to support them and, for good measure, some of the drivers took a hand in the battle; they tied up their mules in a comparatively safe spot, unslung their rifles, and opened fire on the Germans.

After the attack broke through, patrols of 6th Lancers went some miles into enemy territory and another brigade passed through to exploit. There is a description of a night attack by 1/5th Gurkhas:

It was a nightmare trying to call the lads to heel and to point them in the right direction. They were having the times of their lives winkling fat Jerries out of barns and hotting up the less mobile ones with bursts from their tommy-guns. All through the night I kept encountering Jemadar Pitrag Pun, as he roved in the hunt with his revolver in one hand, a grenade in the other, and his kukri between his teeth. (17)

The scene moves on to the R. Sangro, and the story of 19th

Indian Infantry Brigade, who had made the crossing of the
Trigno, catches the eye. They were given an independent role
to the left of the divisional front, to occupy commanding
ground that dominated the sector where the New Zealand
division was to cross the river. 78th Division, on the coast, had
been held up after getting no more than one brigade across,
and once again the weather had been distinctly pro-German
when it was fine down in the valleys, there was a cloudburst in
the mountains.

'C' Coy of 3/8th Punjab Regiment under Captain Girdhari Singh led the way, wading through turbulent floods
up to the men's chests. Wet and shivering they emerged and
began the climb towards their objective. In company with The
Essex they fought bitterly through that day and the next for
possession of the villages of Calvario and Sant' Angelo, but on
the second afternoon after heavy casualties they were ordered
to withdraw. Girdhari Singh felt he had 'a proprietary
interest' in the village and withdrew most unwillingly.

> Convinced that the Germans had taken a beating the day
> before and would not return or counter-attack again, he
> asked permission to re-occupy Calvario and having re-
> ceived permission, climbed the hill again that morning
> with thirty-five men, passing the bodies of their comrades
> who had fallen the day before. The Germans had had
> enough. (17)

The remainder of the battalion, and The Essex on the right,
came forward to consolidate what they had abandoned the day
before: a bridgehead across the Sangro had been established
for the New Zealanders.

Across the Sangro, the division was at first allotted a more
or less static role, charged with deceptive measures to divert
the enemy's attention from the main attacks by the Canadians
on the right and the New Zealanders on the left. To this end
it was decided to build a bridge across R. Moro, 'a comparatively small bridge that became almost a battle cry'. At the
site chosen a right-angled bend in the road made it impossible
to launch from the home bank, and it was suggested that it be

built from the enemy side. Originally intended solely for purposes of deception, on 8 December, due to lack of progress on
either flank, the bridge became an urgent necessity.

> Although it was said 'that the tactical situation does not
> permit work on the Moro Bridge', bulldozers at once
> cleared an area for the bridging lorries, men of 69 Field
> Company crossed the river, swept the enemy approaches
> for mines and cut steps in the enemy bank. Stores were
> waded across and next day a 100 ft Bailey bridge was
> opened to traffic.*

Infantry and supporting arms crossed the bridge which
'remained a triumph for 8th Divisional Engineers and was
proudly known by all the division as "The Impossible
Bridge".'

Throughout December the battle continued: the New
Zealanders and 5th (British) Division were held up in front of
the mountain fortress of Orsogna but the Canadians were
through Ortona and pressing on towards Pescara; 8th Indian
Division had stormed 'the bastions of the Gustav Line'; there
was perhaps now the opportunity to intensify the assault. But
winter intervened. 'On the last day of the year a blizzard
swept in from the Adriatic, with biting cold winds, drifting
snow and driving sleet. Before the wrack of the weather the
offensive slowed to a standstill.'

In the period of inaction that followed:

> Perhaps the most noteworthy if unspectacular achieve-
> ment was that of the Indian Medical Services. Troops who
> had never known extreme cold now fought in frozen fox-
> holes, patrolled in slush and sleet, waded icy rivers, slept
> in snowdrifts, bivouacked in blizzards. Yet such hardi-
> hood had been achieved through adaptability and training
> that serious illness fell to vanishing point and the general
> health was so good that an Indian A.D.M.S.† was able to

---

* *History of K.G.O. Bengal Sappers and Miners* (37).
† Senior medical officer of a division.

boast 'if the general health of India was equal to that of our men in Italy, we should be the mightiest nation in the world'. (17)

The scene now moves to the centre of the Gustav Line where the entrance to the Liri valley is guarded by Monte Cassino. Strategically, it was the door barring the advance to Rome, tactically it is on the short list for selection as the most formidable proposition that confronted any attacker on either side during the whole course of the war. The physical difficulties were enormous and favoured the defender; it was held by two of the best divisions in the German army, and they had an explicit and personal order from Hitler that they must not let us pass; they were lavishly supplied with weapons and they had had four months to improve the defences and stock them with everything needed for a prolonged battle.

The first attack on Monte Cassino was made by the American IInd Corps, the centre of three corps on a twenty-mile front. Recognizing that even this considerable attack might not succeed, and indeed it did not do so, a fourth corps was landed at Anzio, as part of the same operation, in an attempt to turn the whole German position from the rear. To give this landing a chance to establish itself ashore the main attack was to be made two days in advance to pin down German reserves. There was therefore an arbitrary date which, in the event, allowed the Americans too little time for their preparations. They made three separate attacks. The first, more or less head-on, met with no success; the second, further to the north, got across the Rapido; the third coming down from the north, with a division in the valley and a second in the hills above, penetrated along Snake's Head Ridge to within 400 yards of the Monastery walls, but after six days' murderous fighting could get no further. 'They had battled with dourness and gallantry beyond all praise, but they were fought out.'

It should now have been clear that the defences were so formidable that merely to repeat the American plan was to court failure with the certainty of heavy casualties. One of two things must be done, possibly both. Either to attack further to the north and west to avoid the Ridge and come down behind the Monastery on to Highway 6; or, if that was not possible and the attack had to follow the same line as before, to subject the whole of Monastery Hill to an air bombardment of such weight and duration as to paralyse the defenders and allow the infantry to close. The corollary to either was careful preparation, neither could be mounted at short notice.

For the renewed attack, fresh troops were brought down from the Adriatic—New Zealand, 78th British and 4th Indian Divisions. It was unfortunate that it was not possible to provide at least an operational corps headquarters to control an undertaking that was going to need some clear and forceful planning; instead General Freyberg was required to find an improvised headquarters from his own New Zealand divisional resources. The reader will not be surprised to learn that the alternatives outlined above as essential for the success of the new attack represented the views of General Tuker, commanding 4th Indian Division, and in the first outline plan produced by the New Zealand corps it was proposed to move one of the Indian infantry brigades wide of Snake's Head Ridge, with the French to their right also taking part. It was disastrous that at this juncture General Tuker was taken ill and sent back to the main dressing station. While there, he learned that the outflanking move had been ruled out by Fifth Army headquarters; whereupon, although a very sick man, he managed to visit his headquarters, where he met the corps commander, and, to strengthen the hand of the officer temporarily commanding 4th Indian Division, re-stated his conviction that there must be no compromise; if the outflanking movement was ruled out, there must be a co-ordinated and prolonged air bombardment of the necessary intensity. That done, he returned to hospital and was shortly afterwards sent back to Naples.

For the second time Anzio intruded itself upon the scene. Matters there had not been going too well, to the point that there was a possibility that a German counter-stroke might drive the whole corps back into the sea. A diversion was prescribed and, by reasoning which it is not too easy to follow, it was decided that the diversion must take the form of renewing the direct attack on Monte Cassino. Once again this most formidable operation was the outcome of a rush order, with two direct and equally unfortunate consequences: the luckless infantry were committed to action with insufficient time to discover by reconnaissance just what they were being asked to do; and, although a spectacular air attack was delivered on the actual Monastery, it lacked the necessary weight, and no attempt whatever had been made to co-ordinate the strike with action by the infantry, who did not even know the bombing was to take place.

Much discussion has raged round the question of whether we were justified in thus mutilating a sacred building of great antiquity, when the Germans have made great play with their protestations that their troops had been positively forbidden to enter its precincts. This of course is their story, but it does not follow that if the battle had started to run against them, they would not have been forced to go back on their intentions, and indeed their defences were close under the walls of the building, being tactically inseparable from it. Finally there is the point that the implicit threat of this unrivalled place of observation, which seemed to pry into every detail of their daily lives, was having a most disturbing effect on the troops below.

4th Indian Division's demand was for the neutralization by bombing of the whole hill, not of the Monastery alone; and that of course is just where we went wrong. We broke the eggs but we failed to make an omelette.

The lie of the ground imposed two severe handicaps on troops attacking the Monastery from Snake's Head Ridge: the ridge itself was so narrow that, at most, a reinforced infantry brigade was all that could be deployed, and not only deployed, but maintained, for the ridge lay so deep in the enemy position that the supply line was seven miles long—the whole of it in full view of the enemy, and the last part accessible by mule transport only. Over that route everything, down to the last cup of water, had to be carried.

On the relief of the Americans the view was expressed that

the performance of the 34th Division at Cassino must

235

rank with the finest feats of arms carried out by any soldiers during the war. When at last they were relieved by the 4th Indian Division fifty of those few who had held on to the last were too numbed with cold and exhaustion to move. They could still man their positions but they could not move out of them unaided. They were carried out on stretchers. (74)

7th Indian Infantry Brigade took over and found that the Germans held pt 593, the commanding hillock at the enemy end of the ridge, whereas they had been given to understand by American divisional headquarters that it was in our hands. This was a setback of no mean order as it meant that a preliminary attack would have to be made to take it before launching the assault on Monastery Hill. In deference to the demand for haste this preliminary attack was timed for the night of 15 February although the leading battalion, The Royal Sussex, had not had time to reconnoitre the ground that this unexpected commitment would force them to cross.

Immediately in front loomed the rocky crest of Pt 593, with the ruins of a small fort upon its summit. The slopes were shaggy with great boulders, sharp ledges and patches of scrub. These natural hideouts sheltered German spandau teams and bomb squads. Enemy outposts were less than seventy yards distant. The slightest movement drew retaliatory fire. No reconnaissance was possible, nor was there any method of ascertaining the enemy strength. There was no elbow room for deployment, no cover behind which to concentrate effectively, no opportunity to withdraw to obtain space for manoeuvre. 7 Brigade therefore was committed to battle without knowing the lie of the land or the strength of the enemy which held it. Neither artillery nor air could intervene. The infantry must make its way alone. (21)

On the morning of the fifteenth, out of a blue sky, came the air attack on the Monastery. It appears that the monks had been told, the enemy had been told, indeed the world at large knew about it; the only people who did not know were the forward brigade who might perhaps have profited from it, and they had two battalions still back in the reserve area. The Royal Sussex duly attacked that evening with a single company and were heavily repulsed. The next evening the whole battalion attacked, though still limited by the width of the ridge to a company frontage, and again the attack was beaten off with considerable loss. On the night of the seventeenth three battalions attacked, 4th Rajputana Rifles, who had come forward to relieve The Sussex, the 1/2nd and 1/9th Gurkhas. 2nd Gurkhas advanced over a small crest.

> Beyond this false crest aerial photographs had shown a belt of scrub. It was impossible to reconnoitre, but such undergrowth had proved negotiable elsewhere so it was presumed that it did not constitute a serious obstacle. As a result the leading companies walked into a death trap. The scrub proved to be thorn thicket seeded with anti-personnel mines, its outskirts threaded with trip wires linked to booby traps. Behind this deadly barrier storm troopers lay in wait. The leading platoons dashed into the the undergrowth and blew up almost to a man. Colonel Showers fell shot through the stomach. Two thirds of the leading company was struck down within five minutes yet the survivors continued to force their way ahead. Riflemen were found afterwards with as many as four trip wires round their legs, Naik Birbahadur Thapur although wounded in many places managed to burst through the copse and to seize a position in the midst of the storm troopers, Stretcher Bearer Sherbahadur Thapa made sixteen trips across this deadly ground before he was killed. An unscathed handful battled on till ordered to withdraw. Seven British Officers, four Gurkha Officers and 138 other ranks had fallen. (21)

That was out of a total of just over 400; the other two battalions between them lost nearly 450 men. After the fall of Cassino the bodies of Major Markham Lee and Jemadar Maru Ram and a number of men of the Rajputana Rifles were found inside the ruined fort on pt 593. They had died in the heart of the enemy defences, but by dawn the brigade was pretty well back on the start lines. Down in the valley the New Zealand division had been attacking the town. Under a heavy bombardment they had crossed the flooded river and captured the railway station, but their Sappers, after the most prodigious efforts, just failed to get a bridge across before daylight. Tanks and anti-tank guns could not therefore reach the troops who were hanging on in the town, and they fell back before counter-attacks by the enemy's armour.

The battle at the Anzio beach-head was still raging and, though it had, in fact, been won, there was still no certainty about it and it was accordingly decided that the assault on Cassino must go on. It was timed to open on 24 February but the weather broke completely; 'for three weeks winter gales, driving snow and freezing rain pelted the exposed infantry'. It was a most unfortunate start. The troops were deployed and could not be relieved, and the luckless 7th Brigade on Snake's Head suffered as many as sixty casualties a day throughout the three weeks of waiting, till on 14 March the weather cleared sufficiently for the attack to be made.

The weak point about the original plan had been the lack of co-ordination between the two thrusts; it was now decided that the two divisions should attack side by side from the north. Approaching from that direction the attackers were confronted with five distinct tactical features which they must overcome before reaching the Monastery. The town of Cassino consisted of strongly built stone houses that provided ideal cover for the defenders, while on the north-west corner where the slope begins there was an area in the centre of which was the Continental Hotel, giving observation over the rest of the town, which was the scene of some of the bitterest fighting. Above the town was Castle Hill, which dominated the approaches and was the only way by which the troops could pass to continue the advance on the mountain above. The passage across the col which connected Castle Hill to the massif was covered by two strong points which had been built on the northern corners of the loops of the road as it zig-zagged its way upwards; and, lastly, there was pt 435, a jutting platform of rock, so close under the Monastery walls as to be out of view from the building. On it, a gibbet-shaped pylon which had carried an aerial ropeway gave the feature the name of Hangman's Hill.

The plan gave the New Zealand division the task of securing the northern part of the town and Castle Hill. 5th Brigade would take over the hill and continue to advance to, progressively, the strong points on the loops in the road, and then on to Hangman's Hill. It was proposed to subject the town to an air attack during which 1,000 tons of bombs would be dropped over a period of three and a half hours. This was to be followed by an artillery barrage fired by over 600 guns, to open as the New Zealanders left their start line a mile north of the town. There was some initial success, but penetration into the town was held up as it was found that the devastation caused by the bombing was so great that the supporting tanks were unable to make their way through the rubble; and, as if this was not disappointment enough, that night the rain came down again in torrents which intensified the difficulties of clearing a way through the debris and cheated the attackers of the moonlight which they had hoped would aid their progress. The Essex relieved the New Zealanders on Castle Hill; behind them the rear half of the Rajputana Rifles was caught by heavy artillery fire, and the two leading companies unaided did not succeed in reaching the road loops. Nothing daunted, 2/9th Gurkhas made their way through the ruins, found a track that by-passed Castle Hill, and sent two companies on to Hangman's Hill, each by a separate path. With that uncanny aptitude of the Indian soldier for finding his way in impenetrable darkness across a trackless waste, one company did reach Hangman's Hill, though it was not till noon next day that a very weak wireless signal brought news of them. Later the rest of the battalion joined them.

Thus began an ordeal which for nine days made 9th Gurkhas the best known battalion in Italy. Clinging like limpets to their shaggy boss in the shadow of the Monastery, they impelled the battle for Cassino to take shape round them. The New Zealanders considered that in an enterprise in which so many had failed it would be unworthy to desert the few who had succeeded. Hangman's Hill became the focal point of the battle.*

There are books in plenty for the reader interested in the details of those nine days; the street battles of the New Zealanders, meeting tanks with their turrets built in to the lounge of the Continental Hotel; the fury of the counter-attacks by *1st Parachute Division*, perhaps the finest troops in the whole German Army, which kept the Gurkhas on Hangman's Hill isolated; the failure of a tank attack wide to the north of the Monastery.

By the twenty-fourth both divisions had fought themselves to a standstill, and captured diaries and letters reveal that the enemy was in no better shape. It was accordingly decided to call the battle off and withdraw 9th Gurkhas, who were still on Hangman's Hill. It was thought to be too risky to send the message by wireless so one officer from each of the battalions in the brigade volunteered to make the night journey, having memorized the details as to how the actual order for the withdrawal would be given. Each officer carried a carrier pigeon to fly back to brigade headquarters with the news that he had completed his journey. The Gurkhas, on being told that they must withdraw, asked who would be relieving them.

The journey back from Hangman's Hill took three hours and that night, 24–25 March, brigades of 78th Division relieved 5th and 7th Indian Brigades, the relief taking place in a blizzard of unexampled severity which delayed its completion.

> The quickening dawn saw many of us still in the Rapido Valley. Men who had spent long days in foxholes and whose knee joints and muscles had weakened through lack of normal exercise had to move carefully. The blizzard was still just thick enough to hide us from view. As we neared the transport that was to carry us away, the smoke screen cleared and the shape of the now shattered Monastery loomed out dressed in a mantle of snow as if

* *The 9th Gurkha Rifles* (69).

240

Street fighting in Italy

A Sikh and a Pathan bringing an anti-tank gun into action

R.I.A.S.C. mule evacuating wounded from R. Sangro

The Monastery, Cassino, from the north-west

to hide from us her scars of battle. It was a fitting farewell. (21)

On the crest of the shaggy outcrop below the Monastery a
giant boulder today wears the badge of the 9th Gurkhas.

The casualties of the three divisions between 15 and 26
March totalled over 2,100, more than half of them in 4th
Indian Division, which in the six weeks in front of Cassino lost
over 4,000 officers and men. It is not surprising that there is
hardly a single account of the battle that does not pay tribute
to those concerned with the care of the wounded—Corporal
Hazle of The Essex, in charge of the aid post on Hangman's
Hill, who performed major operations and even amputations
with the slender resources of his first-aid haversack; Sepoy
Chet Singh of 4/16th Punjab Regiment who made over a
hundred trips in his jeep and was killed helping a wounded
man to safety; Baz Mir, a humble washerman, who, as a
stretcher bearer, made repeated trips to Hangman's Hill and
won a fighting soldier's award for his bravery.

The regular ambulance units were reinforced by a group of
volunteer ambulances of the American Field Service, an
entirely voluntary organization which had been associated
with the division throughout its fighting in North Africa.

The river crossing—Windy Corner—received an unhealthy amount of shelling. Jeeps did not tarry there.
Yet in full daylight, an American volunteer halted his
ambulance, rescued a wounded man, dressed his wounds,
took him to the advanced dressing station under continuous fire, and classified it as 'all in the day's work'. (17)

The fourth, last and finally successful assault on Monte
Cassino was made under far more favourable conditions: it
was not a fight against time, it was not undertaken in the depth
of winter, and it was a properly co-ordinated part of a larger
offensive. The task was given to the Polish Corps of two divisions, but, even under these more favourable conditions, it
took a week of hard fighting before their final attack cut

through behind the position and joined hands with 78th (British) Division coming up the Liri valley.

General Alexander had decided that to give his troops a reasonable chance of success in forcing the Gustav Line he must have a superiority of three to one in infantry at the actual points of attack, and must therefore deceive his opponents as to where those points would be. He evolved for the purpose an elaborate cover plan for a seaborne landing at Civitavecchia, on the coast some forty miles north-west of Rome, giving the impression that we had given up all hope of breaking through by a head-on attack. The plot succeeded, and Kesselring was forced to keep his reserves mobile to meet three possibilities; the new threat, a break-out from Anzio, or a break through the Gustav Line.

The overall plan then, starting on the south, was for the United States IInd Corps to attack up the coast along Route 7 where they had the advantage of a bridgehead over the river won in the fighting the previous autumn; the other corps of Fifth Army, the French, would make for Ausonia and try to cut in to the Liri Valley from the south. On Eighth Army's left, XIIIth Corps would attack up Route 6 and the Liri Valley, and hope to swing north and cut off Cassino from the south. The Polish Corps would go for Cassino from the north-west on the same line followed by 4th Indian Division's first attempt, but moving much wider to the flank. The attack was launched an hour before midnight on 11–12 May.

XIIIth Corps had available four infantry and two armoured divisions and attacked in the first instance with 4th (British) Division on the right, astride Route 6, and on the left 8th Indian Division, supported by 1st Canadian Armoured Brigade, old friends from the fighting on the Adriatic coast; across the width of the divisional front the passage of the R. Gari was the first major obstacle of the whole operation. The river was about forty feet in width, six to eight feet in depth, and swiftly flowing. Meadows on both banks were marshy and intersected by numerous rhines and drainage ditches.

Behind all this lay of course the usual intricate defence positions based on a network of mines, wire and concrete.

As may be imagined high priority was given to assault boats to get the first waves of infantry across and then to bridging equipment to enable the armoured brigade to move to support the infantry before the inevitable counter-attack. The most elaborate precautions were taken to ensure that the component units of a battalion were allotted to boats so that they reached the far side in the order in which they would most probably be needed, and one battalion order ran to seven pages of single-spaced foolscap typescript, concluding with an artillery time-table and administrative appendix and the crossing table. Nothing had been left to chance. But chance intervened all the same. No one had expected the whole affair to take place in a dense fog. The fog resulted, apparently, from the river mist mingling with dust and cordite fumes from the barrage and with smoke put forth, for some reason, by the enemy. (31)

In terms of its contribution to the battle on the whole front, the outstanding success achieved by the division was the completion of two bridges.

Moving imperturbably among the beach parties were the bridgehead sappers, the men who would win or lose the battle of the clock. Even as the infantry took the water their labour began. Through the blast and crackle of the barrage came the steady chug of the bulldozers as they filled ditches and built up ramps for the launching sites. 'Oxford' bridge grew steadily through the night, but when the darkness thinned the Bengal Sappers needed a few hours more. Again the German smoke screen served well. At 0840 hours, a few minutes before the curtain of fog dispersed, the bridge was completed. Three minutes later the first Canadian tanks rumbled across the Gari. The roar of the armour was music to the infantry as the panzers were expected at any moment. (17)

The bridge at Plymouth, further downstream, was a triumph of mechanical improvisation between 69 Field

Company, the Canadian Engineers, and 14th (Calgary) Armoured Regiment. A tank appeared

> carrying a complete Bailey span on its back, while another
> tank pushed from behind. The leading tank waddled into
> the river carrying one end of the bridge. In midstream it
> submerged; the crew climbed out at the last moment
> spluttering. The rear tank thrust, and the span slid
> across the back of the carrier until it reached the far bank.
> (17)

A single example from each brigade front will illustrate the
severity of the fighting. On the left the two leading companies
of 3/8th Punjab Regiment had crossed the river but had
suffered terribly; one platoon of Sikhs had been wiped out to
a man and was found later lying under the muzzles of the
machine-guns. The support companies crossed to make good
the ground won.

> The advance was pinned down by a sleet of fire from front
> and flanks. Movement meant death. A volunteer was
> called for to deal with a gun firing from the right flank.
> Kamal Ram, a nineteen year old Jat sepoy, in action for
> the first time, crawled through the wire and leapt upon
> the crew single-handed. He shot the gunner and
> bayoneted his feeder, swinging about to kill a German
> officer who sprang at him from a slit trench firing a pistol.
> With the post silenced he pressed on. Having sniped the
> gunner of a second nest, he bombed the remainder of the
> crew into submission. Together with a havildar he
> attacked a third machine gun post and dealt with it in a
> similar fashion. The line was open. The Punjabis moved
> forward to secure their objective. Later, in a forward re-
> connaissance, Kamal Ram wiped out a fourth machine
> gun nest, an unsurpassed day's work which earned this
> gallant youngster the Victoria Cross. (17)

The advance of the right-hand brigade had been halted by
determined resistance from the village of Sant' Angelo which

from a height dominated the whole front; in particular that of the Royal Fusiliers on the right, who found themselves unable to move. The task of clearing the village was given to the reserve battalion, 1/5th Gurkhas, supported by a squadron of Canadian tanks.

The attack began at midday. Fifteen minutes later the leading troops entered the village and then followed some seventy five minutes of desperate hand-to-hand fighting. Major Winstanley was severely wounded but although unable to move continued to direct operations from a stretcher. The Germans resisted fiercely from houses, cellars and dugouts and the scene was reminiscent of the shambles of Mozzagrona. By 1.30 the far side of the hill was reached but isolated pockets of enemy still fought on in the village and it was not till 3 p.m. that all resistance ceased. Even after this, badly shaken Germans in twos and threes continued to appear from odd holes and corners anxiously looking for a kind face to whom to surrender; three such surrendered to the divisional commander in person nearly twenty four hours later. The attack on 'Platform' to the east was supported by two Canadian tanks which by the most admirable driving had succeeded in making their way over the mountain of bricks and rubble that was once Sant' Angelo.

Whether it was the sight of the tanks, whether it was the knowledge of what had happened in the village, whether for this, that or the other, we do not know, but no sooner was the attack under way than 'Platform' bristled with white flags. Thirty seven prisoners were taken. The battle for Sant' Angelo was over. (65)

In fighting and establishing themselves across the Gari, 8th Indian Division performed a notable feat of arms, for it was over the bridges they built that 78th Division crossed to attack north across Route 6 and link up with the Poles.

The story of the fighting round Monte Cassino would not be complete without some account of the work of the Mule Companies of the Royal Indian Army Service Corps who there, and in many other parts of Italy, and under many masters, served under conditions of danger and discomfort which, if no worse, were certainly no easier than those of the forward infantry battalions. Indeed the cry for mules went up only when the tracks were so precipitous and the weather so appalling that all other forms of transport were halted.

When 4th Indian Division relieved American IInd Corps at Monte Cassino two mule companies were rushed down by train, arrived and moved forward by night, only to find when dawn broke they were on a forward slope overlooked from the town and the Monastery. Suffering some casualties they moved at once to a ravine known by the French as 'L'Inferne'. Their arrival brought the total of mules to 1,500, and they found they were sharing the amenities 'with an American battery, armed with a particularly offensive type of weapon manned by men suffering from permanent insomnia, a battalion of French infantry, a main dressing station and some 500 Goums—French Colonial Cavalry—who made P. C. Wren's description of them seem pale and insipid'.

The group was there for nearly a month. The pack trains moved out every night on their ten mile turn-round journey, loaded up, and then crossed the valley and climbed the steep hills to the north-east of the Monastery. The trail was very steep, narrow and most exhausting. Up to 800 animals a night used the same track and great care had to be taken to avoid congestion as the route was under mortar fire and considerable casualties were suffered. Many animals slipped over the side and fell down the *khud*; yet one of the company commanders could write:

The early days in the Inferno were I think very happy ones. A veritable League of Nations had been assembled —Indians, Americans, Tunisians, Algerians, and Italians. Between them there existed a fine spirit of cooperation. In spite of the perils of the mule track, the unburied dead, and the horrible stench, everyone was willing to do his share. In spite of the hard work by night animal management retained its high standard. Mention must be made of parties of three or four men who used to go out by day to collect animals which had broken loose the previous night, braving minefields in these attempts.

A story leaps to the mind from the time when we worked with The Guards Brigade.

'How do your mules react under fire?'

'They lie down, of course.'

After the relief of 4th Indian Division the group stayed on with 78th Division and later with the Poles. They won many awards for gallantry and all told lost 150 officers and men, killed and wounded, and 500 mules in the Cassino area.

During the final attack they provided transport for nine artillery observation parties, each consisting of seven mules carrying wireless equipment. When the pursuit went forward they prided themselves that they could pretty well keep up with the advance of the infantry divisions with their mechanical transport. On one occasion in answer to a sudden call they marched eighty miles in three days in drenching rain through country lanes not yet cleared of mines. 'To say that they retained their sense of humour when, on arrival, they found they weren't needed after all, is the highest tribute that can be paid to their discipline and their morale.'

Among their 'unsolicited testimonials' was one from a battery of Horse Artillery which complimented them on their saddlery and man-management, and another from an American infantry battalion commander who wrote:

The men have exemplified the highest devotion to duty it has been the opportunity of my command to witness. They taught our men the use of the different types of pack and cheerfully climbed the tortuous trail to our positions three and four times daily if necessary. All this was done in weather of the worst type, rain, snow, sleet and sudden thaws, and in spite of the treachery of the terrain and the difficulty involved not one piece of equipment was lost.

CHAPTER FOURTEEN

Italy: The Gothic Line

June 1944–May 1945

With the collapse of the Gustav Line both Fifth and Eighth Armies were in full cry after the retreating Germans. Though the political reward was the fall of Rome, the military object that General Alexander had set himself was the destruction of the German armies, and in this he was less successful. The magnet of Rome attracted to itself more than a fair or necessary share of the divisions breaking out of the Anzio beachhead, very much at the expense of the drive on Valmontone which would have placed them squarely across the line of withdrawal, and a number of enemy escaped who might have been intercepted. But an even more bitter disappointment was in store. High-level plans for a landing on the south coast of France had been under discussion for some months as one of several possible operations that would bring pressure to bear on the enemy from a new direction. It now appeared that this landing was to take place, and that no fewer than seven divisions, three American and four French, would be taken from the army in Italy for the purpose. General Alexander made a most eloquent appeal for their retention.

> I cannot over-emphasise my conviction that if my tried and experienced commanders and troops are taken away for operations elsewhere we shall certainly miss a golden opportunity for scoring a really decisive victory and we

shall never be able to reap the full benefits of the efforts and gains we have made during the past few weeks. I feel strongly that it is of the greatest importance not to let go the chance that has been so hardly won.

His plea was backed by the Prime Minister, but it fell on deaf American ears. The projected operation had no direct strategic purpose but was designed to secure the use of the port of Marseilles to land some forty American divisions that were waiting in America to take part in the fighting in Northern Europe, but which could not be handled through the English Channel ports. There was inevitably a period of delay and dislocation while our armies in Italy were being sorted out, a delay which gave the enemy 'a breathing space to rest and regroup their forces'. General Alexander's object was now defined as being 'to give the greatest possible assistance to Overlord* by destroying or containing the maximum number of German formations in the Mediterranean'. Italy had become a subsidiary theatre of war, and the architects of victory must remain thankful that the fact did not seem to affect in any way the willingness of the soldier to fight and, if needs be, to die in the common cause.

Before resuming the story of the Indian divisions mention must be made of a threat from which the leading troops were never really free even though the enemy was miles away : the danger from the mine. The mine was in the first place devised as a protection against the tank, but it spawned a hundred bastard offspring designed to kill the unwary man. They would be laid to protect a tank minefield and trap the unfortunate sapper in his efforts at clearance ; and they were cousins to the booby trap, well known in the First World War, but now appearing in a score of satanic disguises, a bar of chocolate or a first field dressing.

The sappers, responsible for mine clearance and, in their general omniscience credited with knowing all about anything new that might be encountered, probably suffered more heavily than most. In a single week a Sapper and Miner

* The landings in Normandy.

company lost three officers killed when clearing minefields under shell fire. 'It was nothing unusual for a party to lift fifteen Teller mines at a time, every mine ringed with intricate booby traps and loaded with death.' (37) But death lay in wait for the unwary, whatever his regiment or corps. 'It had been reported that the area was mined and that it was probable that a new type of mine would be found. The pioneer platoon went ahead to sweep the area, with orders not to disarm, but to report any strange mine. Unfortunately, owing to the Gurkha's innate curiosity, four men, who could not resist the temptation to fiddle, were killed, but the area was clear when the battalion arrived.' (63)

If a casualty occurred in a mine-clearing party, the situation was fraught with difficulty because anyone attempting to rescue the wounded man could only too easily be blown up himself, and on at any rate two occasions of this sort there were displays of cold, calculated bravery, different from, but no less worthy of esteem than, gallantry in the heat of action.

During a pause in the battle for Cassino, Subedar Subramanyam of the Madras Sappers and Miners was in charge of a mine-clearing party when the man in front of him trod on an anti-personnel mine of a type with a small initial charge that throws a canister into the air which explodes with great violence. The Subedar realized at once what had happened and threw himself on top of the mine, taking the whole force of the explosion on his body and saving the rest of the party from death, or at least the most serious injuries. The citation on which he was awarded posthumously the G.C. concludes that he deliberately gave his own life to save that of his friends. 'Although he has gone the example of his unexcelled heroism remains; one in accordance with the highest traditions of the Indian Army.'

Even more remarkable is the story of the patrol sent out by the Central India Horse under Lieutenant Graham Young.

When they had almost reached their objective the two leading men stepped on mines. It was pitch dark so the order for everyone to stand still was given, whilst the

position was reviewed. Graham Young moved forward
into the minefield and dug up three German schu mines
with his hands. These are small wooden boxes almost
impossible to detect with a mine detector and very easily
hidden. He reached the two men unharmed but whilst
lifting one of them to carry him back to safety he himself
trod on a mine and both his legs were blown off. It was
useless to do any more before it got light, so everyone lay
as quiet as possible and a man was sent back to guide up
the medical party. Graham Young was still conscious
next morning and had been giving orders from the minefield all night. Unfortunately, through loss of blood, he
died before reaching hospital. (41)

One of the wounded men, a young Dogra sowar named
Ditto Ram, had his left leg blown off below the knee. He
applied a field dressing and then, hearing calls for help from
the other man, he crawled through the minefield to assist him.
He found him with his thigh shattered and, although in the
greatest of pain himself, bandaged his comrade's wound.

He was a very young soldier with only two years' service,
nevertheless, besides showing the greatest personal
courage and disregard for pain by crawling through a
minefield to help a wounded comrade, he set the finest
example of soldierly comradeship and self-sacrifice. He
maintained consciousness only long enough to finish the
bandaging before he died without a murmur of complaint
or a suspicion of regret. (41)

Both officer and sowar were awarded posthumously the
G.C.

By 25 August both Fifth and Eighth Armies were generally in
contact with the Gothic Line, having driven in the outpost
positions which extended anything up to twenty miles to the
south. The Line took advantage of the southern slopes of the
Northern Appennines, and was some 180 miles long, extending from Pesaro on the Adriatic to La Spezia on the west

coast. It was not continuous, as there were considerable mountainous areas which were virtually proof against attack, and the Germans had been able to concentrate on their usual formidable belts of defence works on all the road approaches through the mountains. There was a gap at the eastern end of the line between the hills and the sea, and 4th and 10th Indian Divisions and 43rd Gurkha Lorried Brigade were all concerned in the battles that were fought to clear the gap, capture the port of Rimini, and so open the way for an advance north-westwards to Bologna and the valley of the Po.

4th Indian Division had been relieved on 16 March after its second attack on Cassino and, in spite of the punishing casualties it had suffered, was in the line again by 7 April when it relieved 8th Indian Division on the Adriatic sector. It was in the van of the pursuit up the coast when the enemy withdrew early in June, and for three weeks from the middle of July was engaged in Operation Vandal directed against the centre of the Gothic Line. On 10 August Vandal was called off in favour of the drive directed at the gap between Pesaro and the sea, and the division enjoyed three whole days' rest before trekking forward to take over the left sector of Vth Corps. It found it was to have the doubtful privilege of advancing behind a screen of Italian irregulars. They 'seldom sent in situation reports, and their movements in screen remained vague and unpredictable'. On 25 August, the opening day of the advance, 2nd Sikh Regiment caught up with enemy rear-guards and advanced on a village that had been reported by the irregulars as clear of the enemy; they were met by a withering fire and lost two officers and seventy men. On the twenty-ninth, 3rd Baluch Regiment reached the line of the R. Foglia and, when their patrols reported no resistance, they carried out a night attack, climbed the spur and captured a village which, to their surprise, was empty of the enemy; but any further advance was hotly contested. That night Eighth Army attacked across its whole front, and while 46th Division, on 4th Indian Division's left, made good progress, 7th Indian Infantry Brigade was checked. Three days later a patrol of the brigade entering a village 'was confronted by an eerie situation—a battle position silent, deserted, and apparently untenanted'. The platoon commander placed his men in covering positions and himself worked round the back and found enemy detachments lurking in houses. 'When these hideaways were flushed the main positions opened fire, revealing a carefully baited trap.' The jemadar sent back a report by wireless, called for and directed artillery fire which prevented reinforcements being sent up, and that night two companies of the battalion took the village.

On the night of 5–6 September another brigade drove the Germans out of two villages after 'a slow and expensive slogging match. Two days later there were high driving winds and incessant cold rain, and an icy downpour soaked and chilled the forward troops as they crouched in the battle positions'. At this stage the two British divisions on the right, 46th and 56th, were held up by the bare ridge of Gemmano, which for five days defied their repeated assaults. On the thirteenth it was included in 4th Division's front and after an artillery concentration of terrific intensity the enemy, weakened by the cumulative effect of ten days' fighting, were driven off by an attack by The Camerons. On 17–18 September 1/9th Gurkhas attacked two commanding knolls with steep, cliff-like sides. During this action Rifleman Sherbahadur Thapa with his section commander stormed an enemy strong point. He gained the ridge where, single-handed, he defied enemy counter-attacks. After covering the withdrawal of his platoon, which had exhausted its ammunition, he twice went out to bring in wounded men in full view of the enemy but, as he returned from the second journey, fell riddled with bullets. He was awarded a posthumous V.C.

From the sublime to the ridiculous: three days later the divisional commander, General Holworthy,* was liberating San Marino, the oldest republic in the world.

I was taken to the Governor's Palace and escorted into the sanctum sanctorum. The Captain Regent was seated beside a large table. He wore a tail coat, butterfly collar, pepper and salt trousers and elastic-sided boots. I was in

---

* Major-General A. W. W. Holworthy, D.S.O., M.C.

shorts, khaki shirt, battle-dress blouse and coat duffle. We adjourned to a dining room where I signed my name in the Golden Book. We had some wine. I was asked to state what I desired. I said I wanted headquarters for myself and for brigade, and some stamps. I was allotted a villa and told that all the stamps of the Republic were at my disposal. The Captain Regent expressed his gratitude to the Allies for their restraint in not bombarding the town. We then shook hands warmly and I went back to see how the battle was going. (21)

After the fall of San Marino the German *278th Division* was replaced in the line by *114 Jaeger Division*, 'tough, surly and truculent'. Attacking a position held by them 2/7th Gurkhas lost, in one morning's fighting, 130 casualties, half of whom were killed.

By the 1st October the division's advance slowed and came to a halt. For the last ten days the elements had excelled themselves. Autumnal gales brought torrential rains. On the western flank C.I.H. patrols were marooned on the wrong side of the river; men were drowned trying to rejoin their units. It was now 32 days since the division had opened the battle. Casualties had been heavy, amounting to 1,892 of all ranks. The battle had been of the most wearing type, an unrelenting series of small, bitter clashes, with thrust piled on thrust, in which the evenly balanced strength of assailants and defenders exacted a substantial toll for each acre of gained or lost ground. (21)

The record shows the remarkable recuperative powers of an Indian division, if it is allowed a reasonable pause to recover and reorganize. The story 'is rich in characteristic performance by all ranks, great courage in extremity, inimitable doggedness, quick improvisation, the ability to make war and win through against every stress of circumstances'. (21)

The division was relieved by 10th Indian Division on 3 October and on arrival back in a rest area found, as had happened before, that the unexpected awaited them. They would proceed forthwith to Greece.

To enable 46th and 56th British Divisions to concentrate their attention on the capture of Gemmano, 1st Armoured Division moved into the line on their right; and with the division came the Gurkha Lorried Brigade. Formerly a part of the Indian Armoured Division in Iraq, it had arrived, under Brigadier Barker,* a month before to meet the demand for a higher proportion of infantry to tanks in the armoured divisions. Almost at once it found itself committed to a full-scale attack against a position held by *26th Panzer Division* which had so far resisted Eighth Army attacks.

> On the evening the 12th September the assault battalions moved silently towards the line of the Fosse del Valle, a tributary of the Conca which it was necessary to cross before a start line could be established. The low sky line of the ridge ahead indicated the objective. Along its crest the glow of smouldering fires identified the villages; during the day bombers had plastered key points with incendiaries that would act as guides for the advance. The Gurkhas themselves had left nothing to chance. Air photos had been intensively studied, and the riflemen had been told the number of hedgerows they must count before they closed with the enemy. (17)

When dawn broke the brigade had made excellent progress, but the terrific defensive fire put down by the enemy had brought havoc behind them. They had plastered ceaselessly every crossing over the Fosse del Valle, and the tracks leading down to it, and the two Ark bridges had been knocked out. A long line of blocked transport with guns and armour struggled to move forward in support and, luckily, a part of The Queen's Bays with some anti-tank guns found a crossing and reached the ridge an hour or so before the enemy counter-attacked. 'The ridge had been won, the Eighth Army had elbow room to

---

* Brigadier A. R. Barker, D.S.O., O.B.E., M.C.

continue the battle. Far away in Whitehall the soldier's eye of the Prime Minister had followed the course of the fighting. His congratulations on "this brilliant feat of arms" was a proud tribute to the first engagement of the Gurkha Lorried Brigade.' (17)

Success is a powerful tonic. Across the R. Marano lay another ridge, with both sides racing for possession. Finding themselves well forward, and ahead of their time-table, at two hours' notice the brigade switched their attack from dawn to an hour after dusk, and took the enemy completely by surprise. A whole battalion was wiped out, caught by artillery concentrations as they moved forward, and great booty was taken, including over fifty machine-guns. Once again the inevitable river with a ridge behind confronted them; this time the ridge was five miles away across a wide watercourse, and on it stood 'the fortress of Santarcangelo, with its walled town closely clustered about it'.

While the Gurkha brigade was consolidating its gains, the two flanking divisions had been attacking across the river, the Marecchia, with heavy casualties to The Queen's Bays, but with uncertain success. Contrary to the brigadier's own view of the situation, which was that the enemy was standing fast, intelligence reports insisted that only scattered rearguards remained and that a quick attack would succeed. The order was accordingly given and, although there had been little time for proper reconnaissance, the advance began half an hour after midnight on 23 September. They crossed without opposition but a thousand yards beyond the river ran into heavy machine-gun fire.

> With dawn it became apparent that the intelligence summaries had painted too rosy a picture. The British line of attack was by no means up to Santarcangelo Ridge, and the Gurkha thrust had created a narrow and dangerous salient in a strongly fortified position. Santarcangelo itself was held in force, with self-propelled guns sited well forward to sweep its approaches. The Gurkhas on pt 88 were almost completely surrounded by machine gun posts. (17)

The other forward battalion was in a no better position, and all the indications were that the enemy was sure of his ground and was devoting his resources to ejecting those who had penetrated his defences. Nothing daunted, the brigade commander sent in his reserve battalion, and that evening with the support of tanks of 10th Hussars, and artillery who had managed to cross the Marecchia, the brigade surged forward, the ridge was won, and 2/6th Gurkhas broke into the town. The castle garrison was mopped up and 'the partisans led by the local barber flocked to join the victors. Morning revealed that the Boche had taken his beating and had dropped back across the Rubicon'. (17)

Towards the end of March, 10th Indian Division, commanded by Major-General Denys Reid,* had arrived in Italy from the Middle East. It moved into the east coast sector, alongside 4th Indian Division, and its aggressive tactics in patrol encounters very soon won it the respect of the enemy. Typically, one of the forward posts reported: 'A white flag has been seen waving frantically in the area C279134. Later a man began to crawl towards our lines. He has not yet arrived, but tea for fifty has been laid on.' (17)

Towards the end of June the division moved to Perugia in the valley of the Tiber. It could have been ground of its own choosing.

> During the long years of waiting in Syria the theme of all divisional training had been mountain warfare. The men had lived and worked in the mountains. They had thought and dreamed of them. Mountain warfare is flexible and individual and General Reid had deeply inculcated the basic tactics. The value of high ground and dead ground, of observation posts and hidden approaches, of unobtrusive infiltration and deep penetration—a score of such lessons, learned laboriously in the training area, were now to be tested in actual combat. (17)

Corps orders called for the division to advance along both

---

* Major-General D. W. Reid, C.B., C.B.E., D.S.O., M.C.

banks of the Tiber, through the heart of the mountains. The lateral valleys which feed the great Roman river are of no particular length and after entering the foothills they quickly deteriorate into bush-filled gullies impassable to all but the goat-footed. In an early operation by 3rd Royal Garwhal Rifles

> two companies made a silent and unsupported assault, and after some fighting the enemy withdrew in disorder. This was the first of many quickly staged and silent night attacks which the battalion was to make, and the Germans were never able to find the answer to them. It completely upset his timetable for the withdrawal. He had expected an orthodox approach to the situation and a day-light attack, when the observation he possessed would have given him an advantage out of all proportion to the force he employed. (59)

By a succession of such bold manœuvres on a varying scale, moving wide to a flank over ground the enemy may well have thought impassable, the division made remarkable progress, but there was always a keen appreciation of the risks taken, as on the occasion when reconnaissance suggested that a projected attack was opposed by much greater strength than had at first been thought. During the pause to reconsider, the Germans attacked and captured a ridge behind the companies covering the forming-up positions. The battalion commander of 2/3rd Gurkhas

> quickly appreciated that under cover of the mist the forward companies had been by passed. He managed to get MacGregor (C. Coy) on the wireless and told him to contact the other company commanders near him, with the orders to turn about, to fall on the enemy from the rear and close on Il Castello. He pointed out that, obviously, no artillery support was possible, and finished up by saying, "Get stuck into them like nobody's business". A bloody hand-to-hand battle followed resulting in the complete rout of the German force. The battlefield

was littered with bodies and abandoned equipment. Elements of three different divisions were identified and Intelligence officially established that the Germans had used their corps reserve in an effort to regain this vital feature. (63)

Nor is there any lack of examples of individual gallantry. On one occasion 3rd Mahrattas, determined to regain a lost position before handing over to a relieving battalion, counterattacked. The company commander and six N.C.O.s were killed immediately but Naik Yashwent Gadge charged on and by his single-handed action succeeded, before he was killed, in saving the company. He won the first V.C. for his regiment.

With the decision to transfer the weight of Eighth Army's attack to the coast, the division remained for a time holding the ground at the head of the Tiber and Arno valleys; then on 3 October they moved to take over from 4th Indian Division on the line of the Rubicon.

The terrain was very different from the wooded hills of the Tiber valley; the hills were smaller, the countryside heavily populated, with well-built villages and farmsteads providing ready-made strong points for the Germans. In particular, church towers surrounded by thick, high cemetery walls were likely to be key points of the defence. The division's first task was to thrust westwards to enlarge the gap between the hills and the sea. They cleared a five-mile frontage on the R. Rubicon and found themselves confronted by two high, bare hills. 'On the right Monte Farneto, 1,600 feet high, was protected by a maze of deep water-courses, impassable to vehicles and in wet weather next to unscalable by men. More than 2,000 yards to the west stood Montecodruzzo. This abrupt buttress rose 1,300 feet above the plain, with steep and trackless slopes.' (17) The flexible tactics which had won ground before at low cost were no longer likely to succeed; two strong enemy divisions held the ridges and nothing but a frontal assault would dislodge them. The attack was made by 3rd Mahrattas and 2/3rd Gurkhas in pelting rain and impenetrable darkness, and took the enemy by surprise. The forward positions were not manned, and Monte Farneto was gained with little loss. Only one hour behind the infantry the tanks of the North Irish Horse reached the top and were largely instrumental in beating off the ferocious counter-attacks with which the Germans tried to recapture the ridge. 43rd Lorried Brigade was now under orders of 10th Division and five nights later three companies of 2/6th Gurkhas similarly captured Montecodruzzo, which proved to be of even greater tactical importance than Monte Farneto, but which also was held in the face of determined efforts to retake it.

The record of the division during the closing weeks of the year, when vile weather and wintry gales brought operations to a standstill, is all in the same key, the same readiness to take the chance that, by its unexpectedness, reaps its rewards; and the story is laced with instances of personal bravery from which it is almost invidious to pick out the story of Naik Trilok Singh of the Garwhal Rifles. When under fire from an enemy position with an unusually high proportion of automatic weapons, his platoon ran out of ammunition. He thereupon seized a rifle and bayonet, charged the nearest enemy machine-gun, bayoneted two Germans and brought back the gun and its crew. Sending back his prisoners, he set up the spandau and covered the advance of his platoon. Shortly afterwards he was killed, still firing his captured gun.

In the opening months of 1945 there was little activity other than local operations to secure jumping-off areas for the main attack to be made when the weather improved. Despite overwhelming superiority in the air, and a comfortable margin in armoured formations, we had in fact to husband our resources: the transfer of divisions to the armies in France had left us little better than equal in infantry, and the British formations reflected the general drain on British manpower in the form of changes in organization which reduced their numbers. There was also a shortage of artillery ammunition which imposed severe daily rationing if stocks were to be built up for the spring offensive; for it was certain that, although defeat was now staring the Germans in the face, they were still full of fight, and we should need every man and every gun we had before we finally defeated them.

Operations in the previous autumn had been directed mainly at the capture of the strategic centre of Bologna to which there were two main approaches: from the south through mountainous country, ending up against the elaborate defences of the city itself; or from the south-east over the plains, with four major and three minor rivers to cross. The significant river in that area is the Reno which runs eastwards and attracts most of the tributaries flowing north-east off the slopes of the Appennines. Once over the Reno it was reckoned that we would be advancing over country with few natural obstacles, and be able to cut in behind the German armies to prevent them withdrawing to their National Redoubt in the southern Alps.

We are concerned now with Eighth Army in the south-east, and with no more than a limited sector at that, involving the passage of the Senio, the river up to which our front had advanced as the result of the winter fighting; and over the Senio to the Santerno, the last stream to be crossed before Bastia, where Highway 16 from Rimini to Ferrara crosses the Reno.

The attacker here is faced with an obstacle peculiar to this corner of Italy. The rivers flowing into the Reno receive in spring an immense volume of flood water from the snows melting on the hills, and to prevent the flooding of the densely populated and fertile plain the natural banks of the rivers are reinforced by great dykes standing above the plain. The walls of these dykes had been tunnelled and passaged, and were honeycombed with machine-gun emplacements sweeping the plain to the south against the opening stages of the attack, and taking in murderous enfilade any attackers who captured the first dyke and tried to cross the stream itself. It had, indeed, been considered whether the best course for the attacker was not to secure the near bank first, as a base from which to tackle the river and the northern line of dyke. This course was rejected on grounds of loss of time and surprise, and because the true object of the operation was the passage of the Santerno seven miles further on.

Vth Corps, attacking on the key sector for the drive on Bastia, had the New Zealand division on the left, 8th Indian Division on the right. The date of the attack was 9 April and for ninety minutes that afternoon the whole enemy position was the target of a terrific attack by 825 bombers of the Strategic Air Force; they were followed by timed artillery concentrations lasting till 7 p.m.; then the assault was made. The Argyll and Sutherland Highlanders on the divisional right made good progress, but 6th Battalion Frontier Force Rifles on their left were less fortunate.

They carried the near bank, but the trough of the river was lashed by a score of machine guns, firing from port-holes in both inner banks, and from enfilade positions on the left flank. Sepoy Ali Haidar and two others were all of one platoon to reach the far bank. From thirty yards away a machine gun nest spat death. Bidding his comrades give him covering fire he lobbed a grenade and followed in under it. Although wounded by a stick bomb he closed and destroyed the post. Without pause he charged the next weapon pit. He was struck twice and fell, but he crawled forward, pulled the pin of a Mill's bomb with his teeth, and hurled it into the spandau nest. Weak with loss of blood he pulled himself to his feet, staggered forward and threw himself on the gunners. The two surviving Germans surrendered. (17)

It was the turning point and, through the gap he made, his battalion advanced across the river and took up the chase.

The 3rd Mahrattas, right-hand battalion of the neighbouring brigade, had found themselves in similar straits. It was then that Sepoy Namdeo Jadhao found himself on the far bank with two wounded comrades.

In the face of pelting fire, he half-dragged, half-carried the men back across the stream, struggled up the inner slope and deposited them in safety. Having saved his friends he resumed the battle single-handed. He dashed at the nearest machine gun and wiped out its crew. A bullet tore his hand so he dropped his tommy gun and closed with bombs. Two more enemy posts were silenced in quick succession. Standing on the lip of the bank he shouted his war cry and waved his comrades forward. Three company commanders had fallen but the Mahrattas, responding to such dauntless leadership, swarmed back across the river. With both banks clear they pushed on into the night, to deal with the obstinate garrisons of a number of houses in fields adjoining the river. (17)

They were twin feats of arms for which it is hard to find a match. Two young soldiers, not even N.C.O.s—one a Pathan, the other a Mahratta—within a few hundred yards and a few minutes of each other won the V.C. for acts of gallantry that gained the crossings over the Senio for their division.

While the flood-bank fighting was still going on, jeeps and anti-tank guns were being slung over the river; by dawn the next morning there were three tank crossings over, and when the battle began to sort out in daylight a strong force of British armour was roving between the Senio and the Santerno, on call for the infantry.

For the next fortnight the enemy, although in full retreat, fought as hard as he had ever done. When 20th Brigade of 10th Indian Division reached the R. Idice

they were confronted by floodbanks thirty feet high, the near bank covered by a wide irrigation ditch at the bottom of the slope. For the last time they met Germans of the type they knew so well—fanatically brave fighters, skilled in battle, contemptuous of death. 1/2 Punjabis moved forward to storm the defences and plunged into its bitterest fighting of the war. With great gallantry two platoons of Dogras of 'D' Coy reached the far bank. British armour arrived but the tanks either bogged down in the irrigation ditch or were destroyed by mines and enemy fire. A South African artillery observation officer, Lieut. Spiro, took over command of 'A' Coy and continued to direct the fire of his guns. On the far bank the Dogras fought to the last man, ringed by implacable enemies who asked and gave no quarter; when found the Dogras lay in groups clutching their bloody bayonets.

This ferocious fighting marked the end of organized resistance on the front of Thirteenth Corps. When morning broke any enemy who survived had gone. (17)

As the chase swung north-east, both 8th and 10th Indian Divisions were squeezed out by formations advancing on either side of them. The last to come to a halt was the Gurkha Lorried Brigade which reached Padua where they stayed to hold the ring when the Patriots sought to settle old scores against those Fascists who, to the end, had sided with the Germans.

But before they came to rest they too had fought a last engagement of great individual brilliance. Operating in their true role of lorried infantry as the pursuit column of the Polish corps, they were loosed on their own. Avoiding the main road and bridges, which were heavily defended, they zigzagged across country by lanes and tracks; 2/10th Gurkhas crossed the R. Sillaro at a marshy ford in a remote spot, and over the Ark bridge which they had established 14th/20th Hussars—backed by 2/6th Gurkhas—crossed the river and at dusk attacked on a wide front the key road centre of Medicina, fifteen miles east of Bologna.

Such unorthodoxy caught the Germans, feverishly assembling their defences, by surprise. For the next ten minutes Medicina was Wild West, Balaclava and Stalingrad rolled into one. The leading tanks charged self-propelled guns in the main street, knocking them out at point-blank range. A German *bazooka* man stepped around a corner and hurled a bomb into the tank, a Gurkha subedar followed him round the corner and slew him with the kukri. An ammunition dump blew up with a colossal crash; a self-propelled gun blew up, trapping a number of tanks in the narrow street; the remainder of the Gurkhas arrived in the main square and swarmed over the town, hunting paratroopers to death in cellars, in lofts, and even on the rooftops.*

* *A Gurkha Brigade in Italy: Story of the 43rd Gurkha Lorried Brigade* (18).

The enemy was routed and fled and the two corps on either flank, New Zealand and Polish, who had been held up, were able to continue their advance.

In memory of that evening, men of the 14th/20th Hussars now wear the crossed kukris of the 43rd Lorried Brigade, and the 6th Gurkhas wear the eagle of the 14th/20th Hussars. Nor was it the only occasion of its kind.

There were times in Italy, as elsewhere, when the Indian Army had reason to feel they had been given less than their share of credit by those who were well placed to know how much they had done; but they could afford to be magnanimous for they never lacked tributes from those best placed of all to assess their worth, the men who fought alongside them.

'Everyone is pleased over working with the Indian troops, because it is something to talk about later', ran the war diary of The Westminsters, a Canadian armoured regiment. And the Canadian official history is not content to let it rest at that. 'It was more; it was a strengthening of the happy association of Indian and Canadian soldiers which had begun in November between the Sangro and the Moro and which was to continue to thrive on many fronts throughout the entire Italian campaign.' *

Then there was the friendship formed between the Argyll and Sutherland Highlanders and 6th Battalion The Frontier Force Rifles, formerly 59th Scinde Rifles.

> It was only natural that the battalion after a friendship cemented on so many battlefields should join with the Argyll and Sutherland Highlanders in celebrating the victory and on 6th May in the main square of Costa di Rovigo a huge bonfire was lit. Round this the Indian sepoy and the Highlander fraternised. After the performance of eightsomes and Khattak dances the pipes played "*The 91st and 59th at Monte Cerere*", a march composed by Pipe Major P. McGlin.†

* *Official History of the Canadian Army in the Second World War: The Canadians in Italy* (9).
† *The Frontier Force Rifles* (58).

The friendship was cemented after the war by the gift to The Scinde Rifles of a full-dress breast-plate from the 91st, who received in return a silver statuette of Havildar Tara Singh firing his machine-gun in their support at Monte Cerere.

For the same reasons 1st Battalion 5th Royal Gurkha Rifles decided to present a kukri in an ornamental scabbard to 1st Battalion The Royal Fusiliers.

Always a Fusilier describes their part in the ceremony.

There came the great day of what was to be, in effect, the last parade. The battalion was to be inspected by the Commander-in-Chief, India; and after all it had been in the Indian Army since 'heavens knows when' and fought alongside Indian troops since the war began. But the day was to mean more than that. Between the Fusiliers and 1/5th Royal Gurkha Rifles there had grown up a special friendship, based partly on good relations over a long period of association, but more on the mutual trust created by fighting alongside each other. And never had either battalion anything but complete reliance upon one another. Now that the time was coming for them to part the Gurkhas decided to commemorate these years of comradeship in battle by the formal gift of a kukri, the Gurkha warrior's most treasured personal weapon. Only once before, in 1872, has a kukri been presented to a British regiment. Never before had it been formally presented, with both battalions drawn up on parade. All of this was fully understood by the Fusiliers who cleaned, and polished and drilled in preparation for the great occasion. (31)

General Sir Claude Auchinleck, inspecting the guard mounted to meet him at Perugia Airfield, considered it to be the finest display of any guard he had seen.

With a modesty befitting the donor of a precious gift the Gurkha regimental history records that 'the kukri was handed by the subedar-major on behalf of the men to Lieut.-Colonel Le Marchand who handed it to Lieut.-Colonel Fairclough of the Fusiliers, who in turn handed it to the regimental sergeant major on behalf of his men'. (65)

On the evening of the parade—'a fitting climax,' as Lieutenant-Colonel Le Marchand said, 'to twenty months of comradeship on the field of battle'—the Fusilier officers entertained the British officers of the 1/5th Gurkhas. Simultaneously, the Gurkha officers were entertained in the sergeants' mess. 'Trevor Fairclough and I looked in on the latter party, rather wondering about the language difficulty. We need not have worried. There was a buzz of conversation —all in Italian.'

CHAPTER FIFTEEN

Burma: Taking Stock

Three times between 1939 and 1942, at Dunkirk, in Burma, and in North Africa, our armies were convincingly defeated, and in all three places they duly turned and rent their enemies; but if that is the traditional pattern on which we fight, then nowhere did we run more true to form than in Burma, where the extremes of failure and success were perhaps greater than in either of the other two campaigns. Equally sharp in contrast was the extent to which victory in Burma was won by the troops on the ground, with far less lavish support from modern weapons, equipment and aircraft than was forthcoming in Africa and Europe; which accounts for the fact, maybe, that more intelligent use was made of the support which was available.

There were two other distinctive features. The first was the way in which the Indian soldier, confounding his critics in high places, proved that given reasonable equality of equipment with his enemy, and a chance to learn to use it, he would fight against the Japanese with all the fire and determination which won him victory elsewhere. The second was that, quite apart from the enemy, the physical difficulties of fighting in Assam and Burma were immeasurably greater than elsewhere, so great that to the sophisticated global planners of London and Washington they may well have seemed insuperable.

Along the Indo-Burmese border, in a shallow curve, sweeps the wide belt of jungle-clad, precipitous hills, railless, roadless and, for six months of the year during the monsoon rains, almost trackless. Sparsely populated by wild tribes, disease-infested, and even unmapped in places, much of this great area had been penetrated only by occasional Europeans and then only in the dry season. It could be fairly described as some of the world's worst country, breeding the world's worst diseases, and having for half the year at least the world's worst climate. To move even small pack caravans by the few dry-weather tracks from Burma to India was so difficult that no proper trading route existed. To supply, move and fight great armies in or through the mass of jumbled hills had for so long been regarded as impossible that no serious defence measures had ever been taken on India's eastern frontier. (71)

It is no exaggeration to claim that Fourteenth Army created its own opportunity to defeat the Japanese, and seized that opportunity with both hands.

Field-Marshal Slim, who had been appointed army commander, has observed that, though there was often talk of fighting to the last man and the last round, the Japanese was the only soldier who actually did so. This determination was the outcome of a system of mental conditioning of fanatical intensity which was all the more successful against the traditional background of Japanese life: there is nothing more glorious or desirable for a Japanese to do than to die for his Emperor. And not just go out and die for him tonight or tomorrow morning, but to go on being ready to die for him every day for the next six weeks, under conditions of ever-worsening physical and mental strain, accepting death as inevitable only when it actually comes. It was a characteristic that gave the Japanese soldier the edge over pretty well every other nation in the world. It was this complete disregard for well-being, or personal safety, allied to his ability to live low, and very often live off the country, that made the Japanese outflanking and encircling tactics so very hard to counter. When it was a question of which soldier could keep on fighting longest when away from his base, the Japanese won every time; so much so that his commanders came to accept it as a factor in their planning. Both in the Arakan and at Imphal they committed their troops to battle with a very low margin of administrative safety, banking partly on the fact that their men would fight on, and partly on the near certainty that we should do what we had so often done before when threatened with encirclement, withdraw down our supply line leaving accumulated stocks of supplies to fall into his hands. It was because we at last found the answer to this manœuvre that the risks the enemy took landed him in disaster.

That answer was air supply, a note on which is given at Appendix C. Formations established themselves in all-round defensive localities large enough to be self-supporting and, if surrounded, they stayed put, and supplies of all natures were dropped on them from the air; dropped, that is, if the localities were too small to contain a landing strip. So long as they could withstand the attacks of the enemy, and now it was the enemy who had to do the attacking, the result was only a matter of time.

In terms of fighters and bombers Fourteenth Army had no more than a fraction of the massive air support that covered the armies fighting in Europe, but the R.A.F. did win a comfortable margin of air superiority which kept the skies clear for aircraft employed on supply delivery, troop carrying and the evacuation of casualties. When fighting was at its fiercest, up to a third of the squadrons flying on these tasks came from the United States Army Air Force, a figure which for a brief critical period rose as high as half. It is time to explain just what the U.S.A.A.F. was doing in this theatre of war.

Support for China had been a cardinal point of American foreign policy for many years, and at any rate during the first twelve months of the war against Japan it was important to maintain the flow of supplies which would keep in the field the Chinese armies that were containing Japanese divisions which might have been employed elsewhere. When the loss of the Burma Road put paid to delivery by land, air supply was the only alternative.

The decision as to what supplies were to be sent, and the purpose they would be put to when they arrived, was always dominated by two men who stood at the head of Chinese military affairs. General Chiang Kai-Shek was of course a political figure of world importance, but his influence on American opinion was probably out of all proportion to the practical return he gave for the support which was given him. Promises he would give, usually in return for some further concession, but there was no certainty that the promises would be honoured; and he was quite capable of giving diametrically opposed answers on successive days.

The Generalissimo's chief military adviser was General Stilwell, the redoubtable 'Vinegar Joe', who was sent out to him to fill that appointment in February 1942. He had long experience of working with the Chinese, spoke their language and commanded their respect. He was a man of great drive and courage and, within the sphere of his immediate personal influence, achieved a great deal. He had a low opinion of his British allies, and he was notorious even among his compatriots for being an extremely difficult man to deal with; but with all his faults he was a tough, redoubtable soldier, and the Chinese armies under his personal leadership, with British 36th Division and Merrill's American Marauders under his command, fought with great effect on the left flank of Fourteenth Army. It is no small tribute to the commander of that army that for the co-ordination of these operations in the field General Stilwell agreed to serve under his orders.

The Americans also maintained in China an independent air force employed on bombing Japanese shipping and the Japanese mainland, and the results achieved were sufficient to stir the Japanese armies in the heart of China to advance on the airfields they were using.

While the operational effect of these American activities on the fortunes of Fourteenth Army varied from time to time, they overshadowed the whole administrative background. Supplies could reach China only from a group of airfields grouped round Ledo in the north-east corner of Assam, whence they were flown over 'The Hump', a snow-clad off-shoot of the Himalayas soaring to 15,000 feet. By the middle of

1944, 1,000 tons a month were actually being delivered at Kunming, the Chinese railhead; over and above this was the tonnage needed for the operation of the aircraft, the construction of airfields, the maintenance of the Chinese forces on the northern front and last, but by no means least, the building of the Ledo road itself.

Ledo was at the far end of the Assam railway system, Fourteenth Army railhead at Dimapur was half way up; tonnages were allotted in accordance with priorities laid down in Washington and London, and Fourteenth Army never got a ton more than they could justify on grounds of operational necessity. American reinforcements of staff and rolling stock achieved miracles in increasing the traffic the railway could carry, but they never caught up with the demands placed on it. In the eye of the American public, the American forces in India were there to support the Chinese, or to further their own war effort in the Pacific; we may be grateful that they were there at all, for without the help of their air squadrons the reconquest of Burma from the north would not have been possible.

At the end of the fighting in 1942 the enemy withdrew from the line of the Chindwin, and on our side IVth Corps was content to hold the south-eastern and southern approaches to the Imphal plain. The Japanese had reached the limits defined for the Greater East Asia Co-Prosperity Sphere and lacked the resources to support an attack into India itself; for our part neither the numbers nor the quality of our troops justified our taking the offensive. Chapter Ten gives some account of how India Command tackled the problems of training the individual soldier to a higher standard to fit him for the rigours of the war he was being schooled to fight; complementary to that was the even more difficult business of creating in Fourteenth Army confidence in its ability to defeat the Japanese. Without an understanding of how this was done it is impossible to appreciate the extent of the transformation. Up to the middle of 1943 success after success was conceded to the enemy; not more than six months later we passed to the offensive and, after months of bitter fighting, completely destroyed the Japanese armies in the field and won

In the Arakan. Men of the Rajput Regiment waiting to assault the enemy position 100 yards away

Kohima. The battlefield at Naga village

opposite Kohima. Men of the Royal West Kent
Regiment visit the 161st Indian Infantry
Brigade Memorial:
'The Japanese invasion of India was halted'

Supplies moving up the lines of communication for the Lushai brigade

a race against the monsoon to occupy Rangoon from the north.

It is significant that 'The Foundations' is one of the longest chapters in Field-Marshal Slim's book *Defeat into Victory*; it is in this chapter that he explains how he set about the task.

Before tackling the problem of morale in the abstract it was essential to raise physical fitness to a far higher standard. Better food was the first demand, but with the best will in the world no great improvement was possible. The two things the fighting soldier needs are fresh meat and fresh vegetables— they are more important than all the rest of his rations put to- gether. In the Arakan, where the line of supply was short, the problem was not too difficult, but in Assam British troops were going for months on end without tasting fresh meat; they lived on bully and soya links. The Indian soldier, forbidden these delicacies by his religion, might get no meat at all; nor did he get the extra milk allowed in the ration scales as an alternative.

The army commander's second great problem was health.

> In 1943, for every man evacuated with wounds, we had one hundred and twenty evacuated sick. The annual malaria rate alone was eighty four per cent per annum of the total strength of the army and still higher among the forward troops. Next to malaria came a high incidence of dysentery followed in this gruesome order of precedence by skin diseases, and a mounting tale of mite or jungle typhus, a peculiarly fatal disease. At this time, the sick rate of men evacuated from their units rose to over twelve thousand per day. A simple calculation showed me that in a matter of months my army would have melted away. Indeed it was doing so under my eyes. (71)

The numbers of doctors, nurses, hospitals and ambulances needed to tackle the problem were away below what were necessary; to quote but a single figure there would be at any hour of the day or night one nurse on duty for each hundred patients.

The first thing was to stop men going sick and to that end

anti-malarial discipline, with prophylactic doses of mepacrine, was rigidly enforced. The next was to do away with the time-consuming journeys by road and rail to hospitals in India. For those not seriously ill they were not necessary, and for those who were they might prove fatal. Special forward malaria treatment-units were opened, often quite close behind the fighting troops, for the immediate treatment of malaria. A man would reach one of these hospitals no more than a few hours after falling sick, and he was kept there till he recovered; psychologically, perhaps, an encouragement to improve his anti-malarial discipline when he returned to duty. Complementary to this was the evacuation by air of the seriously ill and the severely wounded. Men were flown out direct to hospitals in India with airstrips located alongside them.

> One such hospital took in during 1944 and 1945 eleven thousand casualties straight, in their filthy, blood-soaked battledress, from the front line. The total deaths in that hospital were twenty three. Air evacuation did more in the Fourteenth Army to save lives than any other agency. (71)

By the end of 1944 the ratio of sick: wounded had dropped to 10:1; in the final campaign it fell as low as 6:1.

To improve morale a properly co-ordinated series of talks to the troops was undertaken, designed to convince the men on three points:

1. That there was a worthy, vital and tangible object before him, to the achievement of which his own personal effort made some contribution. In the light of the army commander's definition of the purpose of the battles he was to fight, it is significant that this object was defined as being 'not to defend India . . . or even to occupy Burma, but to destroy the Japanese Army, to smash it as an evil thing';

2. That he belonged to an efficient unit, and an efficient army, which could hope to achieve the object set before it;

3. That he would get a fair deal, conditions as good as they could be, weapons and equipment the best that could be provided.

The fulfilment of this last condition was something which was largely outside the powers of the army commander, but he records that Fourteenth Army took a fierce pride in overcoming difficulties by determination and ingenuity. From start to finish 'they had only two items of equipment that were never in short supply: their brains and their courage'.

Particular attention was paid to the administrative troops in the rear areas. It was not only that after some far-reaching Japanese encirclement they might, and at Kohima actually did, find themselves in the thick of the fighting, but that the rear areas were 'the filter through which all units, drafts and individuals for the forward units had to percolate', where 'they might become contaminated with the virus of despondency'. By playing on the very natural desire of the individual to feel that both he and the job he did really did matter, a stage was reached where 'administrative, labour and non-combatant units acquired a morale that rivalled that of the fighting units'.

For the fighting troops themselves something more practical than inspiring speeches was of course needed and self-confidence was restored by carefully graded stages.

As the first step to encourage the man that he personally held the upper hand, the rock-bottom need was to achieve a high standard of patrolling, and two random extracts will show how successfully this was done.

> A section met a Jap patrol some twenty strong, with other enemy in close support. The commander attacked immediately, regardless of the enemy supporting strength, himself charging a Jap light machine-gun, killing the gun numbers and capturing the weapon which the section brought away with them in the face of enemy efforts to retrieve it. (53)

> It was now clear that a change of tactics was necessary if contact was to be maintained and more damage inflicted by the small numbers available. A succession of small fighting patrols was sent out. These patrols, named 'Sherforces', consisted of a rifle section less the Bren gun, 4–6 days' rations and 4 grenades a man, with orders

275

to remain out till food or ammunition was exhausted. The tactics were entirely guerilla, no attempt to take prisoners, obtain identifications or hold ground. The idea was to select an ambush position, let the enemy scouts through and then open up with grenades and tommy-guns at short range on the main body. (58)

Once individual confidence had developed, it was extended to the collective proving of battalions and brigades by minor offensives so carefully planned that there could be no risk of failure.

We attacked Japanese company positions with brigades fully supported by artillery and aircraft, platoon posts by battalions. (71)

While all this was going on, the planners had not of course been idle. At the very highest level, conference followed conference: Trident, Quadrant, Sextant, there was never a dull moment. On 25 August 1943, the day after Quadrant ended, it was announced that Admiral Lord Louis Mountbatten had been appointed supreme commander of the newly formed South East Asia Command. With every reason to suppose that sooner or later amphibious operations would have to be undertaken for the recapture of Burma and Malaya, they were kept under review even though their fulfilment might have to await the release of ships and landing craft after the defeat of Germany. Projects ranged from a somewhat ambitious landing, on the north-west corner of Sumatra, to a very limited operation in support of a land advance in the Arakan for the capture of Akyab; but in the end, 'after weeks of discussion at high level the far-reaching plans for the 1943–44 campaign, completed by the Supreme Commander and endorsed at Sextant, came to naught'. (7) Of ten operations which achieved the status of a code name, seven were cancelled.

On 9 January 1944 the commander of Fourteenth Army received his orders. Starting in the north, the North Combat Area Command, the American and Chinese forces operating directly under Stilwell were to advance to Mogaung and

Mytikyina. IVth Corps on the Assam front was to clear the Chin hills as far as the Kabaw valley, dominate the area south of the Tamu-Sittang road between the Yu and Chindwin rivers, and contain Japanese forces in the Kabaw valley. The operations of the Long Range Penetration Group, under the command of General Wingate, were to be planned in conjunction with both these two. In the Arakan, the task set was to clear the mouth of the Naf river, capture Maungdaw and Buthidaung and exploit success to the utmost.

These orders had only just emerged from the planners' cauldron when patrol reports filtering in from IVth Corps made it only too clear that something big was boiling up on the enemy bank of the Chindwin. Although in 1942 the Japanese had rejected the possibility of exploiting their successes by an advance on India, by the middle of 1943 the very considerable overall change in their fortunes compelled them to reconsider the matter. In the south-west Pacific it was only too clear that the best they could hope for was to cling grimly on and avoid further disasters, and a compensating success elsewhere was highly desirable. Burma was the obvious place for it, and that was not the only consideration. General Mutaguchi, commander of *15th Army*, had been impressed by the ease with which the Chindit columns in 1943 had penetrated his defensive layout. He concluded that the only effective counter to the attack on a far larger scale which he might expect in 1944 was to capture Imphal, the base from which it would be mounted. To make Imphal secure he would have to extend his hold to the high ground about Kohima, and he would then be well placed for an advance into India itself. The plan had everything: greater security for Burma, a good chance of a victory over an army whose value he probably did not rate too highly and, above all, the prospect of cashing in on the favourable political situation which, according to Subas Chandra Bose with his Indian National Army, was there waiting to be exploited.

Attractive though it all seemed, there were distinct risks and Mutaguchi had some difficulty in persuading his superiors that they were acceptable. The overall plan which was eventually agreed was to attack with two divisions in the

Arakan a month or six weeks before the main offensive, both to confuse the issue and to tie down reserves; to mask the Chinese armies in the north and in Yunnan; and to allot three divisions for the capture of Imphal and Kohima. One of these divisions in the south, *33rd*, was to start a fortnight before the other two and advance on Imphal along both the Tiddim and Tamu roads with the idea of drawing southwards any reserves that might be watching the northern flank. On D Day, the second division, *15th*, was to move across country and establish itself north-east of Imphal, while the third, *31st*, was to move even wider and attack Kohima. When that division was in a position to hold off reinforcements arriving from India and keep the ring for the other two, they were to attack Imphal itself in a pincer movement from north and south.

The three important hazards on which Mutaguchi, and eventually Kawabe, the commander of the *Burma Area Army*, had to satisfy criticism were: considering the depth of the advance, were three divisions going to be enough? Would the available air support be effective? And what about the supply position? The criticisms were reasonable enough, and events were to prove that on all three counts Mutaguchi had been unjustifiably optimistic. Everywhere the opposition he encountered was far greater than he expected, and when the crunch came he was short of troops. Although the move of a force as large as a whole division to attack Kohima took us completely by surprise, it nevertheless got there just too late, and in insufficient strength to discharge its essential task of holding off reinforcements. The Japanese air force was never on top of its job. It was not able to prevent the air lift of reinforcements and supplies which were the decisive feature that enabled our garrisons to hold out; it never seriously interfered with our fighting troops; and it was not able to prevent the R.A.F. from giving effective and immediate support to our operations, either by limiting enemy movements to the hours of darkness or by low-flying support for our attacks. The supply plan was the biggest gamble of all, as it must have been obvious that the difficulties of maintaining the two right-hand divisions moving wide and deep across country would be enormous. No more than three weeks' supplies were allowed for, after which it was hoped that some of our reserves somewhere would have been captured. No such captures were made and, although the Japanese soldier did all and more than his commanders can have expected of him, fighting on in conditions which would have broken the heart of any other troops in the world, even he was defeated in the end, and the collapse when it came was complete.

CHAPTER SIXTEEN

Burma: The Arakan

There is room for no more than a summary of events in the Arakan to bring them up to December 1943, the month which saw the opening moves in the struggle that, over the whole Burma theatre, went on continuously until the final defeat of the Japanese in August 1945.

The Indian official history describes the scene of operations.

The land of Arakan consists of a strip of country running along the eastern seaboard of the Bay of Bengal. It stretches from the Naf estuary on the southern borders of Chittagong, to within ninety miles of Cape Negrais. On the east, it is bounded by the Arakan Yoma which separates it from the Irrawaddy valley. Along its northern border, its greatest breadth is about 100 miles, gradually diminishing towards the south as it is hemmed in by the Arakan Yoma, until in the extreme south it tapers into a narrow strip which is not more than fifteen miles wide.

In general, Arakan consists of tangled, jungle-covered hills which run down to a narrow coastal strip of paddy-fields and mangrove swamps, a highly malarial region infested with the most virulent type of mosquito. The hills and the coastal strip are heavily intersected by hundreds of streams (*chaungs*) and tidal creeks often many miles long, mostly unfordable and offering few landing points. In 1942, such landing points as existed were strongly defended by the Japanese, and since there was not a single beach along the hundred-mile stretch of the coast from Akyab to Taungup, these *chaungs* constituted the only means of access to the hinterland.

The terrain of Arakan may be divided into four sectors:

1. The COASTAL SECTOR which lies between the Bay of Bengal and the foothills of the Mayu Range. It is up to two miles wide in the northern part of the Mayu peninsula, but narrows to a few hundred yards between Donbaik and Foul Point. Intersected as it is by innumerable tidal *chaungs* and swamps, it makes the deployment of forces in this area very difficult.

2. The MAYU RANGE with foothills on either side, rises to slightly under 2,000 feet and forms the spine of the Mayu peninsula. Its jungle-covered slopes are particularly steep and rocky, constituting a formidable barrier to movement in any direction.

3. The MAYU VALLEY consisting mainly of flat paddy-fields and swampy areas, is intersected by tidal *chaungs* and is completely dominated by the hills of the Mayu range.

4. The KALADAN VALLEY resembles the Mayu valley and lies some thirty air miles to the east of it.

What with the Mayu Range, a jumble of knife-edged ridges and well-nigh impenetrable jungle, the *chaungs* running in from the sea, the tidal rivers, the long monsoon, and the pernicious mosquitoes, the Arakan was, all in all, the most difficult place to fight in the whole of Burma. Compared with Assam, the lines of communication were short, but the difficulties of road construction were enormous, and in October 1942 there was still a stretch of 150 miles from the end of the metalled road in the north down to Foul Point in the south.

The position of the opposing armies at the end of October 1942 was that the Japanese had during March occupied Akyab, the last forward airfield used for the support of the army withdrawing from Burma, and had pushed out covering detachments north of it. We had been content to guard Chittagong with armed police. The enemy had occupied the Andaman Islands out in the Bay of Bengal where there was an airstrip, but losses in the Pacific had caused them to withdraw the bulk of their navy. Neither side enjoyed any decisive advantage in the air, and without air superiority the Royal Navy were not prepared to support landing operations with anything larger than coastal craft.

General Wavell, who, as commander-in-chief, India, was still responsible for the overall direction of the war in Burma, was anxious, if only to restore morale, to prove that we were capable of fighting the Japanese on level terms, and as shortage of troops and administrative resources ruled out anything but local operations in Assam, the Arakan was the only alternative for a trial of strength.

The original orders given to General Lloyd, commanding 14th Indian Division, were to occupy the Maungdaw–Buthidaung area where the only road that crossed the Mayu range passed through the Tunnels; that done, a fully trained amphibious force that had been operating in Madagascar would sail from Chittagong to capture Akyab. When the force failed to arrive in India from Africa, he was ordered to advance the whole way to Foul Point by land to support a far less ambitious attack from the sea to be made by 6th (British) Infantry Brigade. The brigade moved to Chittagong and began to train, but some of the necessary landing craft had to be diverted from the rather meagre total of shipping available for the maintenance of the main advance, with the result that in the early stages administrative difficulties slowed up the whole operation to an extent which was largely responsible for eventual failure.

Under the original plan speed was not important, but for the second it was vital; nevertheless, to ensure that the first attack on the enemy was made in decisive strength, this was delayed until the lines of communication had been improved sufficiently to allow two brigades to be employed. When in early January 123rd Indian Infantry Brigade attacked Rathedaung, and 47th Indian Infantry Brigade attacked Donbaik, the supply position of both brigades so far forward was still precarious, the enemy was found to be well entrenched on the ground of his own choosing, and both attacks failed. We were confronted by a new problem, the Japanese bunker: mutually supporting, proof against artillery fire, camouflaged with such skill as to be invisible at fifty yards and manned by a fanatically determined enemy, the bunker was something that our infantry, who had not been trained for the task, could not overcome. Months later, when the technique of air support, tank support and close artillery support had all been worked out and rehearsed, a direct attack on a position the enemy had had time to perfect never offered much better than an even chance of success.

A second attack was no more successful and, with the realization that the seaborne attack on Akyab was now out of the running, 6th Infantry Brigade was made available to General Lloyd for one last attack on Donbaik. The brigade moved south for an attack that never took place; the enemy struck first. He had moved his battle-tried *55th Division* across from Burma and, positioning it west of the Kaladan river, he cut in behind both the brigades which had been placed to guard our left flank. He then cut the road behind the troops massed for the last attack on Donbaik, causing heavy casualties to 6th Infantry Brigade; and finally he drove us out of the Maung-daw–Buthidaung position, so that we were forced to withdraw to the line from which we had started south of Chittagong.

The plans for the Arakan were too ambitious and were persisted in after it was clear that they no longer offered any hope of success. The verdict of the official historian is that we 'paid the penalty for committing inexperienced troops to a difficult operation at the end of a tenuous line of communication'. (6)

Before the second Arakan campaign was launched the short-comings responsible for the failure of the first had largely been remedied. The troops were more experienced and there was a proper system of command; a whole regiment of tanks was available and there was most effective air support; and the administrative layout was adequate to support the force on to the objective defined for it. Above all, to ensure that we should not be deflected from our purpose by being manœuvred out of our positions, it was everywhere understood that formations which might be surrounded were to stand fast, and that immediate and continuous supply by air would be arranged for them.

The Japanese had taken up their main defensive position

astride the one feature of outstanding tactical importance, the lateral Maungdaw–Buthidaung road, and they had constructed three veritable fortresses, one at either end of the road and one in the middle astride the Tunnels. The first object of XVth Corps, commanded by General Christison,* was to capture this area. 26th Division, which after the end of the first campaign stayed in the line throughout the monsoon of 1943, was relieved by 5th Indian Division under General Briggs—newly arrived from the Middle East—which took over the Mayu range and the plain to the sea; and by 7th Indian Division, under General Messervy, which took the inland sector to the east across the river. Our forward positions were on the approximate line Bawli Bazaar–Goppi Bazaar. 81st West African Division was sent wide to the east into the Kaladan valley to protect our flank and to distract the enemy's attention to that area. On the main front the first major task was the construction of a road to take tanks and medium artillery across the Ngakyedauk Pass, the completion of which very much simplified the maintenance of 7th Division, and enabled one division to reinforce the other.

On 30 December 1943 4/7th Rajputs, of 5th Division, launched the opening attack on the Razabel fortress—which guarded the western end of the enemy's line—with an assault on one of the outpost positions.

> The two leading companies crossed the *chaung* without incident. No sooner had they started to climb towards Point 124 than the Japanese opened fire with mortars and small arms. The resistance was fierce, the enemy well dug in, and our own guns hampered by the proximity of the men to the target, and by the thick undergrowth on the slopes. Though the rest of the battalion crossed the *chaung* by midday they found themselves pinned to the ground unable to advance. More than ninety casualties had been suffered.

> They attacked Point 124 continuously for the next six

* General Sir Philip Christison, G.B.E., C.B., D.S.O., M.C.

days. On several occasions the leading sections reached the triple fence of barbed wire round the top trenches before being driven back down the slope by the hand grenades that the Japanese lobbed at them. Each little scrub-covered hilltop had rings of trenches dug round the summit, and each was covered by the fire of at least one machine gun from another hillock.

A policy of strangulation, starvation and attrition was adopted, but it was not until January 7 that the enemy positions were found to be abandoned. The Japanese had slipped away by night; the sounds of their retreat were covered by the wind and the teeming rain. (22)

The division was now in a position from which it was possible to work round the flank of the enemy position and capture Maungdaw.

On January 6 the West Yorkshires set out, prepared to cross the *chaungs* that barred the way to Maungdaw. 'A' company led the way to where a number of folding boats had been assembled. The men embarked and propelled themselves to the far bank, using the boats as a ferry service. The boats were hauled out of the water, saturated by the first crossing and now doubly heavy, and were carried across two miles of paddy fields to a second chaung. (22)

Very little opposition was met and they chased the 'few remaining Japanese out of Maungdaw'.

Maungdaw presented the grim spectacle of a derelict town. Grass grew over the warped verandahs; half-ruined shacks stood side by side with more solid brick buildings that had been robbed of doors and windows. In every corner among the piles of rubble and fallen beams lay perished rubber gas masks and the oozing contents of food tins that had burst. A little way downstream stood the mouldering steamer station, with its wooden piers bleached by the sun, its little red tin hut rusted and empty, and the muddy water lapping at the green slime level. (22)

And it was of course the steamer station we were after. The divisional engineers rapidly cleared the port of mines, repaired the steamer berths and very soon afterwards 'much of the maintenance of XVth Corps rattled over its ramshackle wharves'. (71)

The battle for Razabel went on.

On 28th January the Dogras attacked 'Wrencat', and its little neighbour 'Wrenkitten' without success. The jungle had been dense bamboo, but the ravages of artillery, mortars and dive bombers had transformed the hillside into one great sand dune, bare and precipitous on certain approaches. The Dogras had virtually to pull themselves up the hill by the remaining bamboo stumps, always in the face of savage fire . . . Major Ghulam Qadir led four separate attacks and won the Military Cross. Again and again the little Dogras climbed slowly up 'Wrencat', through the black smoke of showers of grenades. Each time the men no sooner reached the top than the enemy on the neighbouring hillocks opened fire with mortar and machine-gun and forced them off. (22)

The R.A.F. had been giving close support to these attacks but their bombing was not sufficiently accurate, and even a direct hit by the heaviest bomb had little effect. We had not yet found the answer to the bunker. It was accordingly decided to leave Razabel alone for the time being and to switch the weight of the corps attack across the Mayu range to 7th Division. Over the Ngakyedauk Pass went the medium guns, the tanks of 25th Dragoons, and 9th Infantry Brigade to relieve a brigade of 7th Division which was to pull out of the defences for the attack on the eastern fortress.

At this moment the Japanese launched their all-out attempt to encircle and destroy XVth Corps. Intelligence reports had for some time indicated that the enemy was sending considerable reinforcements to the whole Burma Command and the greater part of a second division was now thought to be in the Arakan. Certain precautionary moves had accordingly been made: 26th Division, in reserve about Chittagong, had been warned that they might be needed, and in a hurry; 36th British Division was coming down from India to replace them; and the air supply units at the airfields east of Calcutta were warned to begin their prearranged programme of packing, and stand by for twenty-four hour working. For all that the strength and depth of the attack, when it came, took everyone by surprise. On 4 February, leaving no more than the smallest force necessary to protect Akyab and to contain our troops deployed against the Maungdaw–Buthidaung position, the Japanese under cover of the morning mist managed to pass nearly two brigades round our left between 7th and West African Divisions. This force captured Taung Bazaar nearly ten miles behind our forward troops, sent a detachment still further west astride the road running south from Bawli Bazaar, and then turned the main weight of its attack against the road over the Ngakyedauk Pass and the rear of 7th Division's brigade areas. It did in fact completely cut that division off from all communication except by air.

The Japanese conception was voiced by General Sakurai when he said: 'As they have previously suffered defeat, should a portion of them waver the whole of them will get confused and victory is certain': unfortunately for Sakurai none wavered.*

Their plan was based on two assumptions that did not materialize: the first was that 7th Division would run true to British form, abandon their positions, and make their way as best they might back to Chittagong, leaving supplies, weapons and ammunition to fall into enemy hands; the second, which followed from the first, was that they need bring no more than ten days' supplies with them. When the first assumption went wrong, so did the second, and when the end of ten days found

* *Golden Arrow: The Story of the Seventh Indian Division* (23).

287

them with their object still unfulfilled, they were facing disaster.

Air supply came into operation almost without a hitch, and thanks to the gallantry and devotion of the aircrews who flew in to drop their loads by day in face of fighter opposition, or by night to avoid it, the division never lacked any essential article of supply right up to the time when the battle was won.

The Japanese attack overran 7th Divisional headquarters but the commander and most of the officers and men succeeded in making their way back to the Admin Box, the centre of the large area where the division's reserves of ammunition and other stores were located. It lay in and around an open area of dried paddy-fields, surrounded by low hills 100 to 200 feet high, covered in dense evergreen jungle. The bulk of the garrison consisted of administrative units of all types—workshops, animal and mechanical transport, supply, ordnance and medical units and stretcher-bearers.

Protecting the Box was part of 24th Light A.A. Regiment, but they were reinforced by two batteries of Indian Mountain Artillery, two squadrons of 25th Dragoons and three companies of the West Yorks. These last of course belonged to 5th Division; they were ordered to the scene at the very last moment when divisional headquarters was known to have been overrun, and the commander of 9th Brigade, Brigadier G. C. Evans,* was made responsible for the defence of the Box and remained in command throughout the fourteen days of the siege. The following day there arrived also part of 4/8th Gurkhas and of 6th Medium Regiment R.A. There is accordingly the embarrassing choice between the two divisional histories, the 7th, whose Box it was, and the 5th who were largely responsible for its defence.

The first heavy attack was made that night when the enemy penetrated the perimeter and, before being driven out, ruthlessly shot or bayoneted nearly the whole of the staff and patients of the main dressing station.

During the night of 8th/9th the enemy had succeeded in

* Lieutenant-General Sir Geoffrey Evans, K.B.E., C.B., D.S.O.

infiltrating with man-handled mountain guns on to a feature on the perimeter, and as soon as it became light opened fire at point-blank range. Their main target was the artillery dump which was set on fire. The enemy guns were soon silenced by our artillery and they and their escorting infantry driven off by counter-attack, but the damage had by then been done; a series of explosions started which went on for hours, making a large part of the area uninhabitable and setting fire to the grass. It was for a time a very ugly situation and there were many un-recorded deeds of cool courage in dealing with it.

From now on till the end of the siege, never a day or night passed without an attack on some part of the perimeter, while enemy artillery kept up continual harassing fire. Every shell landed somewhere in the Box, which was an unmissable target, and though the shelling caused surprisingly few casualties it was, as may be imagined, extremely unpleasant.

From the 10th till the 12th, attack after attack was made. Many of them succeeded in reaching vital hill features overlooking the Box. Each time after a hurricane bombardment by all the available artillery, including heavy anti-aircraft and Bofors guns at point-blank range, and supported by tanks of the 25th Dragoons, the West Yorks went in with the bayonet.

The most dangerous of these attacks was one which captured Artillery Hill, a small but very vital feature held by a composite force of men from various artillery units. At its re-capture were evolved the beginnings of a new technique in tank and infantry co-operation which in months to come was to prove decisive against Japanese suicide squads fighting from positions tunnelled into jungle-covered hillsides.

The 25th Dragoons set to work with high-explosive shells with instantaneous fuse, which stripped the jungle, laying bare the enemy defences, which were then attacked with high-explosive shells with delay-action fuses. As the infantry closed in, solid shot replaced H.E. and such was the accuracy of the fire that the infantry were able to close up on the steep hillsides to within ten to fifteen yards and rush to positions with bayonet and grenade the moment the tanks lifted the fire of their guns and machine-guns. (23)

Although by the nature of things, the ordeal in the Box was the most severe, very much the same events were going on elsewhere in the other defended localities which were standing fast; but so long as they stood fast the enemy had lost the battle. 26th Division came pressing down from the north, 5th Division spared 123rd Brigade to attack the Ngakyedauk Pass from the south, and the dominating Sugar Loaf that overlooked the Box was captured by 2/1st Punjab Regiment on the 22nd.

The troops made a wide and precipitous detour in order to approach from the north. Two parties of Japanese were routed on the way, and many enemy dead found in the jungle proved how effective our bombing and shelling had been. When Sugar Loaf was reached the Japanese offered no resistance. They had fled after a dive-bombing attack and on hearing the distant war cries of 'Allah ki jai!'

The siege of Ngakyedauk was at an end. The Pass had been opened. At two o'clock General Briggs rode up to the command post in a tank, bringing bottles of whisky. And Lomax's* 26th Division from the north had gained touch with the defenders in the Box. (22)

'The hammer and the anvil squarely met and the Japanese disintegrated.' Characteristically, the Japanese persisted in their efforts long after they had overshot the limit of possible success and they paid the penalty. Of the 7,000 men who had struck behind our lines, 5,000 bodies were found and counted; there can have been but a handful of survivors.

* Major-General C. E. N. Lomax, C.B., C.B.E., D.S.O., M.C.

The enemy was given no respite; after no more than a few days to pick up the threads, both 5th and 7th Divisions were again attacking the fortresses on the line of the Tunnels. The renewed attack on Razabel came in from the south as well. Using the new technique of close tank support the honour of leading the attack went to 4/7th Rajputs.

> Never were the faces of Indian Infantry set with such determination. They were out to capture and avenge. But the enemy had realised his untenable position. He was surprised by the encirclement. And during the night he evacuated the fortress.
>
> When the battle was over the scene was one of devastation. Some Japanese bunkers had been smashed to rubble and splintered timber by the bombing. But others had not been touched, or else their depth had saved them from wreckage. Inside the hill the enemy had hollowed out an immense cavern, used for a dressing station, and at one place was a corridor with openings at each end to enable a gun to be fired in both directions. (22)

The Dogras too, had their revenge on Wrencat:

> And with a dash and determination made almost reckless by their anger at having failed twice, the Dogras rushed in to the attack, shouting their war cries in the moonlight and appearing out of the mist with such suddenness that the Japanese turned and fled. (22)

No one is better qualified to sum up the results of the fighting than the army commander:

> This Arakan battle, judged by the size of the forces engaged, was not of great magnitude, but it was, nevertheless, one of the historic successes of British arms. It was the turning-point of the Burma campaign. For the first time a British force had met, held, and decisively defeated a major Japanese attack, and followed this up by driving the enemy out of the strongest possible natural

positions that they had been preparing for months and were determined to hold at all costs. British and Indian soldiers had proved themselves, man for man, the masters of the best the Japanese could bring against them. (71)

Set against the background of his strategy for Burma as a whole the Japanese object in the Arakan had been to distract our attention from his preparations for his advance on the Assam front, and, if not to destroy, at any rate to tie down reserves that might be switched northwards. It was a near thing but, thanks to the R.A.F. and U.S.A.A.F. transport squadrons, he did not succeed in either object. The Japanese advance in Assam began on 8 March; on the twelfth 5th Division was still fighting hard in the Tunnels area; and on the twenty-seventh their leading troops began to arrive in Imphal.

25th Indian Division (Major-General Davies*), which had been training in the Mysore jungles, relieved 5th Indian Division, and shortly afterwards 7th Division was also withdrawn into reserve at Chittagong and eventually sent to Assam. The final clearing of the Tunnels area was carried out by 26th and 25th Divisions. With the battle raging around Imphal there was clearly no prospect of anything but local offensives in the Arakan, so 26th Division was again withdrawn to Chittagong to train for combined operations while 25th Division remained in the line through the monsoon.

XVth Corps tasks for the cold weather in 1944 and 1945 were to advance and seize Akyab island, where the airstrips were needed to shorten the haul for aircraft flying on maintenance tasks for Fourteenth Army as it advanced towards Rangoon. 25th Division was to advance along the Mayu peninsula, with 3rd Commando Brigade acting in very close co-operation. They were opposed by the remnants of the Japanese *54th Division*, totalling less than 2,000 men. 82nd West African Division was to move down the Kaladan river to cover the left flank, and had facing them the *Matsu* group

* Major-General H. L. Davies, C.B., C.B.E., D.S.O., M.C.

of all arms, equal to a weak brigade, whose task was to cover the final escape road back into Central Burma.

Under command of the African Division was 30th Indian Mountain Regiment. There had been numerous small encounters with the enemy and, on the night of 15 December, a section of 33rd Mountain Battery was in a forward company locality of 8th Gold Coast Regiment to counter enemy shelling that had been troubling the division. However at 10 p.m. the enemy put in a strong attack which continued for several hours. The guns were subjected to heavy fire from guns and mortars preliminary to an attack made by two enemy companies. Havildar Umrao Singh, who was in charge of one of the guns, 'so inspired his gun detachment with his personal example and encouragement to fight and defend the gun that they were able to beat off the attack with loss to the enemy. Though twice wounded by grenades in the first attack he again held off a second attack by skilful control of the detachment's small-arms fire, and by manning the Bren gun himself he fired at Japs who had got to within five yards' range'. He was seen in hand-to-hand combat with the enemy before the section was overrun, and when the position was later recaptured he was found beside his gun 'almost unrecognisable with seven severe wounds and ten dead Japanese beside him'. He was the first and only Indian mountain gunner to be awarded the V.C., and the only other rank of the Royal Regiment of Artillery to be so decorated in the years 1939–45.

With the experiences of the 1943 campaign in mind 25th Division planned to make the fullest possible use of sea communications. The flotilla—or, as the divisional history calls it, the regatta—assembled for the move of 53rd Infantry Brigade, was a triumph of improvisation and a tribute to the ingenuity of the divisional engineers. There were 100 powered folding boats and assault boats, another 150 craft from Inland Water Transport sources, and no fewer than 380 country craft. The brigade met an appreciable amount of opposition during its advance but

to belittle the difficulties which it experienced with its boats would detract from the fine achievements of this brigade. Through its tenacity of purpose and courageous enterprise it reached its final objective within the time appointed. The conception of the water-borne advance alone made possible the operation at the speed required.*

The Mayu peninsula was clear of the enemy by the end of the year and the battle for Akyab island was on. 'The Corps Commander, like King Xerxes at the battle of Salamis, took his seat on a high view-point overlooking the waters, and out at sea to the west could see a host of landing craft of all types approaching in neat formation; but the enemy had not waited.' (26) 25th Division occupied the island without firing a shot.

With the object of blocking the retreat of *Matsu* force which was being harried southwards by the West Africans, the division lost no time in clearing the mainland to the east, and after the capture, with the assistance of the Marine Commandos, of the Myebon peninsula thirty miles south-east from Akyab, the waterways the enemy had been using were effectively closed. He would now have to use the road leading east through the Arakan Yomas, and if that also could be stopped, his retreat would be finally cut off. The crucial point was at the village of Kangaw perhaps eight miles north-east of the beaches on the Myebon peninsula. The unexpected approach from the south was chosen, a distance of eighteen miles by water, and at 1300 hrs on 21 January 3rd Commando Brigade landed having achieved complete local surprise. The next day the leading battalion of 51st Brigade, 8th Battalion The Hyderabad Regiment, got ashore and they were joined with some difficulty, as the beach was waterlogged by a high tide, by a troop of Shermans of 19th Lancers. The flat paddy-fields were studded with small wooded hills which rose from 200 to 500 feet above the plain and dominated the landing place. The object now was to strike inland and cut the road, and it was at once obvious that the Japanese were going to fight for it. Without proper time for reconnaissance, the Hyderabad's first attempt to capture a feature called 'Duns' failed against an

* *The Arakan Campaign of the 25th Indian Division* (26).

unexpectedly powerful defence: 'the measure of their disappointment at their failure could be gauged by the fury of their subsequent onslaught'. From captured documents it became known that the enemy was holding the area with two battalions of infantry and an artillery regiment. On 31 January he made a desperate attempt to isolate 51st Brigade, who at high tide were virtually on an island but, after the most bitter fighting and considerable losses on both sides, he failed. 74th Brigade of the division was now brought up and landed to the north, capturing features which had been enfilading the attacks from the south. The battle was finally won after four weeks of continuous fighting.

> Enemy positions were almost fantastically strong, consisting of underground vaults from which tunnels led to infantry and artillery bunkers constructed of whole tree trunks, and a network of deep trenches and foxholes.
>
> There is no doubt that the enemy had been hit in an extremely vulnerable quarter. His defences all faced north except where 'Perth' and 'Melrose' covered the road as it swung east into the hills. He had spent many months preparing to meet a threat from this direction. (26)

By their choice of the unexpected approach the division had surprised the Japanese and won the decisive battle which ended enemy resistance in the Arakan.

After two more operations to capture islands to the south 25th Division was relieved by the West Africans and withdrew to India. In a farewell message the corps commander congratulated them on having to their credit 'the successful accomplishment of probably the most difficult combined operations any British Force has ever attempted'.

Now only 26th Division was left in the Arakan, training for its seaborne operation against Rangoon.

CHAPTER SEVENTEEN

Burma

January–September 1944

If the Japanese had been content to stand fast on what they had won in Burma, Fourteenth Army might well have secured the objectives set them for the first six months of 1944, but it is doubtful if they would have been all that much better off at the end of it. They would have gained the bridgeheads over the Chindwin but, at the cost of extending their lines of communication without having reached an area suitable for development as a new advanced base, they would have been fighting in a most unhealthy and highly malarious area, faced across the river by an unbeaten enemy administratively better placed than they were. It was the enemy's decision to advance which changed the whole picture and created the opportunity that General Slim, the army commander, and General Scoones,* who as commander IVth Corps would be fighting the battle, grasped with both hands.

As soon as the extent of the Japanese plans became apparent, it was clear that our existing dispositions were quite unsuitable for the conduct of the defensive battle.

17th Indian Division (Major-General Cowan) were down the Tiddim road fighting for local superiority in the Fort White area, 20th Indian Division (Major-General Gracey†)

---

* General Sir Geoffrey Scoones, K.C.B., K.B.E., C.S.I., D.S.O., M.C.
† The late Sir Douglas Gracey, K.C.B., K.C.I.E., C.B.E., M.C.

were similarly employed in the Yu valley at the end of the Tamu–Sittang road, while 23rd Indian Division (Major-General Savory*) were in reserve in the Imphal plain. They had been in the area since April 1942. Over most of the 600 square miles of this plain, the only level space between India and Burma, was spread a network of administrative units and installations sited entirely for convenience of working and with no thought that they might be attacked by the enemy from the ground. There was a gap of some eighty miles of wild, tangled, jungle-covered hills between the two forward divisions which were, in fact, out on a limb and positively asking to be cut off and defeated in detail. It was only too clear that, however hard we tried to stop him, the enemy would succeed in reaching the approaches to the Imphal plain in considerable strength.

It followed that there was everything to lose and little to gain from a series of delaying actions up the two roads, during which we should certainly suffer heavy casualties, in the defence of territory that we were going to lose anyway. The decision taken, then, was to abandon that ground and to fight with the corps concentrated on the eastern borders of the Imphal plain, where we could put to advantage our superiority in armoured units and in the air. But the prize at stake was something very much larger than just the repulse of the attempt to capture Imphal and Kohima. The enemy's plan must involve him in considerable administrative risks, and it was his practice to accept such risks; what we must do was to ensure that he paid the price for his temerity. We must repeat our recent success in the Arakan on a much wider scale—in other words, if we could hold out against his initial onslaught, he would become so weakened administratively that we could hope to inflict defeat on a scale that would open the road for a successful advance across the plains of Burma. The crux of the matter was that withdrawal, particularly before battle is joined, is a retrograde step in more senses of the word than one, equally unpopular with the politicians on one hand, and the forward troops on the other. Success would turn on the timing:

---

* Lieut.-General Sir Reginald Savory, K.C.I.E., C.B., D.S.O., M.C.

not to concede territory until it became essential to do so, but not to delay doing so to the point where our troops ran the risk of being cut off.

The Japanese plan was for the *33rd Division* in the south to attack up both the roads in an attempt to isolate our forward divisions and generally attract reserves in that direction. The attack on the Tamu–Palel road was to be pressed to secure the passage through to the plain of tanks and medium artillery. A fortnight later, when it was hoped that we should be well committed, *15th Division* was to move across country on Ukhrul and then turn west and cut the road to Kohima and the outside world; whilst *31st Division*, moving even further to the north, was to attack and seize Kohima and, by preventing the arrival of reinforcements from India, hold the ring while the other two divisions closed the pincers on Imphal from north and south.

The Japanese *33rd Division* began to move at the very beginning of March and for the next five months there raged a battle in which the fury of the enemy was matched by our determination to prevent him from breaking into the plain. Although fighting was often in progress at one and the same time on all the approaches, for the all-too-brief record of this book it will be divided into five parts: the withdrawal of 17th and 20th Divisions from their forward positions; the repulse of the enemy *15th Division*'s attempts to break in north and north-east of Imphal; the siege and battle of Kohima; the battle on the Tamu–Palel road; and the fighting round Bishenpur. During this period the initiative was generally with the enemy. When he had failed in every one of these attempts, there followed the counter-strokes, pursued regardless of the fury of the monsoon and the extreme fatigue of our troops, when Fourteenth Army chased him down the Palel and Tiddim road, reduced his army to a battered wreck, and seized the crossings over the Chindwin which they were going to need for the advance into Burma in the closing months of the year.

On 9 March 17th Division was disposed with 48th Brigade forward of Kennedy Peak, 63rd Brigade behind it, and a detachment of two battalions back about milestone 126 watching the vital bridge over the Manipur River. That day a two-man patrol reported that 2,000 Japanese with guns and animals had crossed the river south of Vangte, but as no verification came in from other sources no action was taken. Events then moved very fast indeed; an enemy column appeared in the Tongzang area, and a second was reported west of milestone 109 where there was a supply dump on which the division was dependent. The withdrawal of 17th Division had been left too late, and when it did begin to move, on the afternoon of the fourteenth, the enemy had established no fewer than four road blocks, with layers of our own and Japanese troops sandwiched in between them.

The most northerly block was about milestone 100, and the corps commander, realizing the need to get the division back into the plain in good order if he was going to fight the battle according to plan, sent two brigades of 23rd Division down the Tiddim Road to help in clearing up the situation from the north.

When 37th Brigade reached Milestone 82 the brigadier found that he was fortunate enough to have anticipated the Japs, but he took one look at the throng of administrative units scattered for two miles along the road and decided that, once his troops were entangled in the mob, beset by rumours of immediate Jap attacks, they would not be extricated in a hurry. He selected a site for his base to the east of the road and there, as darkness approached, he waited for the arrival of somewhat greater protection than his small advanced party could provide. It was 2000 hours before 3/10 G.R. began to arrive after an exhausting day, for there is nothing much more tiring than being jolted from side to side for 110 miles in a tight-packed lorry. 3/5 G.R. were halted for the night 20 miles further back. While the battalion was still on the road the brigadier heard from the general that a company of the Jats (machine gun battalion) was being hard pressed at Milestone 100 and was to be relieved 'at all costs', so he stopped 3/5 R.G.R. to give them time for rest before they were sent straight through tomorrow.*

* *The Fighting Cock: The Story of the 23rd Indian Division, 1942–47* (25).

Next morning 3/5th R.G.R.

reached the Jats when they were almost at their last gasp;
they had been forced to relinquish part of their perimeter
that lay west of the road, ammunition was short and they
must have been overwhelmed during the coming night.
Even after the arrival of the Gurkhas, the position was
dangerous unless the enemy could be thrust back, for he
lay very close to the road.

It was 1730 hrs and an hour of daylight remained to
eject the Japs when 'B' company formed up for their first
battle. A quarter of an hour later the leading platoon
assaulted across the road covered by the Jat machine guns.
The Japs met the attack with all the fire they could bring
to bear. As the Gurkhas began to close upon the enemy,
their losses from machine-gun fire and grenades mounted
until over half the platoon were casualties and the survivors pinned. Without hesitation the company commander, who was conspicuous throughout the action for
his example, ordered his second platoon into the attack.
The determination of the Gurkhas carried the day.
The perimeter was restored.

This apparently insignificant encounter was of decisive
importance. Had the Gurkhas arrived a few hours later,
the Jats would have been eliminated and the road cut
beyond breaching except by a major operation. (25)

It is a fair comment. If such an operation had become
necessary, the battle would have started on the wrong foot and
the initiative might never have been wrested from the enemy.
There was equally savage and determined fighting at all the
blocks as the enemy struggled to consolidate his advantage
and prevent 17th Division from reaching the plain. Of the
final encounter before they broke through, the 5th Gurkha
history records:

It was a real soldier's battle. The opposing sides were too
close to each other to allow of supporting fire from the
rear and the battle was fought out man to man. Their

advance stopped by an overwhelming fire, the Gurkhas not only refused to give up what they had gained: they refused to accept enemy dictation. Despite the fire they continued to worm their way forward, individually, in pairs and small groups, making use of every accident of the ground, every blade of grass even, never for one moment relaxing their pressure; for three hours their pressure mounted grim and remorseless until finally it succeeded. (65)

20th Division had plenty of excitement in their withdrawal but on the whole it went according to plan. Owing to a late change of plan by one of the brigades, two battalions were at one stage cut off and lost most of their transport, but they fought their way back in good order and the division was successfully concentrated about Shenam and Tengnoupal some ten miles forward from Palel. It was to have its fill of fighting before the battle for the plain was over.

When the Japanese *15th* and *31st Divisions* began to move, the situation at once became serious because of the surprise they achieved by moving so wide to the flank, and in far greater strength than either Fourteenth Army or IVth Corps had foreseen. In reinforcing 17th Division to extricate it from the blocks along the Tiddim road, the corps commander had had to draw on his reserve division, 23rd, to such an extent that he had available for the defence of the important communication centre at Ukhrul—where supply dumps had been established —no more than one battalion of 49th Brigade, reinforced by 152nd Indian Parachute Brigade which by great good fortune was at Kohima engaged in jungle training. The brigade had with it 15th Mountain Battery, the mortar troop of 581st Field Battery and a small sapper detachment. Initially the brigade located one battalion forward, dispersed over a considerable frontage and watching the tracks from the east. It repulsed an attack made by a complete Japanese battalion with considerable artillery support, inflicting over 400 casualties, but with the enemy moving wide to the flank and occupying the town of Ukhrul itself, there was no option but to concentrate the brigade further back, where on 22 March a perimeter was established for determined resistance.

The site at Sangshak had two serious disadvantages; there was little or no water, and any attempt to dig trenches struck rock less than three feet below the surface. For four days and nights the small force resisted the enemy attacks.

> Attack was followed by counter-attack by day and by night and although part of the perimeter was overrun that held by the Mahrattas remained at all times firmly held despite the many casualties sustained. When part of the perimeter of another battalion was overrun, leaving in an exposed position the two 3-in mortars of the detachment he was commanding, Havildar Sambhaji Bhuingde jumped from his emplacement and, ignoring heavy fire coming down in the area, organised his mortar numbers in a position of all-round defence, whilst setting an example by firing his rifle and hurling grenades, thus saving his mortars and staving off a complete debacle. Although shot through the chest he continued while lying on the ground and in great pain to encourage the efforts of his men. (53)

Owing to the confined space within the perimeter casualties from artillery and mortar fire were very heavy and after four days' fighting there were nearly 300 casualties lying in shallow slit trenches or in the open. On the twenty-fifth No. 2 gun of the mountain battery had a duel over open sights at 3,000 yards with an enemy gun and silenced it. 'This gave intense pleasure to the infantry.' In an attempt to clear a gun position that had fallen into enemy hands both battery commanders were killed in hand-to-hand fighting, but the No. 1 of the gun, who had been stunned, emerged from the bottom of a trench, seized the ramrod and slew seven or eight of the enemy, and the position was recaptured.

On the evening of the fourth day there was a wireless message in clear from 23rd Division: 'Fight your way out. Go south and west. Air and transport on look-out for you.' The breakout was made that night through the south face of the perimeter with little interference from the enemy, and although about a hundred of the most seriously wounded had to be left behind, many more were brought away. The guns were stripped of essential parts which were carried away by the detachments, and shells were rammed down the barrels 'fore and aft'.

The battery commander's report concludes:

> 2230 hrs. The battery with its walking wounded marched out in a solid block behind 152 Battalion. The Nagas were very friendly and provided guides throughout the journey. (34)

The party consisted of a British officer, two V.C.O.s and forty-three men and they 'plodded on through the jungle without food for four days before reaching the main road'. No one will quarrel with the opinion expressed by their historian that 'the exploits of 15th (Jhelum) Mountain Battery on this occasion are among the best recorded in the Mountain Artillery'. (34)

The brigade had arrested, from 19 to 26 March, the advance of the bulk of the enemy *15th Division* and the left column of *31st Division*; it had delayed the cutting of the Imphal road; and had gained invaluable time for reserves to reach Kohima and Imphal.

After the capture of Sangshak the Japanese lost no time in moving west to cut the main road and threaten Imphal itself, where the second brigade of 5th Division had just flown in from the Arakan. We were forced to abandon the scattered base area at Kanglatongbi, about forty miles north of Imphal, but when they attacked the hill Nunshigum, which offered direct observation over Imphal airfield at a range of five miles, it was time to halt their advance. The hill had been held by a single company of 3rd Battalion The Jat Regiment, which was overwhelmed in a night attack by a superior force, though a counter-attack by another company of the battalion restored the situation. They held out for two more days against a further assault by a complete Japanese battalion, but then they could do no more. The hill was then recaptured by 1st

Battalion The Dogra Regiment, supported by two squadrons of 3rd Carabiniers in 30 ton Lee tanks. After a close support bombardment by three squadrons of Hurricanes, and concentrations fired by the whole divisional artillery, two companies of the Dogras moved off.

At 10.30 a.m. on the morning of the 13th April, the tanks of B Squadron inched their way at one mile an hour up the steep scrub-covered slopes which led to the summit of Nunshigum one thousand feet above them. So acute was the angle of ascent that the task looked impossible and, since the drivers were unable to see the ground in front of them, individual tank commanders had to direct them and were compelled to expose their head and shoulders in doing so. Around the tanks the men of the Dogra Regiment toiled upwards in the great heat, while aircraft of the Royal Air Force hurtled out of the cloudless sky on the enemy positions above.

An hour elapsed before the tanks and infantry reached the near edge of the summit and here they were met by a murderous fire. A knife-edge ridge made it possible for only one tank to move forward at a time and so narrow was the way that one tank reared up and disappeared down the precipitous slope.

Hand to hand fighting ensued with tank commanders, again with head and shoulders clear of the turret, hurling grenades and firing their revolvers at the Japanese trying to close with them.

One by one these gallant officers and non-commissioned officers fell back inside their tanks dead or mortally wounded. The Squadron Commander, Major Sanford, whose father commanded the Regiment many years before, was among the first to be killed.

In a short space of time only one tank-commander remained alive—Squadron Sergeant-Major Craddock—while in the two companies of the Dogra Regiment all the British officers were casualties and Subedar Ranbir Singh had assumed command.

In this critical situation these two courageous men

made their plans together and, after further fierce fighting of over an hour, their efforts met with success. The enemy fled leaving over two hundred and seventy dead on the hill top.

This account of the battle is taken from the citation which is read to The Carabiniers when they parade each year 'to commemorate the battle of Nunshigum'. The squadron commander of 'B' Squadron reads the citation, and the squadron parades without its officers, being commanded by the squadron sergeant-major.

The colonel of the regiment records that after this action the regiment was assigned a company of 1/4th Bombay Grenadiers for protection against snipers.

The most intimate and close relationship was built up between the tank crews and the sepoys of the Grenadiers. I believe it was quite unusually close despite difficulties of language, even to the extent of feeding from the same mess-tin or arranging suitable 'burra khanas' (special dinners) in bivouacs.

After 5th Indian Division, newly arrived from the Arakan, had fought the battle of Nunshigum, 23rd Division took over the responsibility for watching the northern flank. There were grounds for supposing that the Japanese *15th Division* was feeling the strain, so they sent their 1st Brigade north towards Sangshak, where 'they chased divisional headquarters through the jungle'. After a hard battle fought by the Seaforths, 1st Patiala Infantry attempted to capture an adjacent village. After some initial success the enemy counter-attacked:

. . . there was no time to take up fire positions; the company commander charged with his reserve at the on-coming Japs; he fell in a hand-to-hand grapple, but his action checked the enemy for the moment. Five minutes later the Jap came again farther down the ridge and was held by 'B' company; a nine minute interval and he came

a third time between 'B' company and battalion headquarters. Colonel Balwant Singh did not hesitate; as one
of his officers had done a few minutes earlier, he charged
magnificently into the fray at the head of his H.Q. The
Japs were halted at last. The Patiala account of this
tremendous affair runs: 'Balance of the battle from
1425 to 1455 hours simply hanged round the gutts, it
was anybody's battle during this time'. (25)

To the north the Japanese *31st Division*, moving even wider to
the flank, was closing in on Kohima. The little town lies

among the hills five thousand feet above the sea, surrounded by precarious cultivation on terraced slopes. The
villages had been built on promontories, and to those who
had just hurried from the bright heat of Arakan this
beautiful land of wooded hills hardly seemed to be a
potential battle-field. It was hard to convince yourself
that this arrival in Kohima was not the beginning of a
hard-earned leave on the edge of the Himalayas. You saw
a village perched on the very peak of a sharp ridge, and
built substantially of timber with red corrugated iron
roofs. From afar the Nagas, with prodigious calf muscles,
could be seen trotting up the steep paths, with their loads
supported by a band across the brow. (22)

To the casual eye Kohima did not differ vastly from any
other small staging post on a line of communications, but it
sprawled along the dominating ridge where the road climbed
up from the railhead and base at Dimapur, and then dropped
eastwards to the Imphal plain. Geographically, it was the keystone of the whole Japanese plan: block the road there, they
argued, the road block to end all road blocks, and IVth Corps
in the plain below, cut off from reinforcements and supplies,
could not hope to hold out against the attacks of *15th* and *33rd
Divisions*. They closed the road, but success did not yield the
major advantages which they had hoped for. They completely
miscalculated the extent of the air lift which not only brought

5th Indian Division up from the Arakan before the battle had really started, but also kept IVth Corps supplied with ammunition and essentials throughout the long four months that it remained cut off.

It was perhaps typical of their mentality that they stuck rigidly to their plan and failed to take the final risk of all: to leave a brigade to watch Kohima and press on with the rest of the division into the plain to capture Dimapur. It was a move that might well have been decisive.

Failing to appreciate the possibility that a complete Japanese division would move so wide and so deep, Fourteenth Army had done very little to provide a garrison for Kohima, and nothing at all for Dimapur. The stand by the Parachute Brigade at Ukhrul and Sangshak had delayed the enemy for ten days; all that now confronted the *31st Division*

> was one battalion, the newly formed Assam Regiment, with detachments of the Assam Rifles, the local armed police, pushed out some thirty miles to the east, to cover the approaches to Kohima. The main weight of the enemy advance fell on this battalion, in the first battle of its career. Fighting in its own country it put up a magnificent resistance, held doggedly to one position after another against overwhelming odds, and in spite of heavy casualties, its companies although separated never lost cohesion. The delay the Assam Regiment imposed on the Japanese Division at this stage was invaluable. (71)

At Kohima desperate efforts were in hand to clear back the non-combatants and hospital patients, to organize convalescents and those who could fight into units, and to work on the defences. In the last days of March, when the whole of the enemy *31st Division* was about fifteen miles away, 161st Brigade of 5th Division completed its fly-in from the Arakan, and reached Dimapur. It was at once sent up the road to Kohima but, owing to an unfortunate confusion as to the relative importance of the two places, it was ordered back to Dimapur, and then sent forward again. In consequence, only the leading battalion, 4th Battalion The Royal West Kent

Regiment, actually joined the garrison. The other two battalions formed a defensive box at Jatsoma two miles short of the town, harbouring 24th Mountain Regiment which gave invaluable support during the siege. The enemy now cut the road twice; between Jatsoma and Kohima, and again west of Jatsoma, and it was a fortnight before relief arrived from 5th Infantry Brigade, the leading brigade of 2nd (British) Division which had been rushed up from South India.

The garrison, apart from The Royal West Kents, numbered under 3,000 men; some were non-combatants, others had already been fighting in the rearguard actions which had delayed the enemy to the east of the town. Ranged against them was a complete division, which in the fourteen days of the siege put in twenty-five major attacks. Inevitably the space inside the perimeter grew smaller as the days passed.

Of the wounded, sniped, shelled, and mortared as they were in their all too shallow trenches, many were killed or wounded a second time. Some lay in individual trenches, and some in pits that held half-a-dozen wounded soldiers. The small operating theatre which was to receive two disastrous direct hits, lay in an open dugout, covered by a tarpaulin. Here John Young and his surgeons, whose numbers dwindled as a result of the shelling, carved, chopped, hacked, stitched and healed men. And they gave of their best to cheer them and inspire them, even when the days and nights seemed black beyond compare. (22)

The water ration was half a mug a man a day.

When the second brigade of 2nd Division, the 6th, arrived, 161st Brigade was released to relieve Kohima, and on 18 April 1st Battalion 1st Punjab Regiment, supported by tanks, cleared the road up to the hospital and joined the garrison.

And the old comradeship between British and Indian soldier was heartening; the battered hillside rang with shouts of 'Shabash, Royal West Kents!' from the

Punjabis, and 'Good old Johnnie, everything teak hi now, eh?' from the British. (22)

Four days later 6th Brigade took over the defences from the garrison, but the greater part of the ridge remained in enemy hands. They held an immensely strong position, the natural strength of which had been reinforced by cleverly concealed field-works, 7,000 yards long astride the road, both flanks resting in high and difficult country. 2nd Division was faced with a formidable obstacle and it took them another six weeks to overcome it; and, but for the valiant resistance put by the small original garrison, it would have taken even longer. The next three weeks of desperate fighting at Kohima belong to 2nd Division who had four brigade commanders killed or badly wounded. There was little in terms of ground gained to show for all their gallantry and determination, but the enemy had given up his counter-attacks, a sure sign that his losses, and the precarious administrative situation behind him, were beginning to tell. About the middle of May, 7th Indian Division arrived by air from the Arakan and one brigade was placed under command of 2nd Division for a renewal of the attack. 1st Battalion The Queen's Regiment and 4th Battalion 15th Punjab Regiment were the leading battalions, preceded by the

most terrific artillery concentration imaginable. After twenty minutes the concentration ceased and the assault went in. It was magnificent. Through the smoke-screen which the gunners were putting down during the initial assault the leading companies stormed the first bunkers, firing from the hip as they went in. The Japs fought back desperately. It had seemed that no living thing could remain on the two hills after that mighty bombardment, and it testifies to the efficiency of the enemy's field works and to his tenacity and courage that he was able to survive and to defend his positions with such fierce determination. Fighting was now bitter and almost hand to hand. Seen from tactical headquarters what looked almost like a snowball fight was taking place on the west end of the crest. The snowballs however were not white; they were grey and burst, and when they burst men fell. . . . (23)

After the collapse of the enemy's resistance at Kohima, the pursuit was taken up by 2nd Division, with the tanks as the main striking force down the road, and 7th Indian Division moving through the country to the left of the road. General Slim remarks that this arrangement suited the peculiar characteristics of each, 'the ability of 7th Division to operate on pack transport away from roads': it is worth taking a closer look at what 'away from roads' meant.

2nd Division reported strong opposition to their advance along the main road, and it began to look as though the Japanese were pulling themselves together and that another spell of heavy fighting was imminent, unless 4/14th could turn the position quickly. Fighting patrols of company strength were employed in the search for a way round. These patrols had to slither down the steep mountain-sides to the valley bottoms, where the mon-soon-swollen streams made the going difficult and often dangerous, and then make their way south till the commander found a promising route to some feature which appeared likely to provide a base of operations in rear of the enemy. The patrol then had to climb laboriously up the mountain-side, often steep enough to necessitate the use of hands, hoping their progress had not been observed and that the enemy were not preparing an ambush for their reception. Apart from the terrific exertion involved, the great variation in temperature from the turkish-bath atmosphere of the valley bottoms to the cold, clammy mists of the mountain-tops was extremely trying, but eventually one of the patrols secured a suitable base and preparations for the attack were made. The enemy, however, quickly became aware of the threat and pulled out, leaving a small rear party which was wiped out with trifling loss to our troops. (23)

The Tamu–Palel approach was of particular significance to the Japanese as it was the only road by which they could hope to move the tanks and heavy artillery that they knew they would need to force a decision if they gained a footing on the Imphal plain.

> They attempted to break through Shenam Pass by frontal attacks supported by powerful artillery and medium tanks. The features known as Crete West and Scraggy now became the forward defences. They marked the limit of the Japanese advance on the Tamu–Palel road and were destined to be the scene of fighting during the next three months. There can have been few places during the war the possession of which, in proportion to their size, was more costly in human life. (7)

Two stories show how savage the fighting was.

> The Japanese, determined to make a final bid to reach Palel in strength, were throwing fresh troops into the battle. The biggest and most dashing attack of the campaign in this sector came on the night 24th May when the Japanese in a night attack stormed the Rajputana Rifle position on Gibraltar. With grenade and light machine gun fire the enemy first attacked 10 platoon of 'B' company and stormed the platoon position, killing or wounding eighteen men out of twenty one. The only survivors were Lance-Naik Karrora Ram and two others. Karrora Ram being desperate to save the situation asked Subedar Bhima Ram, the company second-in-command, for reinforcements. As there were no men to spare he had to return alone and man the machine gun. When he fired the enemy located him and opened fire. He sat tight the whole night making the enemy believe he was alive with his whole section. If this position had been taken 'B' company would have been forced to retire. (54)

On another occasion 1st Gurkhas were in the thick of it.

At about 0530 hours a new plot seemed to be hatching to
the accompaniment of much jabbering and waving of
swords. No. 7 platoon reported that a party of twenty men
were trying to place a Bangalore torpedo under the wire.
This was the most battered part of the perimeter where
ammunition and grenades were running low. The
platoon commander, Havildar Minbahadur Rana, saw
this at once and shaking off those who tried to hold him
back he seized two sand-bags full of grenades, found an
equal fire-eater in medical orderly Narbahadur Thapa
eager to help him, and led the way over the parapet to the
threatened wire. There standing up alone and fully exposed he flung grenade after grenade on the bunch of
crouching enemy.

Above the screams of the Japanese wounded and the
detonations of his own bombs he shouted orders to his
2-in mortar and brought his Bren guns to bear on the
enemy which he alone could see in the flashes of the
explosions. His last bomb thrown he was about to return
when he was struck down by a sniper's bullet and killed
instantly. Narbahadur picked off the sniper and, in
defiance of orders to get back under cover at once,
picked up and brought back the havildar's body. (61)

The story concludes that

by then the Madrassi signallers had at last managed to
get through by wireless after vainly trying for three hours
to summon help from the battalion. These men earned
everyone's praise, unmoved by the inferno, and imper-
turbable even when two percussion fuses, with shells
attached, penetrated their trench and hung perilously
over their heads. (61)

Very much in evidence also were those old friends of North
Africa and Cassino days, a detachment of the American Field
Service with their ambulances, who 'cheerfully insisted on
coming forward again and again beyond their true beat to
speed up the evacuation of casualties. They drove through

Japanese attacks and heavy shelling with their lights blazing and hooting defiantly'. (61)

The remaining major battle area was the junction of the Tiddim road and the Silchar track, about eighteen miles south-west of Imphal. After the successful withdrawal of 17th Division through the screen formed by 23rd Division, the enemy had found his advance up the Tiddim road blocked, and he turned his attention to an attempt to capture Bishenpur and the track junction by moving across country and coming in from the west. It was for him an attractive proposition, quite apart from the threat to Imphal itself for, if he could secure control of the track to Silchar, he could raid down into India and cut the railway line to Dimapur and Ledo. His *33rd Division* was deployed on this front, rated by our own 17th Division as by far the best he had, and there was much bitter fighting.

> Five thousand feet up on the Silchar track on what was christened Wooded Hill the Northamptons and 8th Gurkhas guarded the precious route which led to the plains of India. Here a company of the British battalion with 8th Gurkhas fought an incredible action at night, in which tanks, which had climbed 2,000 feet to a peak up a twisty and corkscrew track the last part of which was hewn out of solid bamboo jungle by Sappers, turned on their headlights to assist the defenders. The Japanese suicidal attacks were beaten off and the track safe-guarded.*

The 1/4th Gurkhas record

> that the Jap continued to fight desperately to secure the Silchar track but the battalion held on grimly to the ground it had gained and every attack was beaten off. The key point of the battalion's position was the Water Picquet. It became the objective of a number of attacks

* *History of the Gurkha Rifles* (68).

313

launched against it, night after night with scarcely any intermission. On the night of 12/13 May Water Picquet was once again attacked, but the enemy had given up all hope of taking it, and this last attack was but a feint to cover another more serious attack directed against Scrub Picquet. (64)

The attack succeeded and when the battalion counter-attacked three British officers were killed, the third actually on the wire, and the momentum of the attack was lost.

The battalion, its strength in officers sadly depleted, had almost reached the limit of its endurance. But so too had the enemy. His success on Scrub Ridge was stayed. (64)

The battalion was commanded at the time by Lieutenant-Colonel Wilfred Oldham, his substantive rank that of lieutenant. In an army where courage and competence were the hallmarks of a battalion commander he stood out perhaps for his youth, and for the remarkable hold he established over his officers and men. He was himself killed shortly afterwards and 'his death caused a deep sense of loss, and cast a gloom over the whole battalion'.

His death kindled a fresh determination in his men. They burned to avenge him. Evidence of this new temper was given by a patrol sent out soon after. Emerging on one occasion from the morning mists the men found themselves face-to-face with an enemy working party. Had they acted in accordance with orders they would have opened fire on the enemy and withdrawn, for they had been told not to allow themselves to be involved in battle. But there was no holding them. They charged straight in and in a hand-to-hand battle killed the lot. Nineteen Japanese bodies were left on the ground. (64)

The next phase saw an attempt by both 17th and *33rd* Divisions to surprise each other by bold strokes, either of which, if successful, would have had far-reaching results.

17th Division's plan was to send 48th Brigade wide down the road to establish a road block behind the enemy, and then crush him by moving the other two brigades down from the north. The road block was successfully established and was of course at once attacked. It was held by 1/7th Gurkhas.

> On four successive nights the enemy attacked our position with greater or less strength and on each occasion was driven off with loss. His most determined effort was made on the third night. Whether to intimidate us or to fortify himself, that night he filled the air with an eerie howling as he advanced repeatedly to the attack only to be beaten off. When at last dawn came he withdrew and over 100 dead were counted on the ground.
>
> The night's work which went so badly for the enemy ended in a strange finale. We had not long stood down when a Japanese officer appeared brandishing a weapon to which a bayonet was attached. Apparently disgraced and seeking death, he charged our wire as one demented and there, alone, paid the forfeit of failure. (67)

Despite the success achieved by 48th Brigade 17th Division found themselves thwarted when the enemy had put his own plan into operation. This was a last determined effort to break into Bishenpur, and the situation became so serious that the other two brigades, far from coming south to crush the enemy, had to be reinforced from outside to beat off the new threat. In the fighting round Bishenpur during June four men of the division won the V.C.: Sergeant Turner of the West Yorkshires who, when the enemy concentrated their fire on his platoon in the hope of breaking through, five times made personal and individual counter-attacks so that the enemy desisted and left a hundred dead upon the field; Rifleman Ganju Lama of 7th Gurkhas who, despite three wounds and a broken left arm, carried his PIAT* to within thirty yards of three enemy tanks, destroyed two of them, killed the crews and then went back for more bombs to deal with the crew of the

* Anti-tank weapon.

third tank which had been knocked out by an anti-tank gun.

But the palm must go to 5th Gurkhas, two of whose men won the award on successive days, in fighting which finally and for ever broke the enemy's attempts to capture Bishenpur. A feature known as Water Picquet was by then in enemy hands and a platoon of 5th Gurkhas under Subedar Netrabahadur Thapa was sent up to hold the adjacent Mortar Bluff. Starting at 8 p.m. that night the enemy attacked the position, which was subjected to point-blank fire from 57 and 37 mm guns. Just after midnight there was a second and heavier attack which put out of action most of the light automatics. The subedar:

> with tireless energy and contempt for danger moved from post to post encouraging the young N.C.O.s and riflemen of which the garrison was largely composed. In the morning he took the offensive armed with a kukri and grenades. He received a bullet wound in the mouth and shortly afterwards a grenade which killed him outright. His body was found next day, kukri in hand, with a dead Japanese with a cleft skull by his side. (65)

Mortar Bluff passed into enemy hands and the next day the battalion was ordered to retake it. Despite considerable covering fire the attack was halted short of the Bluff and the men were pinned down in the open. It was at that moment that

> Naik Agansing Rai, appreciating that more delay would inevitably result in heavier casualties, at once led his section under withering fire direct at the machine gun, and, firing as he went, charged the position, himself killing three of the crew of four. Inspired by this cool act of bravery his section surged forward across the bullet-swept ground routing all the enemy on Mortar Bluff. (65)

In the attack on Water Picquet he was again in the lead and 'his outstanding brave and gallant leadership so inspired the rest of the company that in spite of heavy casualties the rest of this important action was never in doubt'.

The loss of Mortar Bluff was decisive and on that day the enemy abandoned the offensive and ordered their leading regiment to withdraw.

On 5 March, just when the Japanese were starting the encircling moves which were to threaten 17th Division down the Tiddim road, Wingate's Special Force had flown into northern Burma to begin their operations against the lines of communication of the Japanese division facing Stilwell's forces coming south from Ledo; with orders also to create as much damage and confusion as possible in Northern Burma. The force was predominantly British and as such its exploits are really outside the scope of this book, but it included four Gurkha battalions, and the Indian drivers and mules of a section of mountain artillery. For the conditions under which it was going to fight it is possible that it would have been better balanced if the proportion of Indian troops had been greater, for a Gurkha battalion records that at one stage of their training they were required to attend for instruction a demonstration by a British battalion on the construction of shelters and the like from bamboos.

> Our men, with their innate good manners, watched the amateur efforts of their British comrades without comment, and then went off to build their own bashas with the skill born of long practice and familiarity. Here and later the Gurkha also demonstrated his uncanny skill in producing fire in all and any circumstances. Many British soldiers had occasion to bless our men for this when sodden wet and shivering they found a Gurkha would come over to them and in no time brew a can of hot tea.*

They stood up to the rigour of those operations just as well, and fought just as bravely, as the British element of the force,

---

* *Historical Record of 6th Gurkha Rifles* (66).

and for an example of their bravery pride of place must go to the engagement where a British officer and a rifleman of the 3/6th Gurkhas both won the V.C. The column to which they belonged towards the end of Special Force operations came directly under Stilwell who ordered them to 'strafe, assault, capture and hold' the town of Mogaung. This came as a shock as it was known that the town was strongly held and fortified with prepared positions, and the battalion was in no way organized for such a task. Later the whole brigade was detailed for the task. The most likely trouble spot was thought to be a brick building known as The Red House.

> The epic feat of arms of Captain Michael Allmand and Rifleman Tulbahadur was chiefly responsible for the successful outcome of the attack. Allmand (who had twice already shown very great gallantry in action) was suffering from trench feet which hampered his movements, but moving forward alone over muddy ground pitted with shell holes he charged a Japanese machine-gun position single-handed and fell mortally wounded.
>
> Tulbahadur's section was wiped out but for the section commander, himself and one other man. These three charged the Red House, but almost at once the section commander and the other rifleman were seriously wounded.
> Tulbahadur seized the Bren gun and continued alone against the enemy although in the dawnlight he presented a perfect target.
> He covered thirty yards of open ground still firing from the hip and closed with the enemy. He then gave covering fire which helped the rest of the platoon to reach its objective. (66)

Another force engaged on a long-range harassing role was the Lushai Brigade, commanded by Brigadier Marindin. It had been formed in a hurry from war-raised Indian battalions and local levies to watch the extreme right flank in the Lushai Hills. It had little equipment, no artillery or engineers, and only improvised signals, indeed there was a story that it had only one map. During the pursuit of the Japanese down the Tiddim road the army commander gave as its task 'completely to dislocate Japanese traffic on the road Tiddim–Imphal northwards, and render it useless to the enemy as a line of communication'. He later paid them this tribute:

> There is no doubt that the enterprise and dash of this improvised and light-hearted brigade was a very real contribution to the pursuit to the Chindwin. It had operated for six months on pack transport, supplemented by an unavoidably meagre air supply, across two hundred miles of jungle mountains, against the enemy flank and rear. Considering the paucity of its equipment and resources, it gave one of the most effective and economical examples of long-range penetration. (71)

One of the first actions that marked the passing of the initiative to Fourteenth Army was the recapture of Ukhrul by both 7th and 20th Divisions, after which 7th Division sent one brigade in pursuit towards the Chindwin.

> Rumours of a general, his staff, and elephants to the east were rife. Three Indian Mountain gunners, having been sent to intercept some Japanese walking down a track towards their position, pursued them for two miles, and after a brief interchange of shots, charged from the hip with Bren, tommy-gun and rifle, killing one, taking prisoner another. A Japanese officer and an N.C.O. after a suicide charge were captured by a patrol. Nagas started bringing in Japanese prisoners too sick to move, filthy skeletons, raving, weeping and gibbering in their madness, the ultimate resistance of their minds broken by the unspeakable hardships to which their bodies had been subjected.
>
> The case of the brigade sadly deteriorated, due to the arduous conditions encountered. Many men and officers were too weak to digest or retain their food, and very

many suffered from chronic diarrhoea, a legacy of the Arakan increased by the exertion of these operations. Rum fortunately was ample and for days on end officers, and those Indians whose religion permitted, lived on a diet of rum and milk, all they could manage. (23)

In August the task of pursuit on the Palel–Tamu road was taken over by 11th East African Division, while on the Tiddim road 5th Division relieved 17th. A comment by a battalion of the latter division shows just how necessary these reliefs were.

> The months of arduous service had told on the battalion. Lack of sleep, lack of nourishing food and any semblance of shelter in appalling conditions of rain and water-logged trenches had brought officers and men to the limit of endurance. Though more than willing to continue the fight they were worn out by fatigue and privation and all were in urgent need of rest. (67)

As the engineer resources did not permit both routes to be repaired and maintained simultaneously, preference was given to the Tamu route which would be used later to support the advance into Burma. 5th Division was therefore dependent entirely on air supply:

> What this regular air supply and support meant in skill and strain to the aircrews only those who have flown among these shrouded hills can judge. Yet throughout the whole of this monsoon the fighters of Air Marshal Vincent's 221 Group flew over our troops every single day. I do not think that such devotion has ever been surpassed in any air force, and I doubt if it has been equalled. (71)

The enemy resisted fiercely but he was kept on the run. One of the first real obstacles was the crossing of the Manipur River and, to take any resistance from the rear, 123rd Brigade was sent down a rough track on the east bank. When the

Mountain Battery O.P. in Burma

19TH INDIAN DIVISION TYPES

British infantryman

British officer of Indian infantry

opposite. A Japanese officer prisoner

Mule transport lines

Signalmen, 5th Indian Division

Indian Armoured Corps. Probyn's Horse and Rajput infantrymen

Q.V.O. Madras Sappers and Miners at Fort Dufferin, Mandalay, after
its capture

Collecting a supply drop—Mandalay Hill in the background

leading troops along the road arrived there was no enemy in sight.

To cross without the assistance of the Sappers was out of the question, so rapid and swollen was the torrent that swirled between the banks. Waves and small whirlpools broke up the surface, and even to those standing on the bank the river presented a frightening spectacle. Its roar was likened to that of a football crowd.

At first it seemed that no boat could cross without being smashed on the boulders round which the yellow-grey waters swirled angrily. But the initial crossing was made by Lieut. Cordon and eleven men in a folding boat. Then a single cable was thrown across the river by means of an attachment to a 3-inch mortar shell, and this line was secured by the men who had crossed by boat. A double cable was fastened to the end of the single one and hauled across. (22)

Later rafts were built, then bigger rafts, until four tanks were taken across in one hour.

The Sappers—Sikhs, Pathans, Punjabi Mussalman, Rajputs, Garwhalis—who operated the rafts had, as a safety precaution, to be lightly clad, in bare feet or gym shoes. In all ten men were drowned in the efforts to bridge this turbulent watercourse. (22)

But it was not till they reached the lower end of the road as they neared Kennedy Peak and Fort White among heavily wooded peaks of 6,000 feet and more that the division met really determined resistance.

For three weeks 2/1st Punjab Regiment were held up by a combination of a determined enemy and almost impossibly difficult country. Then at last, after a daring reconnaissance, the intelligence officer found a possible route and a company was sent to block the track, taking five hours to travel two miles. Next day the battalion attacked, 'D' Coy being responsible for a diversion to the flank. From the citation for the

posthumous award of the V.C. to Subedar Ram Sarup Singh
emerges the story of the fight.

The subedar led his platoon against a position of great
natural strength, with every approach covered by machine-
guns sited in bunkers. He at once charged the position, which
so bewildered the enemy that they fled, but he was wounded
in both legs. When the enemy counter-attacked he led a charge
against them. He was again badly wounded but he bayoneted
four Japanese and killed two more before he was mortally
wounded by machine-gun fire in the chest and neck. He died
exhorting his men to fight on.

That morning, before the battle, he had shaken hands with
his company commander and said 'Sahib, either the Japs or
myself today'. His action had a profound effect on his men,
and when volunteers were called for to bring in his body under
heavy fire, the entire company volunteered.

> A week later 3/2nd Punjab Regiment were unable to
> advance so they sent out two reconnaissance patrols to
> investigate the possibility of placing one company on each
> side of the corner and thus isolating the enemy posted
> there. Seen through glasses the approach to the objective
> seemed impossible even to the small patrol, let alone a
> company encumbered with ammunition, radio equipment
> and other stores. But both patrols were entirely successful
> and as a result of the information brought back it was
> decided to place the companies in position at dawn on
> 2nd November. During the night both companies bivou-
> acked 500' below their objective. The following morning
> 'A' Coy was the first to reach their objective. The
> men charged in with the bayonet and captured the
> position with the loss of four killed and four wounded.
> (52)

With pressure so brought against them from every angle,
and subjected to softening up by the R.A.F. and Mitchell
bombers of the U.S.A.A.F., the enemy could hold out no
longer and by 4 November we had taken Kennedy Peak and
driven them back to the river in confusion. On the thirteenth

a 5th Division patrol met a patrol from 11th East Africa Division and they entered Kalemyo together.

> In the course of its advance down the Tiddim road the division had killed 1,316 Japanese—fresh corpses counted on the ground. It had wounded 533, and had taken 53 prisoners. Our own losses during that period had been 88 officers and men killed, 293 wounded, and 22 missing. This had been an outstanding advance in the face of not only an enemy fighting a stiff rearguard action, over nearly 200 miles, but of very serious diseases, the worst furies of the monsoon, mud and steep places on a tortuous road, and a host of administrative difficulties. (22)

Shortly afterwards the division was flown out for a brief and well-earned rest at Imphal.

CHAPTER EIGHTEEN

Burma

October 1944–August 1945

While the clearing of the Imphal plain and its approaches was still going on, the planners at their various levels were busy with projects for the campaigning season from November until the monsoon began in the following May. There were two broad possibilities, with some variation of detail within each. The first was to concentrate on securing north Burma, but always with an eye on the main American purpose for doing so which was to increase the flow of aid to China. The second was to make a seaborne landing at Rangoon and recapture Burma from the south. This latter depended on the release, from the European theatre, of naval support, shipping and assault landing craft, and made heavier demands for supporting aircraft which would have to be diverted from the supply route to China. It did not find much favour with the Americans, who always suspected that our motives for re-capturing Burma were entirely imperialistic, and, when its advantages cames to be debated at the highest level—where these decisions were taken—it suffered somewhat from the fact that its advocate was the Prime Minister. Although altogether in favour of seaborne operations, Mr Churchill leant towards something far more ambitious than the landing at Rangoon for which he was briefed by his service advisers.

What eventually emerged in the form of a directive to the supreme commander, dated 16 September, was:

1. Your primary object is the recapture of all Burma at the earliest date. Operations to achieve this object must not, however, prejudice the security of the existing air supply route to China, including the air staging post at Myitkyina, adequate protection of which is essential throughout.

2. The following are approved operations:

(a) The stages of operation 'Capital' (Capture of Mandalay) necessary to the security of the air route and the attainment of overland communications with China;

(b) Operation 'Dracula' (Capture of Rangoon from the sea). The Combined Chiefs of Staff attach the greatest important to the vigorous prosecution of operation 'Capital' and to the execution of operation 'Dracula' before the monsoon in 1945, with a target date of 15th March.

3. If 'Dracula' has to be postponed until after the monsoon of 1945, you will continue to exploit operation 'Capital' so far as may be possible without prejudice to preparations for the execution of Operation 'Dracula' in November 1945. (7)

A month later, when the end in Europe was still not in sight, Dracula was abandoned as a possibility for the following spring, and replaced by a much smaller combined operation, Romulus, in the Arakan, designed to capture Akyab, Myebon and Minbya. This advance would dispose of the Japanese threat in the Kaladan valley, release forces for training for Dracula, and secure airfields for the support of the advance into central Burma.

It is worth contrasting the somewhat cautious terms of the directive—and it was a vast improvement on the first one dated two months earlier—with the interpretation the commander of Fourteenth Army put on the orders he received. The emphasis there rested on securing Burma down to a line Mandalay–Pakokku in conjunction with the American advance to Maymyo and Lashio; but if the Japanese armies were left in undisturbed possession of the country south of that line, they would in time recover from the beating they had just taken; then, with better communications behind them, they would have had the initiative in attacking from the flank our extended lines of communication running forward from Imphal. We might well have beaten off these attacks, but the outcome would still not have been decisive.

The crystal ball at Fourteenth Army headquarters had the picture in rather sharper focus. There was first of all the selection of the means by which the end was to be attained. The object which General Slim set before his army a year earlier had been not to re-occupy Burma but to destroy the Japanese army; the battle of Imphal was fought as the first step taken towards that object, and the commander now set himself the problem of how to complete that destruction. Until it was done the outcome would remain inconclusive; when it had been done all territorial gains would follow as a matter of course.

It is clear from *Defeat into Victory* that the problem General Slim always kept in mind was not how to capture Mandalay, but how to defeat the Japanese in battle. Further, assuming that the object of the exercise was to deliver warlike stores from America to China, why go on using the roundabout route by sea to Calcutta, some 1,300 miles over the Assamese railway system, only to start the long trail forward again by road from Ledo? How much more practical to open the port of Rangoon and have done with it! The book reveals the existence, as early as July, of 'an unofficial, private plan' for an advance south to Rangoon just as soon as Mandalay had been captured. It was known as 'Operation "Sob"—Sea or Bust'. The planners may well have failed to realize what a knock the enemy had taken; they may have been appalled by the logistic difficulties of an overland advance to Rangoon from the north; but they were lucky to be served by a commander who put such a very forthright interpretation on his orders.

General Slim's first choice of a battle-field was the Shwebo plain, north-west of Mandalay, where the open country would allow us to exploit the superiority we enjoyed in armour and in the air; there was also the advantage that the enemy would be fighting with his back to the loop formed by the junction of the rivers Chindwin and Irrawaddy. From his knowledge of his opposite number, General Slim felt that, despite this hazard, General Kawabe would stand and fight rather than surrender so much territory without a struggle. Planning accordingly went forward on that assumption; on the assumption also that the northern and Arakan fronts between them would do their part in drawing off their share of the enemy divisions available in Burma. Even so his army of one British and three and two thirds Indian divisions would be taking on over five Japanese divisions. He writes:

> A year ago I would not have looked at the proposal. Even now, it was not so much our advantage in the air, in armour, in greater mobility in the open, which gave me confidence to go on with my plan, but the spirit of my troops, my trust in their experienced commanders and in the high fighting value and hardihood of them all. (71)

Under the original plan XXXIIIrd Corps on the right, consisting of 2nd British and 20th Indian Divisions, was to cross the Chindwin at Mawlaik and Kalewa and move on Shwebo; IVth Corps with 7th and 19th Indian Divisions was to cross at Sittang and capture Pinlebu and then turn south on Shwebo. A brigade of 20th Division led the advance in the south, crossing through Mawlaik bridgehead on 3 December; the next day 19th Division in the north broke out at Sittang. 19th Division, the 'Dagger' division commanded by Major-General Rees, was new to battle—for nearly two years they had been training in the jungles of South India—and they were very much in the mood to win their spurs. On the sixteenth they captured Pinlebu, a rate of advance so rapid as to arouse the suspicions of the army commander. The Japanese rearguards had fought well but neither they, nor the positions they had occupied, indicated quite that determined resistance that might have been expected if *Fifteenth Army* was around Shwebo, where it was supposed to be. The question at once arose: were they there, or had they changed their plan?

Not surprisingly, vacancies had occurred among the Japanese

high command: Mutaguchi had been replaced by Katamura, commander of one of the divisions in Burma; and Kawabe at Burma Army Command had been recalled to Japan, his place taken by Kimura, about whom not a lot was known except that he had the reputation of being one of their best generals. Feeling, perhaps, that their personal copybooks were clear of the blots of the past eight months, the new commanders had taken a more objective view of the situation. They saw that if their army was to have a reasonable chance to recover, refit and absorb its reinforcements, it could only hope to do so if protected by the Irrawaddy; so the decision was made to withdraw south of the river and to dispute the crossings, with a division north-east of Mandalay, another at Sagaing, and a third at Pakkoku.

To crowd all his four divisions into the comparatively restricted triangle formed by the Chindwin and the Irrawaddy, and then to be faced with an opposed river crossing would clearly not achieve General Slim's object of destroying the Japanese army. There was just time to recast the whole plan while 7th Division was still west of the Chindwin.

> An opportunity becomes apparent. A few senior officers are summoned to a basha in the jungle, a short informal talk takes place, and almost within a matter of hours the first moves are made in a plan which in a few months was to destroy three Japanese armies. It sounds very easy, and it is too, provided you have the commanders able to see the chances and the skill and courage to seize them. (23)

What General Slim planned to carry out was a remarkable scissors-switch of his two corps. IVth Corps, leaving behind 19th Division and taking with it only 7th, passed behind XXXIIIrd Corps, moved up the Gangaw Valley—which climbs south from Kalemyo—and passed over the watershed at the southern end to debouch on the Irrawaddy roughly about Pagan. 7th Division's task then was to cross the river and establish a bridgehead from which 17th Division, still back in India resting, would break out to drive on Meiktila—

the Clapham Junction of all the Japanese communications in Upper Burma. There were two essentials for success. The first was deception and secrecy. These were achieved by means of a dummy headquarters from which IVth Corps ostensibly remained in control of 19th Division in the north, strict security measures, and, finally, a tight fighter cover by the R.A.F. over the Gangaw valley lest some intruding Japanese plane detecting a suspicious cloud of dust, and deciding to investigate it further, should spot tanks moving south in a place where no tanks ought to be. The second essential was timing. The drive on Meiktila must not begin until the three divisions—19th, 2nd and 20th—convinced Kimura that they constituted the main threat and persuaded him to commit his reserves against them by crossing the Irrawaddy to the north-east. It was equally important that, as soon as he realized the real threat was to his rear at Meiktila and started to move troops to meet it, XXXIIIrd Corps should redouble their pressure. The Japanese, shuttling wildly from crisis to crisis, must be given no breathing-space to regroup and make a con-certed attack on IVth Corps.

Before going any further a word must be said about the length of lines of communication behind the battles about to be fought. As far as Kalewa, which was 300 miles from railhead at Dimapur, both corps shared the same road, of which only the first two thirds was all-weather. From there, supplies for XXXIIIrd Corps crossed the Chindwin by Bailey bridge and had another 190 miles to travel to the Mandalay area; that is, where the corps would be before the serious fighting began. After the capture of Meiktila, supplies for IVth Corps were to go by river from Kalewa—in a fleet of craft built by army engineers entirely from the timber growing on the banks—downstream to Myingyan, where it was hoped to be able to put the 60 miles of railway to Meiktila into running order. In addition to what the roads could bear, there was the air lift carried by the R.A.F. and U.S.A.A.F., without which opera-tions would have been impossible; and to take advantage of its flexibility, the air lift was used to maintain troops who, for operational or other reasons, could not be supplied by road, or to meet the unforeseen crisis of the moment.

I really believe that the heroes of this time were the men
who kept the wheels turning and the wings flying—the
Indian drivers who, two to each three-ton lorry, drove
night and day in shifts over hundreds of miles of crumbling roads; the Sappers who built up those roads almost
between the passing wheels; the I.E.M.E. men who
worked incredible hours to turn the vehicles round
again; the Air Force mechanics, stripped to the waist, who
laboured in the sun by day and in the glare of headlights
by night to service the planes. All of them were magnificent to watch. They identified themselves utterly with the
troops ahead; they were and felt themselves to be a part,
and a vital part, of the team. They had the pride and
bearing of fighting men, for they were one with them.
(71)

To return to the advance of 19th Division: after three weeks
the divisional commander was able to say, in a special order of
the day sent out on Christmas Eve:

We have been given the honour of operating independently of a land L of C on what amounts to a dagger
thrust at the enemy's vitals. We are entirely on air supply,
making our own airstrips; and I want officers to explain
to ALL ranks the hazards of this method, the inherent
necessity for strict economy in all commodities (especially
petrol).

You have crossed the Chindwin; you have dug, fought
and driven 19th Division at speed over 260 miles of some
of the most difficult country in the world, overcoming
both physical obstacles and those effected by the
enemy.

Amplifying two phrases in that order, 'at speed' meant that
a battalion marched thirty-one miles over mountainous tracks
in sixteen hours, and 'most difficult country' had entailed
letting mules down over a precipice on ropes.

The divisional commander continued:

330

(a) The pursuit will continue to be conducted with all the dash, speed and determined endurance of which we are capable.

(b) I wish all ranks of all arms, services and staffs to realise the situation, to appreciate its possibilities, also the fact that we have got the Japs on the run, and if we can keep driving after him it will prevent his getting re-organized and dug in and so save us many casualties. Risks will be taken freely and without hesitation.

(c) All ranks will be informed that we may well go short of things, (incl. food) at times; but I know we will all accept that cheerfully.

It would, of course, be wrong to suppose that 19th Division enjoyed any monopoly of the qualities of dash and determination. The extracts are taken rather to show that by careful training they achieved the standards set by others with months of active service behind them.

As a fitting reward for their efforts they were the first troops to cross the Irrawaddy. After The Welch Regiment had had a small patrol over, 98th Brigade crossed with 4/4th Gurkhas at Thabeikkyin in country boats. Any idea of enlarging this bridgehead had to be abandoned when it was discovered that the enemy had established a position on the west bank at Kabwet which the brigade was ordered to deal with to cover the flank of the main divisional crossing at Kyaukmyaung. As all supply was still by air, artillery ammunition was very short and the Kabwet operation was supported by seven squadrons of Mitchell bombers and Thunderbolts, dropping 1,000 lb bombs, with a squadron and a half of Hurribombers and Spitfires. There was some severe fighting, but as the brigade report concludes: 'the period served as very good training and toughening for the hard fighting which was to follow in the capture of Mandalay'.

The numerous feints and crossing by patrols up and down the river left the Jap mystified and uncertain, and 64th Brigade was able to cross at Kyaukmyaung and establish a company of 5th Battalion The Baluch Regiment on Pear Hill, a feature which dominated the whole bridgehead. An account that appeared in S.E.A.C. newspaper on 24 February took the form of a letter to the wife of a gunner forming part of the observation post which went up with the company:

> For nine sleepless days and nights he was with an observation party on top of Pear Hill, most vital point of the whole three weeks' struggle to enlarge this spearhead on the eastern shore of the Irrawaddy. A tangled mass of bamboo and scrub swamp, miniature lakes, low hills, and scattered Burmese houses and white pagodas are the setting of this picture. With his officer and another gunner from his regiment he went in behind two companies of Punjabis and Dogras. The Japs were caught napping. It was as well, because the slow climb from matted bamboo thickets at the bottom and the slow climb from boulder to boulder up the steep rocky slopes was gruelling enough.

However, once the enemy had decided that this was what he had been expecting—a drive to link up with 36th Division coming down from the north—he acted with characteristic vigour and determination, and Pear Hill was the scene of fighting as bitter as any there had been for the past year. After paying tribute to the magnificent support given by the artillery throughout, 64th Brigade's account of the battle reads:

> One incident may serve to illustrate the severity of the night's fighting. 'C' Company on the southern perimeter had met the major part of the assault, and in the morning it was found that the garrison of one section post had been wiped out to a man. The section commander, Lance-Naik Jog Raj, was found dead outside his post clutching his rifle with its bloodstained bayonet, while round him lay eight of the enemy bayonetted to death. Casualties on both sides had been heavy but whereas The Baluch had suffered the loss of five killed and eleven wounded the bodies of four Jap officers and forty-seven men were counted in the perimeter.

20th Division on the right of XXXIIIrd Corps was the next to cross at Allagappa on 12 February. The river here is 1,500 yards wide, there was a three-knot current, and the banks were steep enough to make the clearance of vehicles difficult. There were no assault craft and the passage was made in ranger boats, towed in a train, with outboard motors of doubtful reliability. Great care had been taken to ensure surprise and the actual crossings of both 32nd and 100th Brigades attracted very little opposition. Once they were across the Japanese reacted very sharply to what they no doubt considered to be a thrust which might, and in due course did, drive south-east and cut off all their troops in the Mandalay area. The bridgeheads were barely established before they were the scenes of heavy fighting. 14th Frontier Force Rifles, who had crossed on rafts constructed by 481 Field Company from captured enemy equipment and powered by outboard motors, soon found themselves in trouble:

> It was now observed that the enemy were in some strength and heavy firing was taking place. From 11.30 p.m. to 1 a.m. the enemy under cover of heavy mortar, grenade and machine gun fire charged the position many times, twice penetrating the perimeter. In each case he was beaten back and fierce hand-to-hand fighting took place. Due to severe wireless jamming communication with 10th Field Regiment, who were responsible for the inner line of defensive fire, failed.
>
> The main brunt of these fierce attacks fell on 'C' Coy. Jemadar Parkash Singh, No. 8 Platoon commander, had been wounded early on in both legs and Lieut. H. H. Khan assumed command of his platoon. When Lieut. Khan was wounded Jemadar Parkash Singh went forward dragging himself on his hands and knees. He was wounded again three times but continued to direct the action of his platoon.
>
> At one time he held one sector of his platoon area single-handed, firing the Bren gun himself, although mortally wounded and in great pain. (58)

He was finally killed by a grenade which struck him in the chest, and was awarded a posthumous V.C.

Elsewhere, at Talingon, 4/10th Gurkhas were in the thick of it:

> The savagery of the fighting at Talingon was unforgetable. We were holding a front which was over a mile long, in long pampas grass which made mutual support between companies and platoons very difficult.*

At one time during the final and critical night the company commander brought down our own defensive artillery fire on to his positions, and this undoubtedly saved the situation. After the war the battalion commander met General Tanaka, commander of the enemy infantry division in this battle, who told him that the regiment involved lost 953 men out of a total of 1,200. In fact, it ceased to exist.

The final crossing on XXXIIIrd Corps front was made by 2nd Division on 24 February about half way between Allagappa and Sagaing, which is where the river turns westwards below Mandalay. There was of course very much less possibility of achieving surprise on this occasion but, although there were losses of boats holed by machine-gun fire in the early stages, the division made a remarkable recovery and, after a week, had extended their bridgehead to link up with 20th Division on their right.

Before leaving the corps front, mention must be made of one of the most useful formations they had. Known originally as 268th Lorried Infantry Brigade, they were raised as part of an armoured division. As an independent brigade they were somewhat of a Cinderella in the matter of transport, which is recorded as consisting of mules and bullocks and, for some considerable time, even elephants. Their composition was unorthodox: a battalion, The Mahendra Dal, of the Nepalese Army; 4th Battalion The Madras Regiment, whose recruitment between the wars had been very much restricted; and 1st Chamars, an 'untouchable' class, which was more than something of an innovation. They were never left idle and 'it was

*Bugle and Kukri: The History of 10th Princess Mary's Own Gurkha Rifles (70).

334

common talk in the brigade (and no doubt a matter on which the men prided themselves) that the most difficult country fell to them more often than to any other formation'. In the opening stages of the advance they covered the gap between 19th and 2nd Divisions, and before the latter crossed the river the brigade took over the task of containing the Japanese troops in the bridgehead at Sagaing.

With absolute secrecy a factor of the first importance, the concentration of 7th Division in its forming-up area on the north bank was in itself a major operation. The road south from Kalemyo had to be remade to carry traffic as heavy as the tank transporters, and the first step was to dislodge the last Japanese rearguard still holding out at Gangaw, a task for which artillery was needed. The divisional engineers in fifteen days improved 180 miles of road to take field artillery, and the 25 pdrs were in action by 27 December to support the attack. This was made first by the Lushai Brigade, then relieved by 28th East African Brigade, with the idea that, if the enemy obtained an identification of the troops opposing him, he would not attach any significance to the presence of formations known by him to be in the area.

> The track before long was a foot deep in a fine red dust which rose in dense, choking clouds, and, resettling on the jungle bordering the track, turned everything into a uniform dirty reddish brown.
>
> The only sign of Japanese occupation was a huge dump of abandoned vehicles in Tamu itself, and many more lying derelict along the whole 150 miles of track to Kan. Our own rather limited mechanical transport, endlessly ferrying troops and baggage forward, looked little better than the derelicts, but by prodigious hard work and skill, R.I.A.S.C. and I.E.M.E. workshops kept them on the road.
>
> The advance of the main body of the division from Kohima started on 20th December. By 15th February—fifty-seven days later—the division had advanced 515 miles, driven in the enemy rearguards covering the

selected crossing-points, crossed the fast-flowing one-and-a-quarter-mile Irrawaddy in face of opposition, and established a bridgehead from which within a few days of the crossing the thrust on Meiktila was launched.

The enemy rearguards were not a mere observation screen. When finally driven back to the west bank of the Irrawaddy they fought with the fanatical resolve typical of the Japanese soldier ordered to fight to the last man and the last round. (23)

Against the wider background the crossing by IVth Corps was the most important of them all, the hinge on which the whole plan turned. Not only must it succeed, but there must be no delay; 17th Division behind them must have a clear run to reach Meiktila before Kimura realized what was happening.

There was an unforeseen delay in clearing the enemy covering position on the near bank, so that the landing craft could not be brought down to the forming-up areas in time for a last 'dryshod' rehearsal. This resulted in delay and confusion when things began to go wrong.

> The crossing of the Irrawaddy at Nyaungu was the longest opposed river crossing attempted in any theatre of the Second World War. The river at this point was over 2,000 yards wide and fairly fast flowing. The south bank was sheer for 100 feet, while the north, or taking-off bank, consisted of paddy-fields, devoid of cover, only a few feet above flood level. The roads serving the area were deep-rutted, and every vehicle raised a great column of dust clearly visible from the south bank. (23)

The South Lancashire Regiment, who had had some experience of landings at Madagascar, led the assault. One company crossed successfully, then:

> In the chill darkness of the hour before dawn the rest of the battalion began to embark. From that moment things began to go wrong. Whatever the cause, there was considerable delay in getting into the boats, a delay aggravated

by the fact that it had not been possible to start up the motors beforehand because of noise, and some failed to start. A few boats were found to leak when fully loaded. (23)

The reserve company found itself in the lead but, instead of pushing on, decided to circle and drop into its allotted place, whereupon 'the Irrawaddy took charge' and carried the boats downstream. Machine-guns opened from the far bank and, as for reasons of secrecy there had been virtually no artillery registration beforehand, by 8 a.m. the position was the same as it had been three hours earlier, except that surprise had gone, and a single company of the South Lancashires was across the river on its own.

Downstream at Pagan, 1st Battalion The Sikh Regiment, who had earlier got a patrol across and had discovered some country craft, were attempting to put one company over, but there was a last-minute reinforcement of the defences and, when the little flotilla came under fire, 'the local boatmen panicked and in a matter of seconds the heavy, unwieldy country craft were out of control and being swept downstream'. At that juncture the luck turned. In the midst of deliberations as to the next move a small boat flying a white flag was seen crossing the river. It contained two men of the Indian National Army who said that the Japanese troops of the garrison had left them and gone away upstream, and that they wished to surrender. At the main crossing the engineers were busy refuelling and exchanging engines that had broken down. The brigade commander decided that, rather than wait to reorganize the battalion which had made the first attempt, he would embark a fresh battalion and send them to reinforce the company of the South Lancashires on the far bank who so far had not been attacked.

At 9.45 a.m. the leading company of 4/15th Punjabis moved off under heavy covering fire. In view of the desperate possibilities that lay ahead the parade-like calm of the embarkation was beyond all praise. Two boats grounded on a submerged and treacherous sand-bank, but the men, quite undaunted, waded shoulder deep in a swift current to reach the beaches. At last all the boats grounded and the men swarmed up the cliffs and nullahs to their objectives on the high ground. More and more boats followed, heavily laden with troops, until boats were going both ways in an almost continuous stream. From 1 p.m. onwards the crossing became a procession, and all day the river was full of the noise and crackle of the engines, and the blue haze of exhaust smoke mingled with the acrid smoke of the high explosives. (23)

The enemy had been taken completely by surprise; they had not expected a landing in such strength, they had left the defences to the I.N.A., and they had not enough of their own troops at hand to make an immediate counter-attack.

The army commander has said that he asked his divisions to cross the Irrawaddy on 'a couple of bamboos and a bootlace'. A pardonable understatement, for there is an element of truth in it. Equipment had to be used in turn as each corps had barely enough for one division, much of it was old and worn, and it had all had to travel hundreds of miles forward by road. To supplement it there was much improvisation from captured enemy equipment or from local materials, and indeed there had to be: if Fourteenth Army had waited for what other armies would no doubt have considered to be a reasonable allotment, they would probably be waiting there still.

So great was the urgency to exploit this surprise that 17th Division began to form up in the bridgehead before the crossing of 7th Division was complete. The division had been reorganized while in India on an all-mechanical-transport basis, and a third brigade, 99th, had been added, organized to move by air. This brigade was still back in India waiting to be called forward. As soon as 255th Tank Brigade was safely over the river, the great drive on Meiktila was launched—on 21 February. 7th Division remained in the area of the crossing, covering the administrative tail of 17th Division, and it took several weeks of hard fighting—in the course of which Naik

Gian Singh and Lieutenant Karamjit Singh, both of 4/15th Punjab Regiment, won the V.C.—before the whole stretch of the south bank was clear of the enemy.

A good deal of opposition was met on the road to Meiktila, but the squadrons of 255th Armoured Brigade under command of the infantry brigade were used with great boldness to outflank anything they met, and nothing was allowed to slow up the advance.

> 63 Bde came up from the south late in the afternoon, having fought its way from Welaung. It had 'blitzed' every village with tank and artillery fire and in one encounter had killed 65 Japs.
>
> Division H.Q. were moved on a wide front and for a brief period tore across country. Small bunds, and cactus hedges proved no obstacle—though the former taken at speed tended to make 3-tonners airborne for a while. The triangle between the roads of Mahlaing and Welaung was infested with snipers so the layout of the harbour area for the whole force was delayed, and the dispositions in the case of some units were not occupied till after dark. But the Jap had taken a terrific knock, and well over a hundred had been killed by one battalion alone in this 'snipers' triangle', and a peaceful night ensued.*

By 26 February the force was concentrated at Mahlaing, north-west of Meiktila, with some tanks and a battalion forward at Thabutkon airstrip where work was started to improve it to take the heavy troop-carrying aircraft. The fly-in of 99 Brigade began next day and by the evening a complete battalion had arrived.

We still held the advantage of surprise in the advance on Meiktila, but the local commander had been able to scrape together some 5,000 men, including all hospital patients who could stand, 'even on one leg with crutches', and set about organizing the defences with great skill and vigour, so that it was imperative to capture the place before he was reinforced.

---

* *History of 17th Indian Division* (24).

The divisional commander, General Cowan, made a characteristically bold plan. He sent 255th Armoured Brigade, with a couple of infantry battalions, in a wide circle to the north to come in and attack from the east where the defences were likely to be weakest; 48th Brigade was to attack from the north, and 63rd Brigade from the north-west, each with a squadron of tanks under command.

> Always, throughout this whole battle of Meiktila, the enemy were in very strong bunkers, were very strong in automatic weapons, with some guns and improvised anti-tank mines, and fought fanatically, refusing to vacate a single bunker. They all had to be killed. Several Japs were found with aerial bombs between their knees and a brick in their hand, squatting in trenches waiting till a tank ran over them to strike the bomb detonator with a brick. (24)

At one stage The Royal Deccan Horse, to the east of the town, had a squadron with its headquarters on a cross-roads, and

> troops advancing along the three roads going north, south and west, slowly knocking out bunkers with 75 fire, and finishing them off by tank commanders throwing grenades into them from the turret.
>
> After one hour the objective was considered clear, but infantry were required to confirm this so a squadron of Probyn's with a company of Rajputs were sent up to relieve 'A' Squadron. For an hour 'A' Squadron sat in uncanny silence on the objective. On the approach of the Rajputs with a squadron of Probyn's, hell was let loose in the form of machine gun fire from bunkers not previously located, and caught the Rajputs in the open. Every tank on the Position opened up at everything and nothing, and for ten minutes the situation was what is known as fluid.*

* History of the Royal Deccan Horse (44).

Small wonder that the divisional history should record that 'these were the first major tank operations carried out by the Indian Armoured Corps with large units of tanks and everyone agreed that the dash and efficiency they showed were most marked'.

63rd Brigade were supported by the R.A.F.

from a daily cab-rank of up to six aircraft on call through tentacles either at battalion headquarters or even with forward companies. Dive-bombing and machine-gunning were carried out through these tentacles, targets being indicated by 2″ or 3″ mortar smoke bombs. The effect on the enemy was usually devastating and it was largely due to the timely intervention from the air which landed a stick of bombs directly on the main centre of resistance that the battalion captured Meiktila West with comparative ease.

On 48th Brigade front the final clearing of their area was completed by The West Yorks when 'the last living enemy had been forced to leap into the lake, where they were shot or drowned'.

And that was happening all round the town. In four days 17th Division, ably supported by 255th Armoured Brigade and the R.A.F., wiped out practically the whole garrison of Meiktila. They then had to reorganize to face the inevitable counter-attack. Kimura was perhaps not yet clear just who had hit him, but he knew that it hurt, and that if he did not at once recapture Meiktila, the battle for central Burma was as good as lost. Abandoning all idea of contesting the river crossings, from north, east and south he pulled in everything he could lay his hands on, and all told brought nearly a whole corps together. The saving grace was that it was a scratch side, and by dint of striking relentlessly at his centres of command and communication we prevented him from making the best use of the troops who reached the town. For all that, 17th Division, with a brigade from 5th Division flown in to help them, but with much of their transport back at the river crossing, were fighting hard for over three weeks before, on 29

March, it could be said that the enemy had given up the struggle. Throughout they had been supplied completely from the air.

On 26 February, 19th Division broke out from the bridgeheads north of Mandalay and, leaving pockets of resistance to be dealt with later, two brigades 'drove south, like a rush of waters over a broken dam'. On 8 March, 98th Brigade reached the foot of Mandalay Hill. The first plan was for The Royal Berkshires to attack that afternoon with artillery support, but as the hill was covered with religious buildings held in high veneration by the Burmese, it was felt that they should be spared damage if possible. The task was then given to 4th Gurkhas, who were fresh as they had been carried by motor transport over the last stage of the advance. The attack was made that night.

It is a holy hill covered with temples and pillared courts. The top is reached by a porticoed staircase that reaches its whole length. Tucked in below the north foot of the hill is a wooded monastery and at the south end a mile away is a second monastery close to the moat and the fort. The hill itself is devoid of vegetation and its slopes are bare and rocky. It was a lesser Cassino and, as in the case of Monastery Hill, there was a pious hope that Mandalay Hill might escape the battle.

At one o'clock in the morning of the 9th the three rifle companies and a tactical (battalion) headquarters reached the point from which it was intended to attack the hill. Packs were dumped and the men rested.

At 3 o'clock Damar Singh, the company commander, was called and told to move. There was a small moon in the sky. He started off his leading platoon and waited till it had cleared a deserted village a short way off. There was no sound. He was quite untroubled and said 'We'll get the hill all right now, had there been anything we should have heard it by now'. (64)

He moved off with his reserve platoons and had hardly left

when firing broke out. 'C' Coy was standing by ready to move
if required.

The account continues:

> There was no news from Damar Singh but there were
> more sounds of firing from the hill, grenades or mortar
> bombs were being used. Time passed slowly. We won-
> dered what was happening and then as the sky grew pale
> and the outline of the crest grew clear against the sky we
> could see tiny antlike figures clambering up the topmost
> steps, and through a sharp fusillade of fire a thin distant
> cry of 'Ayo' came floating down to us. (64)

The sounds of battle continued till 'the C.O. when he
heard the racket that was going on above grew anxious and,
calling Damar Singh on the air, asked him if there was anything he wanted'.

'No,' came back the answer, 'only breakfast—out.'

The brigade war history records that by the time the
summit had been captured more than forty dead Japanese lay
in their positions on the slopes and on the summit of the hill,
and seven guns had been captured.

In the morning The Royal Berkshires attacked up the north
face, but it was several days before the whole hill was finally
cleared. The army commander records that he visited the
scene while the clearing of the city was still going on.

> Through all this noise and clatter of men clearing a
> battle-field came a strange sound—singing. I followed it.
> There was General Rees, his uniform sweat-soaked and
> dirty, his distinguishing red scarf rumpled round his
> neck, his bush hat at a jaunty angle, his arm beating time,
> surrounded by a group of Assamese soldiers whom he
> was vigorously leading in the singing of Welsh mis-
> sionary hymns. The fact that he sang in Welsh and they
> in Khasi only added to the harmony. I looked on
> admiringly. My generals had character. Their men knew
> them and they knew their men. (71)

The capture of Fort Dufferin was quite another matter. On the strength of a first report that it was held by no more than fifty of the enemy, 98th Brigade made a tentative attempt to capture it, with orders not to persist if it was held in force.

Fort Dufferin covers an area of about 2,000 yards square. It contained the palace, Government House, the jail, the club, the polo ground and various government buildings. It is surrounded by a moat about seventy five yards wide with a wall on the inner side. Each wall has a main gate set in the centre obliquely to the bridge leading to it and protected from direct fire by a massive buttress on the moat side. The wall is constructed of brick banked up on the inner side and is about thirty feet thick at the bottom narrowing to twelve feet at the top.

Several attacks from the air were made, using a choice of missiles, including rockets, but they caused no significant damage. The guns were very successful: 5·5 in and 6 in howitzers were used firing from as close as 300 yards. Altogether over fifty holes were blasted in the walls. Fuse 321 was used, and a low charge, as otherwise many rounds went right through and burst inside the fort. After some trial and error, fifteen to twenty rounds were needed to make a breach twelve yards wide. Several infantry assaults were made on the breaches but were all repulsed by fire from machine-gun pits dug into the rubble. On the morning of 20 March, just when it had been decided that Mandalay could be left to be reduced at our leisure, the battery commander, before firing began, saw four Burmans with a Union Jack and a white flag come out of the north gate. They were civilian internees, and they came with the news that the garrison had slipped away during the night.

'Once this was realised a frantic race ensued to see which battalion could enter the Fort the quickest. As a point of historical fact the first individual to enter was Captain Britten of 65 Field Company, Madras Sappers and Miners, who some nights previously had entered alone and armed solely with a dagger by way of a partially blocked and narrow drain.' The reconnaissance proved that that line of approach was impossible. However, on the morning of the twentieth:

> Terrific scenes of enthusiasm followed, as first the Punjabis and then the Baluch, the Worcestershires and the Rajputana Rifles burst cheering and shouting into the interior of the Fort. Flinging wide the gates sappers of 65 Field Company admitted a stream of vehicles (with the BBC recording van well to the fore), as Fort Dufferin was given over to war correspondents, photographers and senior commanders. The battle for Mandalay was over and peace had returned to a shattered city.*

19th Division had fought its way firmly on to the map, and others who considered that they had a proprietary interest in being the first into Rangoon were beginning to sit up and take notice.

After 20th Division had joined up the bridgeheads of its two brigades, and had established contact with 2nd Division to the east, it was directed to secure Kyaukse on the railway south of Mandalay. 'This town was of the greatest importance to the Japanese, for not only was it their chief supply centre for a large part of their army, but it was the bastion behind which Kimura hoped to restore some order in his shattered units.' The enemy was beginning to feel the strain of the blows which were raining on him from almost every point of the compass and a battalion leading one of the brigade columns records that:

> It was noted for the first time that the Jap was becoming reluctant to come to grips and on the first day over 60 were killed and an anti-tank gun captured. A bullock-cart with a Japanese officer and some hostile Burmans were intercepted. The officer was killed and some valuable documents and a wireless set captured.

* *64th Brigade War History.*

On the 17th March the advance against the now known enemy position was begun. The tank support on this occasion was a squadron of Lee tanks from a Royal Tank Corps regiment. It was the first time the battalion had had armoured support from a British tank regiment and there were many who doubted the success of the combination. They need have had no qualms.

The objective was taken and heavy losses inflicted.

Everyone got a chance to kill a few Japs, including the C.O.'s escort. His orderly killed a Japanese officer and captured his sword. The sword was presented there and then on the battlefield to the Squadron commander of the tanks to mark the first time he had been in action and the first time his squadron had worked with Indian troops. It was a timely and courteous gesture worthy of the battalion and of the occasion. (57)

The enemy clung to the town to the last in the effort to save some of the great quantities of stores it contained, but on 30 March it was finally captured. The army commander records that:

This break-out of 20th Division was a spectacular achievement which only a magnificent division, magnificently led, could have staged after weeks of the heaviest defensive fighting. (71)

By the end of March, with Kyaukse, Meiktila, and Chauk on the Irrawaddy, which had been occupied by 7th Division, safely in our hands, the enemy had no longer any prospect of stopping us in central Burma. There were still plenty of pockets of resistance and they could be counted on to give a lot of trouble, but he could no longer hope to fight a properly co-ordinated battle anywhere short of the approaches to Rangoon. The problem was to prevent him from doing anything of the sort.

There was really only one course open: to go bald-headed

for Rangoon. There was no half-way house. Maintained from India, the army was already stretched to the limit; to go further and fail, with air support difficult if not impossible in the monsoon, was fraught with danger. There was, however, one form of insurance, Operation Dracula, the capture of Rangoon from the sea, which would eliminate the risk, almost too horrible to contemplate, of the city being held by Japanese suicide squads who could very effectively deny us the use of the port which, for the maintenance of our forces, we simply had to have. In its original form, with the land front hundreds of miles away to the north and four divisions still locked up in the Arakan, Dracula could only have been mounted in sufficient strength to stand any chance of success by drawing troops and aircraft away from the main front. But against a demoralized enemy, with Fourteenth Army jostling at the northern approaches, if indeed it did not arrive first, a much smaller force would be needed.

Fourteenth Army had two possible lines of advance. Down the Irrawaddy, the way the army came out in 1942, was 375 miles; by the railway, through Toungoo, was fifty miles shorter. With the monsoon to be expected by 15 May, and allowing a fortnight to regroup and mop up, it meant an average of ten miles a day, against opposition. It was a task for a mechanized force, with a prayer that the tanks, which had run hundreds of desert miles before they ever reached India, would stay the course. There were administrative resources to support only a single line, so the decision was made to give pretty well everything to IVth Corps, consisting of 255th Armoured Brigade and 5th and 17th Divisions, and send them down the railway, leaving XXXIIIrd Corps, with 7th and 20th Divisions, to come down the Irrawaddy, managing as best they could. 2nd and 36th British Divisions had been withdrawn to India.

The army commander was under no illusions as to the magnitude of the undertaking:

> It was very plain to me—and if it had not been, plenty of people were willing to enlighten me—that this dash for Rangoon by a mechanised force, confined to one road,

347

thrusting against time through superior numbers, was a most hazardous and possibly rather un-British operation. I knew the risks and penalties of failure, but as I checked over the final plans, I was ready to accept them. Whatever the risks, we were winning. My soldiers were out for Rangoon, and anyone who was with them and had seen them fight could not doubt that they would get there. Once more the exhilaration running through the army was a tangible thing that could be seen and felt. I shared it. (71)

There were now three tasks to complete. To reach Rangoon by land before the monsoon broke; to send a seaborne force, also before the monsoon, to ensure against anything short of complete success; and to complete the mopping up of the considerable numbers of enemy who would be brushed aside, to be dealt with later, if the land advance was to have any chance of success.

In completing these tasks the army did nothing that the reader has not watched it doing already; space, and space alone, restricts the story of them to the barest outline.

On 11 April, 17th Division broke the last vestige of the Japanese resistance by a brilliant tactical manœuvre ending in a hard fight at Pyawbwe, and while they were still clearing the battlefield 5th Division went through on the road south. Thanks to the timely intervention of the Karen guerillas, who had been waiting for this opportunity, they entered Toungoo almost unopposed on 22 April. The hunt was up and progress was followed with something of the keenness one associates with the landowners' race at the Peshawar Vale point-to-point. The odds changed daily; then a fourth horse had entered the race, Dracula was to take place on 2 May. Eleven days left and 200 miles still to go. On 25 April, 17th Division, burning to avenge once and for all the events of 1942, took the lead. By 1 May it reached Pegu and then, by the cruellest stroke of ill-fortune, the monsoon broke, a fortnight early. Stranded, marooned by the rising waters, they heard next day that 26th Division had entered the city from the sea.

The capture of Rangoon, the outward and visible prize of

victory, had eluded them, but Fourteenth Army could with no fear of contradiction claim that it was they who had made victory possible. They had proved once again the truth of the old principle—if you defeat the enemy's armies in the field, the geographical spoils of war are there for the taking.

That impartial critic, Major-General J. F. C. Fuller, in his book *The Second World War* (75) sums up the extent of their achievements:

> Burma was reconquered in one of the most remarkable campaigns of the entire war. Remarkable in that few other theatres of the war presented so many obstacles to organized fighting: heat, rain, tropical diseases, mountains, rivers, swamps, and an all but total lack of roads seemed to have marked out Burma as one of the few regions in the world where powerful highly equipped armies could not fight. Yet in this last campaign half a million men were employed and, as we have seen, armies of considerable size freely moved from north to south and west to east over high mountain ranges, across rivers, and through dense forest and jungle at no mean speed. That this was possible was due to many factors, and beside leadership and soldiership, the three outstanding were air power, medical care and engineering.

During the early months of 1945 the planners had kept their pot boiling with a comparatively modest enterprise, Roger— the capture of the island of Phuket, lying off the north-west coast of Malaya and designed to serve as a stepping-stone to Singapore. They could therefore at comparatively short notice recast their plans and dispatch 26th Division by sea to Rangoon. The river approaches to the port had been extensively mined by both sides, so the opening phase of the operation was the capture of Elephant Point by a parachute attack to enable mine sweepers and assault craft to move upstream. Carried in forty Dakotas of the U.S.A.A.F. Air Commando, 2/3rd Gurkhas Parachute Battalion dropped on their objective at dawn on 1 May and by nightfall had secured the defences against little opposition. Next day 36th and 71st

Brigades of 26th Division landed from assault craft on both banks without meeting any opposition. On the third, 36th Brigade moved upstream to take the city. They were met by a sampan containing two R.A.F. officers who told them that the enemy had fled. Flying low on reconnaissance they had seen a notice on the roof of the jail 'Japanese gone', so they landed at Mingaladon airfield, commandeered the sampan, and set off then to meet the troops up from the south.

If the battle-honour 'Rangoon' was won rather easily, no one could begrudge it to 26th Division. They had been the unlucky ones. Pitchforked into the first Arakan campaign when they were a division in name only, it was not really their fault if, with the tide running strongly against them, they failed to halt the Japanese. They held the fort through the monsoon of 1943 until relieved by 5th and 7th Divisions. They played their part in winning the battle of the Box and, by the capture of the central fortress at the Tunnels, wiped out on the ground the reverse they had suffered twelve months earlier. Withdrawn again to train for the amphibious operations planned to follow the capture of Akyab, they had the mortification of seeing 25th Division carrying on with the task they had hoped would be theirs. They deserved a break.

The division sent parties north from Rangoon and made touch with both IVth and XXXIIIrd Corps, so that our troops were in contact along both lines of advance, and well placed to regroup to undertake the task of destroying the enemy who had been swept aside in the drive south.

The Japanese were known to be in three main areas: east of Meiktila, and moving south; in the Irrawaddy valley, trying to break out eastwards; and in the Pegu Yomas, also trying to break eastwards and cross the Sittang. They totalled perhaps 70,000 and their morale was to prove higher than we had expected.

The plan adopted was to establish a cordon of battalion areas from which columns could operate against enemy parties which were discovered. The weather conditions were appalling for them—the monsoon and the floods had converted the whole countryside into one big lake—and the only means of communication was either along the railway embankment or by water transport. Patrols had to wade through waist-high water, 'too deep for Gurkhas' as one division reported.

The Japanese had the alternatives of trying to filter through in small parties, or of making a concerted break-out. Feeling that the former might result in complete loss of control, they decided on a concerted attempt, over quite a wide frontage, on a given day. By good fortune a copy of their order was captured by one of our patrols, and 17th Division, through whose area most of the escape routes ran, was suitably reinforced.

Japanese intelligence, on the other hand, was poor and the breakdown of their wireless made control difficult. Of the force that was in the Pegu Yomas under Lieutenant-General Sakurai, the Indian official history writes:

> Starving, stricken by disease, harassed by the Royal Air Force and active patrolling by land forces, with no cover from the unending rains, any other adversary would have surrendered his whole force. But Sakurai, true to the traditions of his brave race—not unlike the Rajputs of the Middle Ages in India—did not surrender and paid the price. Of his force variously estimated at between 16,000 to 19,000 only about 4,000 to 5,000 reached the east bank of the Sittang. (12)

They considered this battle in July to be one of their worst defeats in the Burma Campaign.

The object of this book has been to show the Indian Army in action; the sum of its individual deeds is proof of the magnitude of its collective achievement. In Burma, as few armies in history have ever done, it wiped the slate clean after the defeat of 1942. Magnificently led, at every level, perfectly clear as to what it was being asked to do, it met the Japanese around Imphal on equal terms and beat them decisively; then, for good measure, exploiting to the utmost its flair for the unexpected, its ability to live hard and fight on scales of equipment and comfort that would have left other armies waiting at the post, it hunted the enemy out of Central Burma and into the sea.

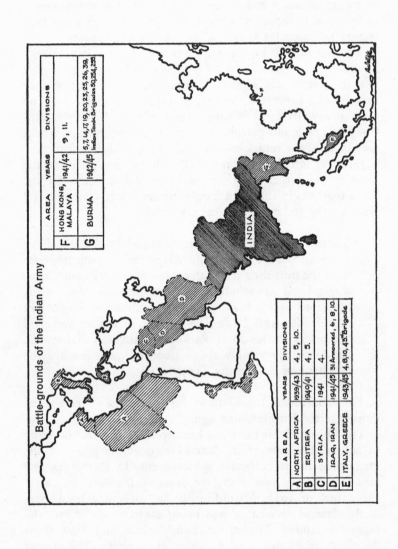

Battle-grounds of the Indian Army

	AREA	YEARS	DIVISIONS
F	HONG KONG, MALAYA	1941/42	9, 11.
G	BURMA	1942/45	5,7,14,17,19,20,23,25,26,39, Indian Tank Brigades 50,254,255

	AREA	YEARS	DIVISIONS
A	NORTH AFRICA	1939/43	4, 5, 10.
B	ERITREA	1940/41	4, 5.
C	SYRIA	1941	4.
D	IRAQ, IRAN	1941/45	31 Armoured, 6, 8, 10.
E	ITALY, GREECE	1943/45	4,6,8,10, 43rd Brigade.

CHAPTER NINETEEN

Tribute

Strictly, this book ends with the surrender of the Japanese armies in August 1945 but, unobtrusive to the last, the old Indian Army had still two last services to render before it disappeared from the scene for ever. They must not go unrecorded. Mention was made in Chapter 14 that 4th Indian Division left Italy to go to Greece where, after the withdrawal of the Germans, civil war was raging between ELAS, the left-wing guerilla faction, and EDES, which was largely monarchist. The role of peacemaker in such conditions is difficult and thankless but by the time the division handed over to 4th British Division early in 1946, to return to India after seven years of war in five countries, Greece had established some semblance of order. There was also an Indian division left tidying up in Iraq, while in the Far East every one of the divisions which had fought in Burma was called on to move further afield to take the surrender of the scattered Japanese garrisons, and to try to maintain order in the uneasy half-way stage between war and peace. A contingent went to Japan, there were divisions in Indo-China, Siam, the Netherland East Indies, Malaya, and two in Burma itself. It was an irksome and dangerous duty and more than one promising career was cut short in discharging it.

The last and perhaps most exacting task fell to the army in the very throes of its own dissolution. The great majority of regiments and battalions were composed of different classes, recruited from both India and Pakistan. Under the partition settlement they were allotted to one or the other of the two new states, and had to tackle the heart-rending business of sending away Hindu or Mohammedan squadrons and companies to units perhaps half-way across the sub-continent, from whom they would receive others in return. The operation was fraught with risk. Whole families, displaced by partition, were streaming both ways across the new frontier that split the Punjab in two, and the most brutal atrocities were being perpetrated on both sides. Fantastic rumours were rife, and there can have been few units that did not hold men whose homes were being uprooted, their families exposed to the dangers which beset the political refugee. The worst of the trouble centred round the railways and it was over the railways that the men moving in exchange had to travel.

The story of just two regiments is typical of what was happening to over fifty others. 19th Lancers were stationed in Peshawar, conquered a hundred years before by the Sikh Maharajah Ranjit Singh whose rule had left bitter memories. The 19th had a Sikh squadron to be sent to a regiment down country and, with half his regiment away on detachment, the colonel was very much concerned for their safety as he had but a handful of Mohammedans available to protect them from the wrath of the local inhabitants. In the very nick of time, the outlying squadron under the risaldar-major returned. Although they had marched up through an area where the most dreadful things were happening between Sikh and Moslem, they never hesitated in their duty, and it was largely to them that the Sikh squadron owed their lives. A plan was made and carried out in such secrecy that not even the police knew until after the squadron was safe across the Indus. 'Thus for the regiment there fell a last shaft of light across the picture of those dark months.'*

Away to the south, in Ahmednagar, the Scinde Horse, destined for the army of India, had much the same problem to solve. Their Pathan squadron was transferred to The

* *The Spirit of a Regiment: The History of 19th K.G.O. Lancers* (46).

Guides Cavalry, in the same station, from whom they received Sikhs in exchange.

> Each man of both regiments removed his regimental cap or pagri badge and handed it over to his opposite number. Thus symbolically did the Pathans of the Scinde Horse pass the custody of the traditions of 'B' Squadron to their new guardians.*

But the regiment's real concern was for their Ranghars, Mohammedans recruited both from India and Pakistan, with homes in the very heart of the troubled areas. Bad tidings poured in, and although regimental parties were sent out to bring back authentic news, many men must have been sorely tempted to take matters into their own hands.

> It is a matter of great pride that there was not a single incident of desertion in the regiment throughout the whole period. Nor was there at any time any display of resentment between members of the two Sikh Squadrons and the Ranghars. At no time was any action taken (to keep peace) other than by the Viceroy's Commissioned Officers on their own initiative and in the normal course of their responsibility for discipline.

> Risaldar Major and Hon'y Lieutenant Niaz Mohammed Khan, (a Ranghar) was an autocrat of the old school. He had seen days when the risaldar-major virtually commanded the regiment, and considered he would be failing in his duty if his commanding officer was bothered with routine with which it was within his own authority to deal. His integrity, moral courage, personal example and bearing were beyond praise in this crisis which affected all. At no time did he entertain or allow to be entertained the idea that outside events were any excuse for friction in the regiment. His vigour and impartiality were perhaps the keystone of regimental discipline at this time. (45)

* *The Scinde Horse (14th P.W.O. Cavalry)* (45).

The taunt has been levelled at the army that it was careful not to enlist officers or men from the politically conscious classes. In those troubled days it would have needed no more than a handful of politically conscious leaders to spark the powder, and the whole country could have flared into a blaze that would have made the mutiny of 1857 look like a tavern brawl. And who would have put out the flames? It was the army's 'finest hour' when the men, led by their Indian officers, stood fast in their loyalty to the British officers who were all too soon to say good-bye to them for ever.

As it began, so the book ends, with a tribute to the Indian Army from a field marshal of the British Army: Earl Wavell, commander-in-chief in the Middle East, commander-in-chief in India, and Viceroy of India, saw the Indian soldier in the round, and in the foreword he wrote for *Fourth Indian Division* this is what he had to say:

The fame of this Division will surely go down as one of the greatest fighting formations in military history; to be spoken of with such as The Tenth Legion, The Light Division of the Peninsular War, Napoleon's Old Guard.

The Division has a claim on history even beyond its fighting reputation. It represents the culmination of one of the finest warrior forces ever created, the old Indian Army, with its mixture of British and Indian units. Between British and Indians there was a true spirit of comradeship, of mutual trust in battle, of fellowship in camp and bivouac.

The old Indian Army, in which all creeds and races of Indians served together with British in mutual trust and concord, is gone for ever. But its memories and traditions will remain, and its proud history in many countries and on many fields.

Appendix A

NOTES ON MILITARY TERMS

RANKS

Indian	*British Equivalent*
Naik	Corporal
Dafadar/Havildar	Sergeant

Viceroy's Commissioned Officers

Jemadar	Second-Lieutenant
Risaldar/Subedar	Lieutenant

The risaldar/subedar-major was the senior Indian officer in the regiment or battalion and the trusted confidential adviser of the commanding officer.

Indian officers holding the King's commission were on an equal footing with those in the British Army.

Chiefs of staff. Orders might reach a commander in the field from several sources. For uniformity, the term 'chiefs of staff' is used.

Planners. All large headquarters (army and above) had a section of the staff engaged in investigating and planning in general terms operations one or two removes ahead of those actually in progress. They are given the general name of 'planners'.

FORMATIONS

A brigade, armoured or infantry, had three regiments or battalions, and a headquarters staff capable of controlling attached units of other arms, when it became a brigade group.

357

(A German, Italian or Japanese regiment was the same as our brigade.)

A division, armoured or infantry, had three brigades and its own artillery, engineers, signals and administrative services.

A corps, a large headquarters, commanded in the field as many divisions as might be given it from time to time.

An army, a larger edition of the corps, had two or more corps; and a wider range of responsibilities, e.g. R.A.F. co-operation, lines of communication, political considerations.

Appendix B

ORDER OF BATTLE OF THE INDIAN ARMY

CAVALRY AND INDIAN ARMOURED CORPS

Unit	*Class composition*
Governor-General's Bodyguard	P.M.s,* Sikhs
Governor's Bodyguard, Madras	Rajputs, Jats
Governor's Bodyguard, Bombay	Mahrattas
Governor's Bodyguard, Bengal	P.M.s, Rajputs
1st D.Y.O. Cavalry, Skinner's Horse 2nd Royal Lancers, Gardner's Horse 3rd Cavalry	Ranghars, Rajputs, Jats, Hindustani Mohammedans
4th Duke of Cambridge's Own Lancers (Hodson's Horse) 5th K.E.O. Lancers (Probyn's Horse)	Dogras, P.M.s, Sikhs
6th D.C.O. Lancers (Watson's) 7th Light Cavalry 8th K.G.O. Light Cavalry 9th Royal Deccan Horse	Jats, P.M.s, Sikhs
10th Q.V.O. Guides Cavalry F.F.†	Dogras, Pathans, Sikhs
11th Prince Albert Victor's Own Cavalry F.F.†	Hindustani Mohammedans, P.M.s, Ranghars
13th D.C.O. Lancers 14th P.W.O. Cavalry, Scinde Horse	Pathans, Ranghars, Sikhs

* Punjabi Mohammedan.
† Frontier Force.

Unit	Class composition
16th Light Cavalry	Jats, Rajputs, Rajputana Mohammedans
17th Q.V.O. Poona Horse ⎱ 18th K.E.O. Cavalry ⎰	Jats, Kaimakanis, Rajputs
19th K.G.O. Lancers	Jats, P.M.s, Sikhs
21st K.G.O. Horse (Central India Horse)	Dogras, Jats, P.M.s

12th (Sam Browne's) Cavalry, 15th Lancers and 20th Lancers were training regiments.

Regiments raised in wartime

43rd Cavalry	Jats, P.M.s
45th Cavalry	Dogras, Pathans, Sikhs

INDIAN ARTILLERY

There were 13 regiments of Mountain Artillery
10 regiments of Field Artillery
9 regiments of Anti-Tank Artillery
16 regiments of Light Anti-Aircraft Artillery and
17 regiments of Heavy Anti-Aircraft Artillery

ENGINEERS

The three pre-war corps were:
Q.V.O. Madras Sappers and Miners
K.G.O. Bengal Sappers and Miners
Royal Bombay Sappers and Miners
each consisting of about six field companies. There are no accurate figures available for war raisings but there were over one hundred by the Madras Sappers and Miners alone. There were also a number of Indian Engineer battalions and Pioneer units not under the aegis of the Sapper and Miner depots.

INFANTRY

Unit	Class composition
1st Punjab Regiment 1st, 2nd, 3rd, 5th	P.M.s, Hazarawals, Rajputs, Sikhs

Unit	Class composition
2nd Punjab Regiment 1st, 2nd, 3rd, 4th, 5th	Dogras, P.M.s, Sikhs
The Madras Regiment	Madrassis
The Indian Grenadiers 1st, 2nd	Jats, P.M.s
The Mahratta Light Infantry 1st, 2nd, 3rd, 4th, 5th Royal	Mahrattas
The Rajputana Rifles 1st (Wellesley's), 2nd P.W.O., 3rd, 4th (Outram's), 5th (Napier's)	Jats, P.M.s, Rajputs
7th Rajput Regiment 1st (Q.V.O.), 2nd (P.A.V.O.), 3rd (D.C.O.), 4th, 5th	Rajputs, P.M.s
8th Punjab Regiment 1st, 2nd, 3rd, 4th (P.W.O.), 5th	Gujars, P.M.s, Sikhs
The Jat Regiment 1st (Royal), 2nd (Mooltan), 3rd	Jats, Mussalman Rajputs, P.M.s
The Baluch Regiment 1st (Duchess of Connaught's Own), 2nd, 3rd (Q.M.O.), 4th (D.C.O.), 5th (K.G.O.)	Dogras, Pathans, P.M.s, Sikhs
The Sikh Regiment 1st (K.G.O.), 2nd (Ludhiana), 3rd (Rattray's), 4th, 5th (D.C.O.)	Sikhs, P.M.s
The Frontier Force Regiment 1st (P.W.O.), 2nd, 3rd (Royal), 4th, 5th (Q.V.O. Corps of Guides)	Dogras, Pathans, P.M.s, Sikhs
The Frontier Force Rifles 1st (Coke's), 2nd, 3rd (Wild's), 5th (Vaughan's), 6th (Royal Scinde) Rifles	Dogras, Pathans, P.M.s, Sikhs

Unit	Class composition
14th Punjab Regiment	Pathans, P.M.s, Sikhs
1st, 2nd (Duke of Cambridge's Own), 3rd, 4th, 5th (Pathans)	
15th Punjab Regiment	Jats, Pathans, P.M.s,
1st, 2nd, 3rd, 4th	Sikhs
16th Punjab Regiment	Dogras, P.M.s, Sikhs
1st, 2nd, 3rd, 4th (Bhopal)	
The Dogra Regiment	Dogras
1st (P.W.O.), 2nd, 3rd	
Royal Garwhal Rifles	Garwhalis
1st (Royal), 2nd, 3rd	
The Kumaon Regiment	Jats, Ahirs, Kumaonis,
1st (Russell's), 2nd (Berar), 4th, and 1st Kumaon Rifles	Rajputs

Regiments raised in wartime

The Bihar Regiment	Ahirs and Rajputs of Bihar
The Assam Regiment	Assamese, Kukis, Nagas, Lushais, Khasis
Sikh Light Infantry	Mazbi and Ramdassia Sikhs
Mahar Regiment	Mahars
The Ajmer Regiment	Rawats, Katats, Minas
The Chamar Regiment	Chamars
The Coorg Battalion	Coorg
The Lingayat Battalion	Lingayats and Mahrattas

GURKHA RIFLES

1st K.G.O. Gurkha Rifles
2nd K.E.O. Goorkhas (The Sirmoor Rifles)
3rd Q.A.O. Gurkha Rifles
4th P.W.O. Gurkha Rifles
5th Royal Gurkha Rifles (F.F.)
6th Gurkha Rifles
7th Gurkha Rifles
8th Gurkha Rifles

9th Gurkha Rifles
10th Princess Mary's Own Gurkha Rifles

All the Gurkha Regiments had two battalions.

All the Infantry and Gurkha regiments approximately doubled their peace-time strength with war battalions, and raised also garrison companies and other units.

The ruling princes of India placed regiments and batteries from their State Forces at the disposal of the Government and they fought in most theatres of war from Italy to Malaya.

Exact details are not available for the following corps but some figures are given of the raisings in the last two years of the war.

Indian Signal Corps	434 units
Royal Indian Army	490 Supply units
Service Corps	10 Air Supply units
	17 Animal Transport units
	79 Mechanical Transport units
Indian Army Medical Corps	over 400 units
Indian Army Ordnance Corps	266 units
Indian Electrical & Mechanical	321 units
Engineers	

There were also over 1,500 other units ranging through Cipher units, Corps of Military Police, Postal units, Remount and Veterinary, Prisoners of War, and Graves Registration and Enquiries.

Appendix C

AIR SUPPLY TO FOURTEENTH ARMY

It is likely that to the absolute finality of Fourteenth Army's victory over the Japanese, air supply contributed more than any other single factor. There must accordingly be a brief account of all that went to build up that complex organization.

In air supply the airman's demands are apparently simple, a base from which to fly and, at the delivery end, a sky reasonably clear of enemy fighters or anti-aircraft guns. But the demand made on the aircrews goes much deeper than that, for the commitment to maintain a force by air supply is final and binding. Operational sorties can be and often were postponed because of bad weather; but failure to deliver the daily airlift leaves the man at the far end hungry, and possibly short of the ammunition and petrol he needs to fight with. Field Marshal Slim paid repeated tributes to the extent to which the R.A.F. and U.S.A.A.F. identified themselves with the army in whose support they flew, and to their cheerful acceptance of the hazards of day-to-day flying over mountainous country in the most treacherous monsoon weather.

Air supply is very far from being just an air force responsibility, and the army will profit from the help it receives to the extent that it discharges its own share of the business in providing three supporting requirements: an elaborate system of control and inter-communication; a highly specialized supply service; and an organization for the construction and maintenance of airfields.

Air Headquarters, India, began investigating the possibilities of air supply towards the end of 1940, the commitment in view being the maintenance of troops which might have to be dispatched to defend the northern frontiers of Iraq and

Iran. Beginning with some rather Heath Robinson experiments in dropping loads from the walls of the Red Fort in Delhi, an organization was set up which was engaged in endless research and trials right up to the end of the war. Air supply to be effective must be all-embracing and cover everything that troops engaged in operations may need; it is not possible to put the awkward load to one side and send it by goods train. Loads sorted themselves out into perhaps five categories:

(a) Those for free-dropping—clothes, flour and so on, which needed only to be packed inside an outer packing cover
(b) The dangerous—ammunition and petrol
(c) The fragile—wireless sets, valves and medicines
(d) The weighty—engineer stores and pieces of artillery
(e) The plain awkward.

It was of course useless to expect a mule to co-operate, and the first one to go down, supported by four parachutes, recoiled in astonishment at the sight of the ground rushing up to meet him, and was so stiff that he could not move for four days after landing. Thereafter each paramule was given an anaesthetic injection before being emplaned, calculated to put him out until ETA + 15 minutes; whereafter he woke up slightly puzzled, but relaxed and unhurt.

Packing material had to be designed for all these things and, since it was non-recoverable, it had to be inexpensive and made from material available in wartime; it must also make for ease of packing. It was also necessary to devise composite loads, as when the engineers wished to deliver 'do-it-yourself' kits of aerial ropeway to forward sappers struggling with streams swollen by the monsoon.

The whole of this vast field of research had then to be codified in the simplest possible terms and applied to the training of air supply companies.

A photo of a typical supply drop at Mandalay Hill faces page 321.

Air supply was tried out on a large scale for the first time in support of the Chindit expedition of 1943, and some of the most valuable lessons of the operation were those learned in this connexion. At the beginning of February 1944, when the Japanese attack in the Arakan was launched, there were four air supply companies on airfields in Bengal and Assam allotted respectively to the West African Division in the Kaladan Valley; Special Force preparing for the 1944 operations; troops round Fort Hertz in the far north; and miscellaneous tasks for IVth Corps in the Tiddim area. They accepted cheerfully, as did the R.A.F. squadrons working round the clock, the rush commitment to supply 7th Division's Admin Box when it was surrounded.

So much for air dropping, a perfectly workable expedient, but extravagant. The weight of parachutes and packing material cut the payload of the aircraft, and both packing and collection and sorting at the receiving end took valuable time. Normal loading was resorted to whenever possible, but endless experiments were needed to discover the best way of dealing with multiple loads to make for speed and tactical convenience. Even bulldozers and bridging materials were successfully 'broken down'.

Normal delivery opened up a completely fresh range of problems in the provision of landing strips in the battle areas. Forward airfield engineer groups were allotted to each axis of advance with the task of providing an airstrip every hundred miles, and a fighter strip at alternate sites. Each group had its mechanical equipment platoon with bulldozers and graders, and quantities of hessian and metal strip for surfaces were free-dropped. But, in general, materials were found locally, and considerable ingenuity was called for in devising mixtures to bind the surface of the soil.

Speed was the essence of the matter and the Americans introduced the multiplex system of air survey whereby contours could be plotted to within a foot from photographs. One group commander was given the ideal site, a dead level except for a small mound six feet high in the middle. Luckily he was able to fly over it before committing his group as it proved to be flooded paddy-fields, with a clump of elephant grass where the mound was said to be. Thereafter he reconnoitred on foot, but engineer patrols moved with the most forward detachments, whether of armour or infantry.

One group in six months built thirty airstrips between the Kabaw Valley and Prome, averaging forty-eight hours as the time for completion: their record—an airstrip in use with control tower built from local teak and all facilities complete within twenty-five hours of reaching the site.

Appendix D

KEY
TO PUBLISHED WORKS FROM WHICH QUOTATIONS ARE TAKEN

OFFICIAL PUBLICATIONS

1. *History of the Second World War: Mediterranean & Middle East*, Vol. I; Playfair; H.M.S.O.; 1954.
2. *ibid.* Vol. II; 1956.
3. *ibid.* Vol. III; 1960.
5. *History of the Second World War: The War against Japan*, Vol. I; Woodburn Kirby; H.M.S.O.; 1957.
6. *ibid.* Vol. II; 1958.
7. *ibid.* Vol. III; 1961.
8. *Australia in the War of 1939–1945: Greece, Crete & Syria*; Long; Canberra Australian War Memorial; 1953.
9. *Official History of the Canadian Army in the Second World War: The Canadians in Italy*; Nicholson; Department of National Defence, Canada; 1956.
10. *Official History of New Zealand in the Second World War: Battle for Egypt*; Scoullar; War History Branch, New Zealand; 1955.
11. *Official History of the Indian Armed Forces in the Second World War: Arakan*; Madan; Historical Section (India & Pakistan); 1954.
12. *Official History of the Indian Armed Forces in the Second World War: Reconquest of Burma*; Vols. I & II; Historical Section (India & Pakistan); 1958, 1959.
13. *Paiforce: The Official Story of the Persia and Iraq Command 1941–1949*; H.M.S.O.
14. *Five Ventures*; Buckley; H.M.S.O.; 1954.

15. *The Tiger Strikes: India's Fight in the Middle East*;
    H.M.S.O.; 1942.
16. *The Tiger Kills: Story of British and Indian Troops with
    the Eighth Army in North Africa*; H.M.S.O.; 1944.
17. *The Tiger Triumphs: Story of Three Great Divisions in
    Italy*; H.M.S.O.; 1946.
18. *A Gurkha Brigade in Italy: Story of the 43rd Gurkha
    Lorried Brigade*; India, War Department, Directorate of
    Public Relations; Bombay, Times of India Press; *c.* 1946.
19. *The Campaign in Italy*; Linklater; H.M.S.O. Popular
    History Series; 1951.

DIVISIONAL HISTORIES

21. *Fourth Indian Division*; Stevens; McLaren & Son,
    Toronto; 1949.
22. *Ball of Fire: The Fifth Indian Division in the Second
    World War*; Brett-James; Gale & Polden; 1951.
23. *Golden Arrow: The Story of the Seventh Indian Division*;
    Roberts; Gale & Polden; 1952.
24. *History of 17th Indian Division.*
25. *The Fighting Cock: The Story of the 23rd Indian Division,
    1942-47*; Doulton; Gale & Polden; 1951.
26. *The Arakan Campaign of the 25th Indian Division.*

REGIMENTAL HISTORIES

30. *The Seventh and Three Enemies.*
31. *Always a Fusilier: The War History of The Royal Fusiliers.*
32. *Proud Heritage: The Story of The Highland Light Infantry,*
    Vol. IV.
34. *The History of the Indian Mountain Artillery.*
35. *The History of the Indian Regiment of Artillery.*
36. *The History of Q.V.O. Madras Sappers and Miners.*
37. *The History of K.G.O. Bengal Sappers and Miners.*
41. *Central India Horse Newsletter.*
42. *History of the 2nd Royal Lancers (Gardner's Horse).*
44. *Royal Deccan Horse: An account of Operations in Burma
    1945.*
45. *The Scinde Horse (14th P.W.O. Cavalry).*

46. *The Spirit of a Regiment: The History of 19th K.G.O.
Lancers.*
51. *The First Punjabis.*
52. *The Golden Galley: History of 2nd Punjab Regiment.*
53. *History of The Mahratta Light Infantry.*
54. *History of The Rajputana Rifles.*
55. *The Sikh Regiment in the Second World War.*
57. *History of the Frontier Force Regiment.*
58. *The Frontier Force Rifles.*
59. *Historical Record of The Royal Garwhal Rifles.*
61. *The History of 1st K.G.O. Gurkha Rifles.*
62. *History of 2nd K.E.O. Goorkhas (The Sirmoor Rifle
Regiment).*
63. *The Regimental History of 3rd Q.A.O. Gurkha Rifles.*
64. *A History of 4th P.W.O. Gurkha Rifles.*
65. *History of 5th Royal Gurkha Rifles (Frontier Force).*
66. *Historical Record of 6th Gurkha Rifles.*
67. *History of 7th Gurkha Rifles.*
68. *History of 8th Gurkha Rifles.*
69. *The 9th Gurkha Rifles.*
70. *Bugle and Kukri: The History of 10th Princess Mary's Own
Gurkha Rifles.*

OTHER SOURCES

71. Slim, Sir William [Viscount]; *Defeat into Victory*;
Cassell; 1956.
72. Tuker, Sir F.; *Approach to Battle—A Commentary:
Eighth Army, November 1941 to May 1943*; Cassell; 1963.
74. Majdalany, F.; *Cassino: Portrait of a Battle*; Longmans;
1957.
75. Fuller, J. F. C.; *The Second World War*; Eyre & Spottiswoode; 1948.
76. Falls, C.; *The Second World War: A Short History*;
Methuen; 1948.

PUBLISHER'S NOTE

A Novel by Eric Linklater, entitled *Roll of Honour*, was
published by Rupert Hart-Davis in 1961.

Index

NOTES

Formations are indexed under 'Brigades', 'Corps' and 'Divisions'; but 'Armies' under their numbers, *e.g.*, 'Eighth Army (Brit.)'. Enemy formations are omitted.

Regiments and technical corps under their names, *e.g.* 'Assam Regiment'; 'Gurkha Rifles'; 'Lancers, 2nd'; 'Royal Deccan Horse'; 'Sappers and Miners'.

Quotations from books under their book titles, which are in *italics*.

'*bis*' or '*ter*' after a page reference means that the subject is mentioned *twice* or *thrice* in separate paragraphs on the page.

'I.A.' means 'Indian Army'.

A.V.G.: *see* American Volunteer Group

Abadan (oil refinery and port): 71, 78

'Abdacom': 151

'Aberdeen', Operation: 194, 195–197

Abyssinia (Ethiopia): 4, 9, 23, 36, 39, 43, 61, 63; Emperor of, 36–7, 41, 61

Acqua Col: 50, 51, 52

'Acrobat', Operation: 183, 184

Ad Teclesan: 60, 61

Addis Ababa: 9, 37, 40, 50, 62, 63

Aden: 23, 39, 62; Gulf of, 61

Administrative serivces of I.A.: 9, 18, 53–4, 61, 174–5

Adowa: 44; Battle of (1896), 36

Advanced dressing station, scene at an: 219

Afghan War, First (1839–42): 3

Afghanistan: 4, 8, 13, 20, 69

Africa, Horn of: *see* Africa, Italian East

Africa, Italian East: 8, 36–67; forces in, 41; final surrender of Italians in, 67

Africa, North: *Aug. 39–Dec. 40*, 22–35; *Mar. 41–Dec. 41*, 102–19; *Jan. 42–Jul. 42*, 183–203; *Aug. 42–May 43*, 204–223

Afrika Korps: *see* D.A.K.

Agansing Rai, Naik, *V.C.*: 316–317

Agedabia: 183, 184

Agordat: 43–7 *passim*; Battle of, 46, 48

Ahwaz: 78

Air evacuation of casualties (Fourteenth Army): 274

Air power: 13

Air supply to Fourteenth Army (Burma): 270, 278, 283, 287, 288, 292, 306–7, 319, 320, 329, 331, 342, 365–8

Airfields and landing strips in battle areas (Burma campaign): 367–8